CROSS AND SWORD

The Political Role of Christian Missions

in the Belgian Congo, 1908-1960

Marvin D. Markowitz

Hoover Institution Press
Stanford University
Stanford, California

The Hoover Institution on War, Revolution and Peace, founded at Stanford University in 1919 by the late President Herbert Hoover, is a center for advanced study and research on public and international affairs in the twentieth century. The views expressed in its publications are entirely those of the author, and do not necessarily reflect the views of the staff, officers, or Board of Overseers of the Hoover Institution.

Hoover Institution Publications 114
International Standard Book Number 0-8179-1141-3
Library of Congress Card Number 75-170209
© 1973 by the Board of Trustees of the
     Leland Stanford Junior University
Printed in the United States of America

To My Parents

Marvin D. Markowitz is Assistant Professor in the
Department of Politics, New York University. He
received his Ph. D. from Columbia University and
was a Research Fellow of the Social Science
Research Council from 1963 to 1965. His articles
have appeared in Africa, Current, Africa Today,
The Journal of Politics, and Africa Yesterday and
Today (Bantam Books, 1968).

CONTENTS

TABLES

Page

ABBREVIATIONS

ABAKO   Association Bakongo
ABFMS   American Baptist Foreign Missionary Society
ADAPES   Anciens Elèves des Pères de Scheut
ASAP   Association des Anciens Elèves des Pères Jésuites
BEC   Bureau de l'Enseignement Catholique
BMS   Baptist Missionary Society
CADULAC   Centre Agronomique de l'Université de Louvain au Congo
c-d-t   contrat du travail
CERS   Centre d'Etude et de Recherche Sociale
CGS   Confédération Général des Syndicats
CPC   Congo Protestant Council
CSC   Confédération des Syndicats Chrétiens
CSP   Conférence Sociale et Philosophique
CUCL   Centre Universitaire Congolaise Lovanium
EAK   École des Sciences Administratives à Kisantu
EJCSK   L'Eglise de Jésus-Christ sur la terre par le prophète Simon Kimbangu
FBEI   Fonds du Bien-Etre Indigène
FEMOCA   Fédération des Moniteurs Catholiques
FGTB   Fédération Générale des Travailleurs Belges
FOMULAC   Foundation Médicale de l'Université de Louvain au Congo
FOREAMI   Fonds Reine Elisabeth pour l'Assistance Médicale aux Indigènes
HCB   Huileries du Congo Belge (Unilever and Lever Brothers)
IIC   Intergroup des Intérêts Chrétiens
IMC   International Missionary Council
JOC   Jeunesse Ouvriers Chrétiens
LOC   Ligue des Ouvriers Chrétien
MNC   Mouvement National Congolais
MOC   Mouvement Ouvrier Chrétien
PLB   Parti Libéral Belge
PSA   Parti Solidaire Africain
PSB   Parti Socialist Belge
PSC   Parti Social Chrétien (Catholic Party)
UMHK   Union Minière du Haut Katanga
UNELMA   Union des Anciens Elèves des Frères Maristes
UNISCO   Union des Intérête Sociaux Congolais

PREFACE

Various writers have taken note of the activity of Christian missions
during the early period of the European exploration and colonization of Africa, but there are few studies of mission political involvement after World
War I, and almost none for the period following World War II, when nationalist movements burgeoned. Taking the former Belgian Congo as my focus, I
therefore set out to explore and determine the depth of the influence and
involvement of Christian missions in the colonial politics and, later, in
the decolonization there.

I had expected difficulty in gaining access to data about what I had
assumed to be a sensitive and limited problem, but very soon I found myself
swamped by the wealth of information available. Instead of the suspiciousness and mistrust I had anticipated from the missionaries, I found, to my
delight, a high degree of openness and friendliness—their archives and confidential files often seemed almost to fly open at my approach.

Unforeseeable events, however, played some havoc with my plans. I arrived in the Congo in January 1964, shortly after a rebellion had broken out
in the Kwilu; by the time I left in September of that year the rebellion had
engulfed most of the eastern region of the Congo. As a result, I had to
limit my research to the Lower Congo region. I did, however, have access to
several central missionary organizations such as the Congo Protestant Council, the Conference of the Catholic Bishops of the Belgian Congo and Ruanda-
Urundi, and the Bureau de l'Enseignement Catholique, and to the files and
archives of certain specific missions and individuals. The resulting study
lays no claim to be definitive or to include all the varied experiences of
the different Christian missions in the vast area that was the Congo and is
now Zaire. All I have sought to do is to outline certain missionary attitudes and policies that appear to have been widely shared during the years
under review.

I could not have carried out this study without the help and advice of
many in the United States as well as in Belgium and Zaire. Above all my
thanks go to the Social Science Research Council which granted me the fel-
lowship that supported my research in Belgium and the Congo and thus made
this work possible. Much information and insight were put at my disposal by
many missionaries with long and varied experience in the Congo, especially
Father Joseph Van Wing, SJ, Father Guy Mosmans, WF, Father Albert Brys,
CSCM, Father Willy De Craemer, SJ, and the Reverend Emory Ross and the Reverend George Carpenter. I owe them a great debt and much gratitude, not
least for their help in gaining access to confidential missionary archives.
This greatly facilitated my research.

In the conception, research, and writing of this study I had the advice
and encouragement of a number of friends and colleagues. Herbert Weiss
shared his experience and understanding of the Congo with me, thus enabling

me to avoid many pitfalls and take advantage of certain opportunities. Others who were generous with their support and criticism were Benoit Verhaegen, Crawford Young, A. A. J. Van Bilsen, Renée Fox, and Guy Malengreau. Thanks also go to Catherine Berry for her diligent editing of the manuscript, and to Ann Guilfoyle, Richard Brof, and Robert Cutler for the tedious work of proof-reading.

To my wife who shared the joys and suffered the pains of this work with me and gave me her criticism, her labor, and her understanding, I give my deepest and warmest thanks and appreciation.

Nonetheless I alone am responsible for all the text that follows.

CHAPTER 1

HISTORICAL BACKGROUND

Christian missions were in the vanguard of European penetration of the Congo as of many other areas of Africa. Catholic missionaries accompanied the Portuguese explorer Diego Cão on his expedition to the mouth of the Congo River in 1484, and some remained behind to evangelize among the Bakongo, the major tribe in that region. In the years that followed additional Portuguese missionaries went to the Lower Congo, where they enjoyed some success and even converted the King of the Kongo.* Subsequently, however, the power of the Christian converts and their Portuguese clergy was gravely weakened by the factionalism and civil war that rent the kingdom, Christianity lost its appeal among the people, and by the end of the seventeenth century missionary activity in the Lower Congo had nearly dried up.[1]

The latter part of the nineteenth century saw a great revival and expansion of missionary work. A rising evangelical spirit took hold of Protestant sects in both Britain and the United States. Many believed the Christian millenium to be at hand, and missions received great public support and burgeoned. Attention was drawn to Africa as a field for evangelization by the writings and reports of David Livingstone and, later, by the accounts of Henry Morton Stanley. An additional and powerful stimulus to missionary activity was the antislavery movement. In both East and Central Africa the slave trade was in the hands of Zanzibari Arabs who spread Islam wherever they went. A blow against the slave trade was thus a blow against Islam also. In addition, the colonization of large parts of Africa by European powers toward the end of the nineteenth century afforded missionaries the modicum of security necessary for their operations.

In January 1878 George Grenfell and Thomas Comber of the Baptist Missionary Society (BMS) landed at Banana at the mouth of the Congo River. After a brief survey they recommended that the society establish a mission at San Salvador (now in Angola) to serve as a base for the establishment of stations upriver. By 1879 the first BMS mission was established at San Salvador in spite of a Portuguese denial of permission to build it. The Portuguese authorities had their eyes set on control of the entire Lower Congo basin, but their claim to this area was not recognized at that time, and the BMS chose to ignore the Portuguese injunction.

————————————

*The Kingdom of the Kongo encompassed most of the region below present-day Kinshasa and included parts of Angola and Congo-Brazzaville. Its capital was San Salvador. For an excellent account of the Kingdom of the Kongo see Jan Vansina, Les anciens royaumes de la savane.

1

The Catholic missionaries in the area reacted swiftly to the establishment of BMS missions among the Bakongo. In 1880 the French Congregation of the Holy Ghost established at Boma on the lower Congo River a mission which, under the leadership of Father Prosper-Philippe Augouard, adopted a policy of aggressive expansion. The congregation also sought to set up a mission to counter the BMS mission at San Salvador. But there it ran afoul of Portuguese expansionist ambitions. The Portuguese saw the French missionaries in the Congo as agents of the French Government laying the ground for French annexation of the area. (In light of the later actions of Father Augouard with regard to the establishment of the French Congo, Portuguese suspicions may well have been justified.) The real threat to their plans, however, lay in another direction.

In 1879 Stanley returned to the Congo as an agent of Léopold II, king of the Belgians. His purpose was to establish a route from the mouth of the Congo to the Stanley Pool* and to set up stations of the Belgian International Association** on the upper river. Seeking to outdistance Portugal and France, Léopold saw in the English missionaries useful instruments for the acquisition of the Congo. Thus, when he became aware of the BMS plans to construct a string of mission stations along the Congo River, he became a subscriber to the society's publication, The Missionary Herald,[2] and carefully cultivated a friendly attitude toward the society itself. This policy was later to yield large dividends.

While Stanley and the French representative, Comte Savorgnan de Brazza, were racing toward the Pool, the BMS sent its own expedition there. Located above the cataracts of the Lower Congo, the Pool marks the start of hundreds of miles of navigable waters and offered an ideal base for penetration of the upper reaches of the Congo River and its tributaries. It was the BMS plan to establish a base at the Pool to support its projected upriver stations. In order to gain the support of the British Protestant missionaries, Léopold instructed Stanley to aid and befriend them. In 1881 BMS missionaries who had gone upriver reported:

> On coming down the river we found Mr. Stanley with his camp, and he most kindly placed a tent at our disposal, and offered to run us down river the next morning to the Isangala Falls. I can not speak in too high terms of Mr. Stanley's kindness to us—his interest in the little journey we had taken, his inquiry after his old friends at Stanley Pool, and his offer to help us with stores if we were short.[3]

While cultivating the support of the Protestant missions, Léopold also attempted to persuade Belgian Catholic missionaries to enter the Congo; the presence of Belgians would further strengthen his hand, if and when the time should come for a decision on the status of the Congo. As early as 1879 he had urged the Scheutist Fathers (the Congregation of the Immaculate Heart of Mary, or the Missionary Sons of Scheut) and the Belgian Jesuits to

---

*A wide expanse of water at the point in the Congo River where Léopoldville and Brazzaville are situated.

**Originally established to promote scientific and humanitarian interest in Africa among the Western powers, this association became merely a front for Léopold's commercial interests.

establish missions in the Congo, but owing to heavy commitments elsewhere they refused the request. In another direction, however, he was somewhat more successful. Cardinal Charles Martial Albemand Lavigerie, founder of the White Fathers (the Society of Missionaries of Africa), was interested in extending his work in Equatorial Africa. When he approached Léopold for support, the king countered with the proposal that he would aid and finance Lavigerie's mission in the Congo, provided that it would eventually be staffed by Belgians and that Léopold himself would select the mission sites. Meanwhile he was using his influence at the Vatican to persuade a Belgian congregation to enter the Congo missionary field. Learning of these moves, Lavigerie accepted the king's offer.*

Léopold's primary concern with any particular mission was not so much its religious identification as its nationality and whether it would help or hinder his claim to the Congo. Thus he fostered British Protestant missions but sought to stifle missionary activity by French and Portuguese Catholics.

During 1884 Léopold opened a new drive to attract Belgian Catholic missionaries to the Congo. The Archbishop of Malines was sent to Rome and obtained permission from the Propaganda to establish an African seminary in Belgium to train priests for work in the posts of the Belgian International Association in the Congo. It was opened two years later at Louvain University, with aid from Léopold. In the same year the Propaganda, responding to pressure from Léopold, announced that French missionaries would leave the Congo when enough Belgians became available to replace them. The Scheutist Fathers sent a mission to the Congo in 1887. The following year saw the establishment of the Apostolic Vicariate of the Congo.[4]

In 1891 the Belgian Jesuits agreed to establish a mission in the Congo; two years later they set up their first station. Soon afterward many other Belgian orders began sending missions—among them the Trappists, Redemptorists, Premonstrants, Dominicans, and the Sacred Heart of Jesus.** The 1880s and 1890s witnessed the expansion in the Congo of Protestant missions also.

---

*As a result of his dealings with Léopold, Lavigerie had become aware of the king's plans for the Congo. In a letter to Cardinal Prefect of the Sacred Congregation for the Propagation of the Faith (the Propaganda) he wrote:

> I feel obliged to confidentially make Your Eminence aware that the King of the Belgians appears to have designs on the center of Africa that are not merely humanitarian but political. He has begun to form a small army destined, no doubt, for conquest, under the leadership of Stanley, the American Protestant explorer. It is unfortunate that this [Catholic] Prince puts himself into the hands of the Protestants for such an undertaking (J. Perraudin, "Le Cardinal Lavigerie et Leo II," p. 916).

**By the end of the nineteenth century the Roman Catholics had seven congregations in the Congo, with seventeen stations staffed by 139 missionaries and Sisters (Alfred R. Stonelake, Congo, p. 128).

The Berlin Conference
and the Congo Free State

In 1884 Britain negotiated a treaty with Portugal which promised British support for Portugal's claim to the mouth of the Congo River. This would have facilitated the extension of Portuguese rule over the entire Congo basin. The treaty was opposed, however, by Léopold, the BMS, France, and Germany. The reason for Léopold's opposition was obvious: he wanted the Congo. France and Germany, both with territorial interests bordering the Congo, did not wish a close ally of Britain to control the area. And the BMS, representing the opinion of Protestant missions in the Congo, feared Portugal's belligerently anti-Protestant attitude. Voicing these fears, W. Holden Bentley made it plain that they preferred the king of the Belgians to the king of Portugal.[5]

Léopold's offer to make the Congo a free-trade zone, under the International Association, attracted commercial and missionary interests in Britain and the United States. A BMS petition to the House of Commons against ratification of the treaty with Portugal had the support of the English chambers of commerce; as a result of this and other opposition the treaty was never ratified.

The agents of Léopold, on the other hand, were completely successful in gathering support for his bid for the Congo. Playing on French fears and on the German desire to keep Britain out of the Congo and at odds with the French, Léopold was able to get both powers to recognize the flag of the International Association before the opening of the Berlin West African Conference which was to deal with the claims and counterclaims of European powers in the Congo basin. By the time the conference met he had gained the backing of France, Germany, the United States, and an important segment of British public opinion. He was almost assured of a favorable outcome. BMS representatives at the conference pressed the British envoys to support the claims of the association. They also played a role in drafting article VI of the General Act of Berlin, 1885 (see appendix A) which assured freedom of religion in the area governed by the association and committed the signatories to "protect and favour all religious...institutions and undertakings."

The General Act of Berlin established the Congo Independent State (also called the Congo Free State) but failed to define all its borders. To support a legal claim required effective occupation. Aware of the ambitions of France, Britain, Germany, and Portugal in Central Africa, Léopold was anxious to rapidly expand the area of the Free State.

During the period 1884-1885 Grenfell of the BMS explored the upper reaches of the Congo and its tributaries. As he progressed, he came into contact with the Arab slave traders, at that time the strongest force in the eastern regions of the Congo. Faced with the Arab threat to their program of expansion, the British Baptist missionaries hoped that the Free State would impose its rule over the Upper Congo so that they could proceed with their work in relative peace. Once again the interests of the Protestant missions and the political aims of Léopold meshed.

In the late 1880s the Arabs, under the leadership of Tippo Tib, had grown so powerful above the Stanley Falls that the Free State had had to withdraw some of its posts from the Upper Congo. At first the Free State pursued a policy of placating the Arabs, but from 1887 on, conscious of its increasing strength, changed its attitude from a conciliatory to an aggressive one. This shift in policy was in part due to the action of the

Catholic Church. In the same year the Scheutist Fathers left for the Congo, and the Vatican began an antislavery movement (whose Belgian branch was La Ligue Antiesclavagiste Belge) in an attempt to win public support for a campaign against the Arabs in Central Africa.[6] Also in 1887 Stanley returned to the Congo as leader of the Emin Relief Expedition—a thinly veiled design to overthrow the power of the Arabs in the eastern Congo and put the region under the effective control of the Free State. The campaign was successful; by 1892 the power of the Arabs had for the most part been broken.

Once again Léopold had effectively exploited the support of the Protestant and Roman Catholic missions on the pretext of humanitarian claims that were merely a cloak for political aims: the underlying calculation was that the fall of the Arabs would allow a more rapid expansion of the missions and the state. He was trying to maintain his friendship with the Protestant missionaries while seeking to counterbalance their influence by the expansion of Roman Catholic missions.

Meantime Léopold was finding the Congo, vast storehouse of natural wealth though it was, a financial disaster. Accordingly in 1891 he issued a decree (never published in the Bulletin Officiel of the Free State) instructing officials of the Ubangi Uelle and Aruwimi districts to gather ivory, rubber, and other products for the state.[7] By the mid-1890s the effects of this secret decree were becoming apparent. Rubber and ivory were being obtained by forced labor. Africans were overworked, underpaid, and underfed. Protestant missionaries began to send home reports of the atrocities taking place under the rubber regime. In 1895 the American Baptists appealed to the State Department about the situation in the Congo,[8] and Sjöblom, a Swede working for the American Baptists in the Congo, sent accounts of atrocities to the European press. The anti-Léopoldian campaign, as it came to be called, was gathering momentum, Britain and the United States being the major centers of activity. It was not, however, to reach its peak until the first decade of the twentieth century.

In spite of the growing opposition to the Léopoldian regime among Protestant missionaries, the BMS refused to join in the attack or to make public charges. It had cooperated closely with Léopold almost from the start of its Congo mission, and even in 1900 it still maintained cordial relations with his regime.* It was Léopold's hope that the BMS would defuse criticism of his regime by other Protestant missionaries. Thus, while other Protestant missions were denied land concessions and were burdened with heavy taxes, the BMS received free land grants and tax relief. And when in 1896

---

*W. Holden Bentley of the BMS wrote in 1900:

Happily the relations between our mission and the Government have been very cordial. Mr. A. H. Baynes, has always received the kindest consideration in any matters which have been arranged with the Central Government and have required his personal attention or presence in Brussels. On several occasions His Majesty the King has received him very graciously and expressed his appreciation of our work. The high officials in the Congo have also been very cordial, and have in no way hindered our work. By the General Act of Berlin liberty of worship was guaranteed to all, and this has been faithfully carried out by the State (Pioneering in the Congo, p. 425).

Léopold established the Commission for the Protection of the Natives in an attempt to quash charges against his regime, Grenfell of the BMS was named chairman—only to resign later in protest against the commission's impotence. Léopold's policy did not avert disaster, but it may have postponed it. The BMS believed that the situation in the Congo was not of his making but was the unscrupulous work of certain Free State officials. They were sure that, if the king were privately made aware of the conditions in the Congo, he would institute reforms, and they felt that public agitation would only make it more difficult for him to take such action. Here the BMS completely misjudged Léopold's character and aims.

In 1900 several Protestant missionary societies in the Congo decided to call a conference of Protestant missions for the year 1902. The General Conference of Protestant Missions met at Léopoldville on January 18, 1902, thirty-four missionary representatives from nine societies attending. This first attempt to evoke a spirit of cooperation between the various Protestant missions in the Congo was spurred by the pressure being exerted on them by the state. Their taxes had been raised, and land concessions had been denied them.[9] A petition to the governor-general sought tax relief and raised the questions of land concessions and treatment of the Africans. In reply the governor-general refused any tax relief and informed the petitioning Protestants that the state had decided not to grant them land but would agree to rent it for a ten- to twenty-year period.[10] On the question of native rights they received no satisfactory answer. Bentley and Grenfell, the BMS representatives at the conference, took the position that the missions should be patient with the state.*

The year 1903 marked the zenith of the rubber regime in the Congo; it was also the year that opposition to it grew formidable. The report in 1903 by Roger Casement, British Consul at Boma, capital of the Congo Free State, caused conditions in the Upper Congo to become a public scandal and the British House of Commons to pass a motion on the Congo situation. It also changed the attitude of the BMS toward the Léopoldian regime. In face of the powerful evidence against the agents of the Free State, the BMS felt compelled to lend its weight to the reform movement. Missionaries, American and British, actively supported the reform movement. In 1903 the General Assembly of the American Presbyterian Church (South) appointed a

---

*An interesting question raised by the conference was whether or not the Protestant missionaries should accept appointments as state officers. By a royal decree of December 28, 1888, religious associations in the Congo could obtain civil authority (Th. Heyse, Associations religieuses au Congo Belge et au Ruanda-Urundi, p. 5). The missionaries present expressed mixed feelings on this problem. The Rev. T. Moody of the American Baptists thought "the office a desirable one...as by doing this for the State we do ourselves a good turn by increasing our acquaintance with the people, and by that, our influence over them. We also avoid the hindrances that apparently, necessarily accrue to the establishment of a regular government centre in the immediate neighborhood of the station" (United Missionary Conference on the Congo, 1902, p. 50). Others believed that missionaries should not assume government posts, except perhaps that of registrar. It was left up to each society to make the decision it deemed best.

committee to present a report on conditions in the Congo to Secretary of State Hay; in November of that year it met with President Roosevelt to discuss the problem.[11] In 1904 Edmund D. Morel, who had been campaigning in Britain against the rubber regime, established the Congo Reform Association there; a United States branch was founded the same year. In December 1904 Senator Lodge introduced a resolution in the U.S. Senate calling for the amelioration of conditions in the Congo.

As a result of this campaign Léopold increased the pressure against Protestant missions and attempted to replace them with Catholic missions which would be more amenable to his policies. In response to the part the British Protestant missions had taken in the campaign against him, he asked that an English Catholic mission be sent to the Congo. In 1904 the Mill Hill Fathers established a mission there. The depth of his concern over Protestant activities is evidenced by the fact that he even went so far as to set up a fictitious organization, the West African Missionary Association with headquarters in Brussels, to grind out statements contradicting the accusations of the British and American missionaries.[12] This sham was, however, soon exposed.

The king's policy of favoring the Roman Catholic missions in the Congo deeply embittered the Protestants. The state was preventing the expansion of their missions while aiding the growth of Roman Catholic missions. The Catholics, well aware of the situation, not only were loath to attack the source of their sustenance but even gave the state material aid. At the 1907 General Conference of Protestant Missions one missionary made the accusation that "up the Kasai [River] the Roman Catholic priests and the State worked together, with the result that the Roman Catholics had a large amount of power. The priests arranged the portage for the state, and a large rubber plantation, the property of the Kasai Company, was really worked and controlled by the priests."[13] The Catholics were also accused of trying to encroach upon areas actively being evangelized by the Protestants. Emile Vandervelde, the leader of the Belgian Socialists, recounts how, during his travels in the Congo in 1908, the Jesuits attacked the Protestant missions: "The Jesuits claim that the Protestants are enemies of the State, who foment rebellion among the natives."[14] There were some Catholic clergymen in Belgium who criticized the Léopoldian system;[15] but for the most part the Catholic clergy either remained silent or gave outward support to the Congo regime.

On May 26, 1906, a concordat was signed between the Congo Independent State and the Holy See. Under the terms of the treaty Catholic mission schools were to receive state subsidies. They were to be under state jurisdiction, but religious training was to be strictly under the missionaries running the school. In addition, the governor-general was to be informed of the appointment of the Superior in charge of each school. The missions were also required to do geographic, linguistic, and ethnographic studies for the state. The state on its side was to allot to each Catholic mission or mission station 100 to 200 hectares of land, inalienable and to be held in perpetuity.[16] The concordat was an attempt by Léopold to ensure Catholic support and to force the Protestant missions to withdraw from the Congo.

Two years earlier pressure of public opinion had compelled Léopold to appoint a commission of enquiry to investigate conditions in the Congo. The commission spent four and one-half months in the Congo collecting information for its report, much of it provided by Protestant missionaries.

In 1905 it published its findings. They were highly critical of the methods employed by the Congo Free State and called for reforms.*

As a result of this report Léopold was compelled in 1906 to decree a program of reforms, which was instituted the next year. Conditions were ameliorated, but the rubber regime continued. Quotas for rubber were lowered, and compensation was slightly raised; but the basic injustices of the system remained. Léopold's hope that the reforms would quell the wave of criticism against his regime proved vain. In England, missionaries Morel and H. R. Fox-Bourne, secretary of the Aborigines Protection Society, continued the campaign with unremitting vigor. By 1907 both the United States and Britain were actively pressing for Belgian annexation of the Congo Free State.

In Belgium members of the Catholic party and the Liberal party for the most part supported the move for annexation; the Socialists opposed it. At that time the Catholic party was in power, and one of its prime considerations was the future of the Belgian Catholic missions. A considerable investment of men and money had gone into support of the missions, and the government undoubtedly feared that, if another power should gain control of the Congo, the Belgian Catholics might be forced out. There was also the question of the vast sums of money that the government had loaned and granted to Léopold and the Free State.** Brussels had no desire to forfeit this investment. Private interests that had built commercial organizations in the Congo also pressed for annexation. In addition, Belgium's prestige had been diminished by Léopold's venture, and many felt that it was her duty to take over the Congo and thus redeem her honor. In 1908, spurred by this combination of religious, financial, and patriotic interests and by international pressure, Belgium annexed the Congo.

Jules Renkin, the first minister of colonies, continued Léopold's policy of favoring the Roman Catholic missions. He denied that religion was a factor in this policy and claimed that he was favoring the Catholic missions only because they were "national missions." Renkin felt, as did many other Belgians, that the presence of English and American Protestant missionaries in the Congo was detrimental to Belgian interests, and that their role in the anti-Léopoldian movement had shown them to be potential troublemakers. Their ability to get political support from the U.S. and British governments irked the Belgians, especially since Great Britain did not immediately recognize the Belgian annexation and was pressing the Belgians to grant new sites to the English missions. To Catholics like Renkin the Protestants represented an alien and hostile creed that was seeking to encroach upon what they considered to be their territory.

In an attempt to displace the Protestant missions, Renkin encouraged the interest of Belgian Protestants in the Congo. Henri Anet, head of the Eglise Chrétienne Missionnaire (an independent church with no ties to the

---

*It did not however publish the evidence it had collected, upon which the report was based. There was much pressure for the publication of these data, but they have not yet seen the light of day.

**Between 1887 and 1907 Belgium had loaned 110,376,630 Belgian francs to the Congo Free State (Emile Vandervelde, La Belgique et le Congo, p. 125).

Belgian government) and one of the few spokesmen in Belgium for the Protestants in the colony, wanted the Belgian Protestants to set up a mission in the Congo. Another group interested in Congo missions was the Synod of the Evangelical Churches of Belgium, led by Paul Rochedieu. This church was in receipt of state subsidies. In 1909 Rochedieu proposed to Renkin that his church act as the agent for the foreign Protestant missions in the Congo in their relations with the Colonial Ministry. A proposal was also made that Belgian Protestant missionaries be trained to eventually displace all foreign Protestant missions.[17] Renkin was naturally interested in this plan; but it was rejected out of hand by most Protestant missions in the Congo. In any case it is doubtful that the Belgian Protestants had either the men or the resources for such a task.

In 1909 the Colonial Ministry instituted the prosecution of William Morrison and William Sheppard, two American Protestant missionaries who had been indicted for libel of the regime. They had publicly attacked the methods employed by the Compagnie du Kasai to collect rubber within its concession. The law under which they were tried had been enacted by Léopold to discourage criticism of his regime by Protestant missionaries. Why the Colonial Ministry chose to prosecute is perplexing. One would have expected it to be to the government's interest to avoid publicity at that time. However, the ministry seems to have sought to demonstrate to the Protestant missionaries that the Belgian government would not stand for public exposure of grievances that the missions might have against colonial policies. Another purpose may have been to discourage the further influx of Protestant missions. At any rate, from the state's point of view the trial was an utter failure. Vandervelde defended the two missionaries, both of whom were acquitted. The trial merely intensified the public demand for continued reform.

The Protestant missions kept up the struggle for reforms, and by 1911 many changes in treatment of the Africans had been instituted. There remained, however, the problems of excessive taxation and of the attitude of the Roman Catholic missionaries and the state toward Protestant expansion. The latter issue was particularly exacerbating. The close relationship between the Colonial Ministry and the Roman Catholic missions struck the Protestants as unfair and illegal.* At the 1918 General Conference of Protestant

---

*With encouragement from the state, the Catholics increased their activity. State subsidies to the Catholic missions in 1911 were 50,000 Belgian francs, and for the period 1914-1918, 31,000 francs a year. This figure increased to 72,000 francs in 1919 (D. Fr. de Meeus and D. R. Steenberghen, Les missions religieuses au Congo Belge, p. 133). Available statistics giving the number of Catholic converts in the Congo during the prewar period vary considerably. One source states that there were only 70,000 Catholics in 1912 (Ruth Slade, English-Speaking Missions in the Congo Independent State, 1896-1908, p. 394), while another says that there were over 100,000 (Kenneth S. Latourette, The Great Century in the Americas, Australasia and Africa: A.D. 1800-A.D. 1914, p. 422). The figures for Catholic converts may have included students and catechumens. It is difficult to establish how many Protestant converts there were during the same period, but the General Conference of Protestant Missions in 1904 reported 8,812 communicants (eight societies reporting).

Missions a delegate remarked that "Catholic priests parade throughout the country boldly asserting that they and the Government are one. Frequently the decisions of Government officials proclaim the boast a fact."[18] It was contended that the state had abrogated the key provisions of the General Act of Berlin and the Penal Code of the colony, treating them "as mere scraps of paper."[19]

The Léopoldian regime had sown the seeds of collaboration between the Catholic missions and the state. These were to germinate and flourish in the colonial atmosphere of the Belgian Congo. On the other hand, the role the American and British missionaries played in the anti-Léopoldian campaign and their continued pressure for reform during the years immediately following annexation created in the Belgian Colonial Administration feelings of lasting bitterness and mistrust toward the Protestant missions.

CHAPTER 2

THE MISSIONARY PHILOSOPHY AND METHODS

The values and attitudes of the missionaries and the methods they developed and employed to promote evangelization helped to transform the traditional structures and functions of African institutions. The missionaries
urged and in some cases forced Africans to accept new modes of social, economic, and political organization and behavior.

Symbiosis with the Government

After the annexation of the Congo by Belgium the new Colonial Administration, headed by Jules Renkin, continued the policy of favoring the Catholic missions.* Its reasons were much the same as Léopold's had been: fear
and suspicion of Protestant motives, the policy of consolidating Belgian
control over outlying districts, and the need for the training of semi-
skilled labor. Moreover, the Act of Annexation had included recognition of
the concordat of 1906 between the Independent State and the Holy See.

In addition, annexation had introduced new problems. The Congo was no
longer the personal fief of one man. The attitudes of the Belgian people
and its representatives in the parliament had now to be taken into account.
There had been much opposition to annexation, and it had been decided that
the colony must pay for itself. Thus throughout most of the fifty-two years
that Belgium ruled the Congo successive governments allowed, encouraged, and
aided the missions to invest money and manpower in areas they themselves
were either unable or unwilling to enter. In spite of the fact that large
subsidies were paid to the missions the savings in money and personnel were
enormous. Another reason for the continuation of the policy of favoring the
Catholic missions may be found in their preemption before annexation of such
fields as education and medicine. Here again the question of men and money
made itself felt. Lastly, the main support for annexation had come from the
Catholic and Liberal parties in Belgium. The former was especially

---

*In recognition of this policy one missionary noted that "the attitude
of the Congo Independent State and of the Belgian Government, thereafter,
has always been inspired by a desire for effective, frank, and spontaneous
collaboration with the missions and from the outset, this was proclaimed to
be a principle of government" (Deuxième conférence plénière des ordinaires
des missions du Congo Belge et du Ruanda-Urundi, Léopoldville, June 16-28,
1936, p. 69).

interested in the position and future of Catholic missions in the Congo, while the latter saw in them a stabilizing and educative force which could aid private enterprise. The mixture of religion and politics in Belgium and the ethnoreligious conflict it produced had a profound and continuing effect on the formulation of policies regarding the Christian missions.

Belgian policymakers conceived of the missions as agents of social control. They hoped that the feelings of respect, fear, and subservience that the missionaries instilled would make it possible to govern most areas of the Congo with a fair degree of peace and a minimum of effort. This was especially important for a small nation such as Belgium. Emile Tibbaut, vice president of the Belgian House of Representatives in 1926, gave a succinct statement of this objective: "While introducing the principles of Christian society into indigenous society, it [Christianity] contributes a new element of security to the colony."[1]

Tibbaut also mentioned two other problems which concerned him, Islam and Pan-Africanism. Islam, although not widespread in the Congo,* did pose a problem for the Belgians in that they had found in the Maniema** the greatest resistance to their efforts at colonization. The campaign against the Arabs had been one of the most difficult problems encountered by Léopold in his attempts to consolidate the Congo. The obvious solution seemed to be in the isolation and, if possible, conversion of the Moslems in the Maniema.

Fear of the nascent Pan-African Movement in the early 1920s, more particularly of Marcus Garvey's movement,*** stemmed mainly from a Belgian belief that the ideas of Pan-Africanism had influenced Kimbanguism and other messianic sects that sprang up in the Congo during this period (see below chapter 13). Here again increased missionary activity seemed to be a likely antidote. Succeeding Colonial Administrations pursued a consistent and conscious policy of continued collaboration with the missions. There can be little doubt that both parties felt that they benefited from this arrangement.

At the second plenary conference of Catholic bishops held in Léopoldville June 16-18, 1936, the rewards of this close relationship were clearly recognized by one speaker who noted that "whenever the spirit of collaboration has presided over the relations of missionaries and colonial officials, that collaborative effort has been crowned with success."[2]****

---

*About 1958 it was reported that there were 115,500 Moslems in the Congo (Inforcongo, Belgian Congo, vol. 2, p. 171).

**Located in the northeast corner of the Congo and mainly inhabited by the Azande.

***The Universal Negro Improvement Association, which called for the erection of a black African state, the decolonization of black Africa, and the return to Africa of American and Caribbean blacks, was at its height during the 1920s. It attracted a substantial following in the United States and gained wide attention at that time.

****This point had not escaped the administration. Martin Rutten, vice governor-general of Katanga and later governor-general of the Congo, was certainly aware of missionary aid to the Colonial Administration when he noted:

One must substitute in the minds of the blacks other commandments for those basic tenets of custom which have been destroyed. Whatever our

What better instrument existed for territorial occupation and the inculcation of discipline into Congolese minds!

Rural Romanticism

The attitudes that the missionaries brought with them to a great extent determined their approach to the African, to his culture and society, and to the entire question of social change. These attitudes easily allowed them to act as agents of social control for a Colonial Administration that viewed Congolese as children.

Many Protestant missionaries, especially those from the United States, had grown up in an evangelical tradition that favored pietistic Christianity and eschewed rationalism and cosmopolitanism. Although they rejected many aspects of their own cultures as un-Christian or corrupt, they nonetheless retained an ethnocentric view of African civilization.[3] In their eyes their own nations had failed to become Christian societies and were irredeemable. Their hope was that in Africa (or Asia or Oceania or elsewhere) Christianity would come to full fruition.* For many missionaries, therefore, more was at stake than the conversion of the heathen. The convert often became the vehicle for the fulfillment of the missionary's own dreams and for the resolution of his psychological and social conflicts. If an African Christian failed to live up to the principles, values, and ethics of Christianity as conceived by the missionary, he was not merely harming himself; in the eyes of the missionary, he was betraying a much deeper trust. Converts thus came to be burdened—often unbeknownst to themselves—with an impossible responsibility.

Their own antiintellectualism and anticosmopolitanism also led many missionaries to become exponents and supporters of African provincialism. They idealized African village life and rejected such aspects of modernity as urbanization and industrialization.** To them rural life was the epitome of virtue while the city was filled with evil and atheism. In its extreme form this rural romanticism led to rejection of the accoutrements of Western civilization and to cultural asceticism. One missionary described rural life as simple, primitive, and Christian and noted that "the coming of any external influences into Arcadia strikes us as almost indecent."[4] The Protestants in particular tended to shy away from the cities and towns and to center their efforts on the countryside.

---

philosophical points of view may be, whatever credit we attach to dogmas, we must recognize the perfection of the Christian ethic, the influence that it has had, and that it still maintains in regard to the development of civilization in the world. To deprive ourselves of this means of uplifting the black race would be a blunder that we will not commit ("L'Avenir du Congo," p. 399).

*Bronislaw Malinowski notes that the missionaries who went to Africa had "a passionate desire to realize the Christian ideal in its pristine purity" ("Native Education and Culture Contact," p. 499).

**Missionaries had no monopoly of this attitude which was shared by many colonial administrators and anthropologists.

Many Catholic missionaries had similar attitudes. Some deplored the fact that the mines drew large numbers of Africans and turned them into a proletariat; they considered that this development contributed to a break-down in community life, the spread of disease, and the danger of rebellion.[5] One Catholic bishop, while pointing to the need for greater missionary action in urban areas, remarked that "the [Catholic] missions often considered the [urban] centers as Babylons from which it was their duty to keep their flocks."[6]

The missionaries were part of Western civilization, yet they saw themselves apart from it. They desired its benefits both for themselves and their converts, but desired them devoid of the tensions and conflicts that Western nations often experienced. They apparently failed to realize that the innocence of the pastoral life could not persist when confronted by the modernizing process of which they themselves were a part. Their desires were at once romantic and irreconcilable.

Methods of Evangelization

The need to rationalize the evangelical approach and methods began to be apparent with the arrival in the Congo of the first wave of Catholic missionaries. Their small numbers and ignorance of the country, combined with the lack of trained Congolese catechists and the inhabitants' hostility or lack of interest, all had a part in dictating mission policy.

An early experiment was the ferme chapelle system instituted by the Jesuit missionaries in the Kwango. The failure of their initial attempts at mass evangelization had convinced them that their only hope of success lay in modifying the basic social structure and customs of the Africans.[7] The revised plan was to take the children out of the parental milieu and place them in a new setting which would allow the inculcation of new habits and customs. In essence it amounted to an attempt to establish a new society by incubation, that is, by careful control of the social atmosphere and prevention of external contamination. Thus the ferme chapelle system, as it was called, was established. This ferme chapelle system—or modified versions of it—was adopted by other, though by no means all, Catholic missions in the Congo. The children belonging to the ferme chapelle were closely supervised, either by African catechists or by the missionaries themselves. Stress was laid on the catechism, prayer, propriety, and work in the fields. Two later out-growths of this system were the écoles chapelles and the villages chrétiens. The former emphasized vocational training rather than agriculture, while the latter were villages established by the missions for those who graduated from the fermes chapelles or écoles chapelles. The missionaries feared that if these new converts returned to their native villages and attempted to reintegrate themselves into village society, they would soon "sink into paganism."[8] In addition, some Africans, especially former slaves, wished to remain under the protection of the missionaries.*

---

*Recruitment for the fermes chapelles had come from three sources: (1) former slaves, either purchased out of slavery by the missions or assigned by the government; (2) "orphans" gathered by the missions and the government; and (3) children placed by their parents. In many cases the "orphans" placed with the missions were orphans only in the eyes of the white man, not to Africans accustomed to an extended family system.

14

As the missions became more firmly established, however, and gained a better understanding of the people, a new policy of evangelization was instituted. The _ferme_ _chapelle_ was gradually abandoned in favor of a system stressing mass evangelization. From 1914 on the Catholics opened rural schools in increasing numbers and encouraged Christian families to return to their native villages to form Catholic nuclei. The major instrument of this new policy was the African catechist.

The catechists enjoyed various degrees of training and preparation for their tasks, and those with the most fervor were not necessarily the most knowledgeable. They were utilized in various ways by the missions: some taught at mission stations, others itinerated, and others again settled in villages. Some taught only religion (the catechism and simple doctrinal concepts); others established village schools and taught fundamentals (reading, writing, and so forth) as far as they themselves had grasped them. The catechist often became one of the most important figures in the village. He was the villager's interpreter of the often bewildering European world, and his advice was sought by village society at every level. Many became scribes and close advisers to the chiefs. On their side, the chiefs and their people looked for tangible political benefits from the presence of the catechists whom they had allowed to establish themselves in their villages. Many hoped that the presence of a representative of the Catholic missions would temper the demands and actions of the local administrator.[9] Often the catechist's appeal lay less in the religious message he bore than in the worldly power he represented. He was a political as well as a religious and social force.

Attitudes to Social Change

The policy of mass evangelization provoked an examination of missionary aims and methods. This dialogue was muffled by World War I, but it resumed in 1919 and continued throughout the twenty years between the wars. It coincided with a period of rapid expansion of the missions.

Two basic schools of missionary thought emerged at the end of World War I. One group of missionaries saw African culture as essentially backward and unenlightened, and therefore in need of an almost complete transformation. This approach was nothing more than a continuation of the prewar view of colonization which saw the civilization of the white man as being indisputably superior to that of the African, and even questioned the existence of an African civilization. The other school of missionary thought evolved from a colonial philosophy that had emerged after World War I. Respect for minority rights and self-determination had been promoted during the war and recorded in the Treaty of Versailles. Article 22 of the Covenant of the League of Nations, vague though it was, did foster the idea that the development of the peoples in the colonial and mandated areas was primary and was a responsibility of the colonizing powers. In addition, British development of indirect rule and emphasis on respect for customary institutions excited favorable comments from some Belgian colonial writers.

One result of these various influences was the development of a theory of evangelization based upon what may be termed cultural selectivity. The customs, mores, and institutions of the Africans were placed in two general categories: those which were "bad" or harmful, and those which were "good"

15

or helpful. These designations provided no solid criteria by which to judge whether particular institutions, customs, or mores were either good or bad, or whether they were to be retained, transformed, or totally discarded. In the last analysis, the decision had to depend on the values, attitudes, prejudices, or whims of the missionaries involved. The African, for his part, had little or no say in the selection process. This theory rested on the naive assumption that it was possible to destroy an integral component of a society without affecting that society's remaining foundations or superstructure. It paid no regard to the fact that the forms and institutions which make up a social system are interwoven and interdependent, that a change in one area cannot but affect other parts of the system.*

This new policy of evangelization, whatever its shortcomings, did serve to provoke in many missionaries a self-conscious and self-critical attitude. One of the spokesmen for the new theory was Father Joseph Van Wing, S J, a leading Jesuit missionary and scholar. In an article, which appeared in Congo under a pseudonym, he called for a slow and careful attempt, based on greater understanding of African institutions, to lead the Africans toward "civilization." He was critical of missionaries who strove to Europeanize the African: "Missionaries are often enthusiasts who are quickly convinced that a native Christian is similar to [a] European." And his criticism of missionary methods led him to ask: "Is Catholic evangelization..., either in principle or in fact, destructive—and, if so, to what degree—of the religious, social, and familial organization of the Congolese?"[10]

Here was an awareness of the impact that the missions had had on African institutions and of the need to modify it in some way. The attempt to reconcile the conflict between the policies of mass evangelization and of respect for African institutions led to tortuous qualifications. Van Wing advocated that the missionaries respect traditional African institutions "so long as they are not contrary to religion, justice, and good morals."[11] Msgr. V. Roelens, apostolic vicar of Haut Congo, made the qualification that such respect should be accorded "if they did not endanger the principles of true civilization"; among the dangers he cited were "primarily the religious ideas of the blacks."[12]

Roelens' qualification indicates how difficult it was for missionaries to conceive of a theory of evangelization which would preserve the societal

---

*Malinowski puts this point very clearly:

While it may seem easy to replace a custom here and there or transform a technical device, such a change of detail very often upsets an institition without reforming it, because...beliefs, ideas, and practices are welded into bigger systems. When we come to the integral institutions of a trible or a nation, matters become extremely complicated. And the reason for this is that an important institution like the family or chieftainship, ancestor worship or agriculture, has its roots in all aspects of culture. It is connected with so many cultural realities, some of which it is by no means easy to alter, that nothing except a complete transformation of the whole society can provide a painless change, free from maladjustment (The Dynamics of Culture Change, p. 52).

cohesiveness of the Africans. The contradiction is apparent in the qualification: if one is not neutral on questions of religion, justice, and good morals which are at the very heart of the social system, then what is left? The theory of cultural selectivity almost unconsciously involves an assumption of institutional exclusivity, which rarely, if ever, exists in any society. Interdependence is the keynote of social institutions. If an outsider is to come into an area and induce the indigenous peoples to change their society according to his decisions, he must have the certainty, genuine or assumed, that what he offers is better than what they already have. The theory underlying missionary methods formulated during and after World War I, while paying homage to African societies, was still based on an attitude of cultural superiority and self-righteousness.

Van Wing took the position that it was not the effects of evangelization that destroyed African society; rather, it was the destruction of tribal institutions, the weakening of the chiefs, the growth of prostitution, and the increase in the number of the déracinés and disoriented—caused not by the missionaries but by the government and the commercial enterprises: "If the missionaries had been the only ones to exercise a civilizing influence among the natives...neither dying communities nor run-down institutions, bound for destruction, would be found there."[13] There is something to this view. Had the missionaries in the Congo come exclusively under their own auspices to evangelize among a people who were independent and self-governing, whatever changes they introduced would have tended to be primarily the choice of the Congolese. There would have been no external constraint in the shape of a colonial administration or commercial interests. And, perhaps even more important, the pace of absorption and change would have been slower, thus allowing time to achieve social integration and synthesis.

Catholic missionary work in the Congo started with government aid and encouragement. The Belgian colonial system operated on the basis of an interdependent triumvirate of missionary, administration, and commercial interests. The missions provided the government with a measure of social and territorial control,* and they educated and trained Africans for work on the plantations and in the mines. In return they received subsidies, protection, and land. At their behest, the state would at times introduce laws that the missions felt they needed to further evangelization, for example, a law

---

*The Catholic missionaries were well aware of the service that they rendered the administration, especially in the area of social control: "If there are no longer any revolts," one missionary noted, "it may primarily be attributed to the fear inspired by the state, but equally to the fact that within native communities there are Christians who are on the alert and could report things to the whites" (Stanislas De Vos, "La politique indigène et les missions catholiques," p. 642). For this service Msgr. Roelens demanded that the government aid the evangelical aims of the missions: "The right to freedom of conscience and religion inscribed in the Colonial Charter must be firmly guaranteed to all of the natives in the colony in the sense of having the right to be instructed in the Christian religion and to practice that religion. Any custom which tends to deprive the native of this right must be considered as contrary to the public order and combated by the government" (V. Roelens, "Le respect de la coutume indigène," pp. 644-645).

designed to discourage polygamous marriage by taxing surplus wives.* The collaboration between the missions, especially the Catholic missions, and the administration was mutually satisfactory. The philosophy, methodology, and attitudes of the missionaries meshed nicely with the needs of the administration. At least until the end of World War II the missions could work toward their own aims while fulfilling those of the colonial government, without overmuch strain or conflict.

Thus the attempt by some missionaries to lay the blame for the weakening of African institutions at the door of the administration and the commercial firms cannot be fully reconciled with the relationship that the missionaries enjoyed with them. Had it not been for their close ties with the administration and the commercial interests, the missions' position in and influence on Congolese society would in all likelihood have been quite different.

---

*Missionary pressure was directly responsible for the Decree of April 4, 1950, which severely proscribed those who had already contracted polygamous marriages and forbade any new marriages of this nature (Pierre Peron and Jacques Devos, Codes et lois du Congo belge, pp. 196-197).

CHAPTER 3

BELGIUM AND THE CONGO

The political role of the missions in the Congo can be fully understood
only when viewed against the background of the social and political forces
operating in Belgium itself. The Catholic missionaries, being preponderant-
ly Belgian, were deeply involved in the tensions and conflicts of the metropolitan culture. These affected both their attitudes and their actions.
But most important of all was the fact that these conflicts enabled the
Catholics to exert significant political power and influence in regard to
the Congo.

Public Apathy

During the interwar period Belgium was concerned mainly with internal
problems and paid scant attention to the Congo. There was little of the
economic dissatisfaction or lack of opportunity at home that spurred many
British, Italians, and others to seek their fortunes outside their native
countries. In spite of Belgium's dense population most Belgians could find
satisfaction of their needs within the confines of their own borders. The
dissatisfied could seek an outlet in neighboring countries, especially
France whose great losses in World War I had left her with a shortage of
manpower.
The Belgian people's lack of interest in colonial questions caused dis-
appointment and chagrin among some of those concerned with the Congo and its
problems throughout the interwar period, World War II, and much of the postwar era. Although World War I had pointed up the economic importance of the
Congo, interest in the colony or colonial questions remained superficial.
Anton F. Marzorati (a former vice governor-general of the Belgian Congo, a
member of the Colonial Council, and one of the most astute critics of Belgian colonial policy) noted that the public showed little awareness or concern for the colonial responsibilities that Belgium had assumed in the
Congo.[1] In the other nations of Europe which had colonial possessions in
Africa, especially in Britain and France, criticism of colonial policy by
the left wing opposition was nearly continuous. But in Belgium there was
almost none. Almost to the end the Socialist party remained virtually mute
on colonial issues. Such criticism as there was came from a small circle of
missionaries, financiers, politicians, academicians, colons (white settlers),
and colonial administrators. It was a case of the experts talking amongst

themselves, with virtually no public involvement.*

This attitude toward public criticism on colonial matters may be traced to a number of factors. Belgium, a small nation, feared that larger powers had designs on her colonies in Africa. Her past experience seemed to offer some grounds for this apprehension. During the time that Léopold II ruled the Congo Independent State it was believed that Britain, France, or Germany desired to take over the Congo—a fear that had been enhanced by the participation of American and British Protestant missionaries in the anti-Léopoldian campaign. Later, both during and after World War II, there was some fear that the United States wished to wrest control of the Congo from Belgium. Aware of their small-power status and conscious of their history as the battleground of Europe, the Belgians could not easily allay their anxiety.

There was, in addition, the problem of disunity within the métropole. The period after World War I witnessed increased discord at home. The conflicts between Fleming and Walloon, between clerical and anticlerical, and between political Left and Right made for a preoccupation with domestic concerns.** When national unity is at stake, it is difficult to turn to the problems of overseas colonies. For the people and the political parties of Belgium the politics of compromise was paramount; if national disintegration was to be averted, divisive issues would have to be avoided or suppressed. Frank discussion of colonial problems and policies would certainly have added to these difficulties.

This situation suited certain groups and individuals interested in the Congo. Such large financial concerns as the Société Générale de Belgique and the Banque Lambert were no doubt pleased that their investments and influence in the colony did not come under forceful attack. Attacks by the Socialist and left wing press on their role in the Congo had little effect. The population was apathetic, and, in spite of their verbal assaults on these interests, left wing politicians tended to play the game of compromise and accommodation so necessary to the preservation of national unity. This may help to explain why the left wing in Belgium did not follow an anticolonial line to the same degree as its brethren in France and Great Britain. It was, however, the Catholic missions that benefited most from this situation. The anticlerical attacks upon them were seldom, if ever, translated into action. The attitude that prevailed in the métropole is well exemplified by the oft-repeated statement that "anticlericalism is not an article of exportation."[2]

If there was any popular sentiment about the colony, it was a feeling of national pride. Many felt that it was an honor that little Belgium should be bringing civilization to a large area of Africa. The missionaries were thought of as the agents of that civilization, and families with little real

---

*Not until 1954, when Professor A. A. J. Van Bilsen made public his thirty-year plan for Congolese independence, did substantial and general criticism of colonial policy appear. Even then many regarded his critique as betraying Belgium and apt to subvert the national interest. (See Van Bilsen, "Pour une nouvelle politique de mouvement en Afrique," pp. 395-411.)

**Val R. Lorwin has noted that Belgian politics has been and continues to be dominated by these three major factors (see his excellent article on Belgian politics, "Belgium: Religion, Class and Language in National Politics," pp. 147 ff.).

interest in and even less knowledge of the Congo would pride themselves on having a son or daughter go there as a missionary. It was said that "the average Belgian is only interested in the Congo in terms of business or evangelization, but remains indifferent to political problems."[3]

Party Attitudes

In face of so pronounced a public apathy, what were the attitudes toward colonial questions and in particular toward the Catholic missions of the three major parties in Belgian politics: the Catholics (Parti Social Chrétien—PSC), the Socialists (Parti Socialiste Belge—PSB), and the Liberals (Parti Libéral Belge—PLB*)? Their attitudes were in large part determined by the socioeconomic structure of their following, which in turn reflected the basic conflicts, such as that between Fleming and Walloon, that existed—and still exist—in Belgian society.

The Catholic party traditionally derives most of its membership and support from the Flemish regions of the country and contains a large segment of the Belgian population: farmers, the industrial and commercial bourgeoisie, some professionals, ordinary workers, and even some members of the landed aristocracy.[4] What holds this amalgam together is the glue of strong Catholic loyalties. The Socialist party finds its greatest support in Walloon districts but also draws heavily from the urban industrial areas and from Brussels and Antwerp, which is Flemish. Most of its members are salaried workers and clerks who are also members of the Fédération Générale des Travailleurs Belges. In addition, it attracts areligious, antireligious, and anticlerical elements of the population.[5] The Liberal party, the third and smallest of the major parties, comes mainly from middle- and upper-class merchants and businessmen, though the party has also managed to attract a very small portion of the white collar vote through the Confédération Générale des Syndicats Libéraux. Traditionally anticlerical, it draws the majority of its votes from urban Walloon areas.

Belgian political parties, because of their composition and because of the social, religious, and linguistic conflicts of Belgian society, have often found themselves in paradoxical positions and unlikely alliances. On religious questions there is a clear dichotomy between the clerical position of the Catholic party and the anticlericalism of the Socialists and Liberals, who can act in concert when this issue arises. On other questions the social composition of the parties makes for a more muddied picture. The position of the Catholic party is the most complex: pluralistic in nature, it relies heavily on a social-democratically oriented proletariat, a conservative peasantry, and middle-class elements. It could on occasion find a basis of compatibility either with the Socialists, who could align themselves with the left wing social democrats within the Catholic party, or with the Liberals, who could identify with the economically and socially conservative middle class and the big business proclericals.

---

*In 1961 the PLB changed its name to Parti du Liberté et Progrès. In this study, which does not go beyond 1960, the earlier name of the party has been retained. Prior to 1946 the PSC was formally known as the Catholic Party.

Rarely can any one party gain a clear majority in the parliament; since the end of World War I coalition governments have dominated Belgian politics. From November 21, 1918, to November 6, 1958, there were thirty-two governments, the longest enduring four years and one month, and the shortest fifteen days. During this forty-year period the Catholic party was excluded from the government for a period of only five years and nine months; during the interwar years it participated in every government (see table 1). In any coalition the Catholics were in a strong position to demand the ministerial portfolios which interested them most. The distribution of portfolios in a coalition government was determined not only by the necessity of balancing parties but also by religious, linguistic, ethnic, and social considerations. Ideological principles were often watered down or sidestepped.

In the trading for portfolios the Catholic party, one of whose major concerns was the promotion and protection of Catholic missions in the Congo, would invariably try—usually with success—to gain control of the Ministry of Colonies (see table 2). In coalition governments composed of Liberals and Catholics they could get this ministry in exchange for the promise not to press hard for increased state subsidies to Catholic schools in Belgium. The Liberals, who included among their members men with large investments in the Congo, took an essentially conservative position on colonial questions and could easily go along with this arrangement. It was not until the mid-1950s that the anticlericalism of the Liberals in the métropole came to be reflected in political action regarding the colony. Even when Louis Franck, a Liberal, was minister of colonies (November 21, 1918, to May 11, 1924) during a Catholic-Liberal coalition government, he played the game of favoring Catholic missionary interests.

When the Socialists participated in coalition governments which included the Catholics, they were willing to accept Catholic domination of the Colonial Ministry in exchange for concessions on social reform and for a moderation of the Catholic drive for state subsidies for Catholic schools in Belgium. Domestic issues were of more importance to them than their ideological stand against colonialism or their anticlericalism. Indeed, until a very late date the Socialists paid comparatively little attention to colonial policies and made few real attempts to change them.*

Virtually without opposition on colonial questions, the Catholic party was able to control the formulation and administration of colonial policy throughout most of the years that Belgium exercised sovereignty over the Congo. Thus it was in an excellent position to strengthen and protect the interests of the Catholic missions.

Colonial Administration

According to the Colonial Charter, the Belgian parliament exercised a number of functions in regard to the colony. It defined the public law (articles 2 and 3); voted the budget and expenses (article 12); and approved treaties of commerce and cessions, exchanges, and additions of territory (article 27). Cessions of more than 10,000 hectares, and concessions of more than thirty years' duration and over 25,000 hectares in extent also had to

---

*A possible exception here was Vandervelde. But he failed to evoke his party's interest.

TABLE 1

PARTY ALIGNMENTS OF BELGIAN GOVERNMENTS, 1918–1958

Govern-ments	One-Party[a]			Coalition						Totals
				Two-Party[a]				Three-Party[a]		
	PSB	PSC	PLB	PSC-PLB	PLB-PSB	PSC-PSB	PSB-PLB	PSC-PSB-PLB	PSC-PSB-PLB	
Number	1	5	0	8	1	3	3	9	2	32
Dura-tion (in months)	.5	54.5	0	97	49	41	19.5	159.5	10	431[b] (35yrs., 11 mos.)

SOURCE: François Perin, La démocratie enrayée, pp. 252–253.

[a]PLB = Parti Libéral Belge; PSB = Parti Socialiste Belge; PSC = Parti Social Chrétien.

[b]Does not include the Belgian Government-in-Exile located in London during World War II.

TABLE 2

PARTY AFFILIATIONS OF MINISTERS OF COLONIES,1908-1960

	Party Affiliation[a]	Date Assuming Office
Jules Renkin	C	October 30, 1908
Louis Franck	L	November 21, 1918
H. Carton de Tournai	C	May 11, 1924
Baron Marcel Houtart	C	May 20, 1926
Edouard Pecher	L	November 15, 1926
Henri Jaspar	C	November 22, 1927
Baron Marcel Houtart	C	December 29, 1927
Paul Tschoffen	C	October 19, 1929
Henri Jaspar	C	December 26, 1929
Paul Charles	C	May 18, 1931
Paul Crockaert	C	June 6, 1931
Paul Tschoffen	C	May 23, 1932
Paul Charles	C	November 20, 1934
Edmond Rubbens	C	March 23, 1935
Ch. Du Bus de Warnaffe	C	April 24, 1938
Albert De Vleeschauwer	C	May 15, 1938
Gaston Heenen	C	February 22, 1939
Albert De Vleeschauwer	C	April 16, 1939
Edgard De Bruyne	C	February 12, 1945
Robert Godding	L	August 2, 1945
Lode Craeybeckx	S	March 13, 1946
Robert Godding	L	March 31, 1946
Pierre Wigny	C	March 20, 1947
André Dequae	C	August 15, 1950
Auguste Buisseret	L	April 23, 1954
Léon Pétillon	C	July 5, 1958
Maurice Van Hemelrijck	C	November 6, 1958
Auguste de Schrijver	C	September 3, 1959
Raymond Scheyven	C	November 17, 1959

SOURCE: Inforcongo, Belgian Congo, vol. 2, p. 35.

[a]C = Catholic; L = Liberal; S = Socialist.

NOTE: Beginning with Pétillon, the title of the office was changed to Minister of the Belgian Congo and Ruanda-Urundi.

have parliamentary approval. In spite of these powers, the parliament tended to treat most colonial matters lightly and failed to make full use of the controls that it possessed.[6]

Budgetary control was the parliament's most powerful instrument for influencing colonial policy. It was, however, little used. In theory the colonial budget had to be submitted and approved by the parliament before the beginning of each fiscal year, but in practice this was rarely done. In consequence, the minister of colonies had wide discretion in the allocation of funds,* and could carry out his policies with little fear of control or censure by the parliament. Most colonial ministries being dominated by the Catholic party, policies favoring the Catholic missions could be implemented with little or no resistance. In the light of the sociopolitical dynamics of Belgian politics the parliament's lack of assertiveness on colonial questions is readily intelligible.

Within these limitations, the Congo was governed by decree under the supervision of the minister of colonies. The decrees were submitted for approval to the fifteen-member Colonial Council, headed by the minister of colonies.[7]

As of 1933, the administrative chain of command for the Congo was as follows:

        Minister of colonies
        Governor general
        State inspector
        Vice governor general (later provincial governor)
        Provincial commissioner
        District commissioner
        Territorial administrator
        Commissioner of an urban district[8]

In 1935 the administrative staff for the entire Congo consisted of the following 684 officials attached to the colonial service:

District commissioners		18
Administrators		197
Agents		469
	Total	684
	On leave	82
	Net total	602 [9]

---

*"The estimates prepared by the Governor-General and reviewed by the Minister of Colonies seldom reached the floor of the parliament before the beginning of the fiscal year, thus rendering inoperative the provision of the charter stipulating that at least four months prior to the beginning of the fiscal year a draft project of the budget will be printed and distributed to the members of the Legislative Chambers. The yearly submission of a budget extraordinaire allowed the minister to supplement the funds already approved by the Chambers in accordance with his current needs. Finally, he enjoyed discretionary powers to transfer budgetary allocations from one item to another. In short, although technically responsible to the parliament for the administration of the colony, the minister was left with wide discretion in the regulation of his policy" (René Lemarchand, Political Awakening in the Congo, p. 56).

In the same year there were in the Congo 1,255 Catholic priests and Brothers, and 1,071 nuns, that is, a total of 2,326 Catholic missionaries or about four times the number of the officials in the colonial service.[10] The area of the Congo is 905,062 square miles. To a local administrator who might have to oversee an area nearly twice the size of Belgium the collaboration of the missionaries, many of whom were in the bush and in constant contact with the Congolese, was of great importance. Also significant was the fact that the missionaries accounted for a substantial portion of the total white population of the Congo,* and represented the largest proportion of non-Africans in the bush.

As the Colonial Ministry was largely dominated by Catholics, so was the Government-General, as is clear from the list of those who served as governors-general and from their religiopolitical affiliations (see table 3). This does not mean that the actions of a governor-general with regard to questions affecting the missions were uniformly dictated by his religious affiliation or lack of it. Personality, depth of religious identification, and the specific question involved all played their part. It is fair to assume, however, that a Catholic governor-general would tend to be more sympathetic than an anticlerical to Catholic missionary needs and demands, especially in view of the fact that he had to respond to the pressures and direction of the colonial minister.** Out of ten governors-general who served between 1908 and 1960, seven were Catholic; while of the other three, one was a Liberal, one a Socialist, and one unaffiliated.

During the early 1950s, according to one analyst, 90 percent of the key positions in the Government-General were occupied by Catholics (see tables 4 and 5). In the absence of adequate data it is difficult to estimate the proportion of clericals to anticlericals in the lower echelons of the colonial service; all indications suggest that both factions were well represented. But in the upper echelons it would seem that the Catholics held sway for most of the time that Belgium ruled the Congo. There can be no doubt that this increased the influence and effectiveness of the Catholic missions. In the two decades between the wars the Catholic party controlled the Colonial Ministry almost continuously. There was only one significant break: the period of the Franck ministry (1918-1924). But even during these six and a half years the ministry tended to collaborate with the Catholics. In effect, for the entire two decades the Catholic missions wielded great influence in the

---

*In 1936 there were 18,683 whites in the Congo, of whom 12,654 were Belgian and 6,029 were foreigners; in that same year there were 3,200 missionaries: 2,475 Catholics and 725 Protestants ("Le Congo en 1936 d'après le rapport annuel aux chambres législatives," Congo 1: 181-182 and 205). By 1958 there were 113,671 non-Africans (including 1,582 Asians) in the Congo, of whom 24,758 were foreigners and 88,913 Belgians (Inforcongo, Belgian Congo, vol. 2, p. 13). Included in this calculation were 7,557 missionaries, of whom 5,904 were Catholics and 1,653 were Protestants (Ibid., p. 164). As of January 3, 1958, the total non-African work force was 46,441; of these 7,131 were missionaries, accounting for 15.4 percent of the total (Ibid., p. 13).

**The governor-general was appointed by the minister of colonies, usually from the ranks of the colonial service. Political considerations nearly always played an important part in such appointments.

TABLE 3

RELIGIOUS AND POLITICAL AFFILIATIONS OF GOVERNORS-GENERAL, 1908-1960

	Dates of Office	Religiopolitical Affiliation
Baron Theophile Wahis	1908-1912	Catholic
Félix Fuchs	1912-1916	Catholic
Eugène Henry	1916-1921	Catholic
Maurice Lippens	1921-1925	Anticlerical Liberal
Martin Rutten	1925-1927	Catholic
Auguste Tilkens	1927-1934	Catholic
Pierre Ryckmans	1934-1946	Catholic
Eugène Jungers	1946-1952	Nonaffiliated
Léon Pétillon	1952-1958	Catholic
Hendrik Cornelis	1958-1960	Socialist

SOURCE: Inforcongo, Belgian Congo, vol. 2, p. 35.

27

TABLE 4

KEY GOVERNMENT-GENERAL POSITIONS HELD BY CATHOLICS, EARLY 1950s

	Number of Positions	Number of Catholic Incumbents
Governor-general	1	1
Vice-governors-general	2	2
Secretary general	1	1
Provincial governors	6	4
Provincial commissioners	7	7
Chef de cabinet	1	1
Administrator of the Sûreté	2	2
Totals	20	18

SOURCE: Camille Huysmans, "La tribune de l'amicale socialiste au Congo, les rongeurs de la politique."

28

TABLE 5

JUDICIARY POSITIONS HELD BY CATHOLICS, EARLY 1950s

	Number of Positions	Number of Catholic Incumbents
President of the Court of Appeal	2	1
Counselor	5	4
Acting counselor	2	1
Prosecutor general	2	2
Deputy prosecutor general	3	3
President of the Court	7	7
Prosecutor	7	6
Judges and deputies	74	68
Totals	102	92

SOURCE: Camille Huysmans, "La tribune de l'amicale socialiste au Congo, les rongeurs de la politique."

29

Congo and could in most instances expect virtually unquestioning support from the Colonial Ministry in Belgium and the Colonial Administration in the Congo.*

Not until the late 1950s did the issue of colonial policy become a public concern in Belgium. For most of the colonial period the Congo was ignored in the métropole. Yet it played an indirect part in Belgian domestic concerns and politics. To some extent it served as a safety valve for Belgian social and economic conflicts; it helped, for example, to delay for some years the conflict between clericals and anticlericals over state-subsidized parochial schools in the métropole, thereby enabling the Catholic party to dominate colonial policy. In consequence, the Catholic missions, sure of the support on most issues of the Colonial Ministry in Brussels and the Government-General in the Congo, became a power to be reckoned with in the colony.

---

*Colonial administrators who were seen as hostile by the missions often found themselves transferred to other, less desirable, districts. (From interviews.)

CHAPTER 4

THE MISSIONS AND ADMINISTRATION POLICY, 1910-1927

The basic outlines and tenets of Belgian colonial policy, especially on
the vital question of political administration, were formulated during the
1920s and 1930s. In the debate concerning the various approaches and methods by which the people of the Congo were to be governed, the missions took
an active part. Perceiving that the outcome would directly affect their objectives and ambitions, they were not at all reluctant to enter the fray.

From the days of the Congo Free State on, the administration had replaced many African customary chiefs because they were either uncooperative
or had "abused" their powers. Many of the individuals appointed in their
stead had no customary right to the position, and tended to become mere ex-
tensions of the administration from which they derived their power and position.*

On May 2, 1910, the Belgian Government issued a decree which sought to
regulate the status and function of the chief.[1]** The decree recognized all
traditional chiefs as agents of the government. The first session (May 15-
June 1, 1911) of the Permanent Commission for the Protection of the Natives
reviewed the effects of this decree and came to the conclusion that "the
native chiefs, as we have known them, are deprived of authority and, with
rare exceptions, they are incapable of getting their subjects to carry out
the various responsibilities which have been imposed upon them."[2] The second session of the commission, which met at Banana from December 26, 1912,
to January 14, 1913, noted that the chiefs appointed to the chefferies*** were
not always chosen by custom, as called for in article 9 of the decree; that
in many cases the district commissioner appointed chiefs who were not recognized by the population over which they were placed. While conceding that

---

*Often former noncommissioned officers of the Force Publique or even
the faithful servants of whites were placed in chieftaincies (Antoine Rubbens,
"L'Evolution administrative et politique de la colonie," p. 507).

**This decree was also an attempt on the part of the Belgian adminis-
tration to lay to rest the criticisms which had been leveled at Léopold II's
Independent State. Ostensibly it was a recognition of traditional African
social structure and an attempt to preserve it, but in reality it enabled the
colonial government to tighten and formalize its control over traditional
authorities.

***Under the Decree of May 2, 1910, the chefferies and sous-chefferies
were the lowest administrative units in the Belgian colonial system.

31

there were occasions (as for instance when the customary chief led a revolt) when such a course of action was necessary, the commission on the whole was critical of the practice of government-appointed chiefs.[3] The commission, which was dominated by Catholic missionaries,* expressed its approval of the policy of retaining customary authorities (i.e., the chiefs) but clearly indicated that they should be closely supervised and that their powers should be limited by the state. The reason for this proviso was the fear that the chiefs might lead their people back to the old way of life which included practices, such as polygamy and trial by poison, that commission members found repugnant. The missionaries on the commission undoubtedly feared that any such development would make evangelization more difficult and might even lead to a loss of converts.

The attitude adopted by the missionaries, as expressed in commission reports, is especially interesting in light of the philosophy and methods of evangelization formulated by the missionaries after World War I, and the lack of solid criteria for their policy of cultural selectivity. The findings of the commission in regard to the Decree of May 2, 1910, point to the conclusion that the choice between "good" and "bad" institutions or customs was really a choice between those that aided and those that hindered the progress of evangelization. This criterion, whether consciously or unconsciously applied, was almost certainly in constant operation. This view appears to be amply supported by the position that Catholic mission spokesmen took in the 1920s and 1930s regarding administration policy.

Lippens and the Missions

During World War I the African campaign, economic problems, and isolation from Belgium had interrupted the movement in the Congo toward rationalization of administration and consolidation of rule. After the war, however, a new administration began to grapple with these problems once again.

From 1908 to 1918 the portfolio of minister of colonies had been in the hands of Jules Renkin, a member of the Catholic party. In 1918 a Liberal, Louis Franck, took over. The consequent shift in policy was notable. One of Franck's aims was to tighten up the administration so as to give greater control over policy to the Government-General in the Congo. This policy had its opponents. Prominent among them were those in charge of colon interests in Katanga. Desiring to shake off the domination of Boma (at that time still the capital of the Congo), they demanded autonomy for Katanga which had lost its semiautonomous status under a 1914 reorganization. Franck's campaign for greater administration control over colonial policy was attacked by Martin Rutten, acting governor-general, and Msgr. Jean de Hemptinne, apostolic

---

*The commission in 1911 included four Catholic clergymen, one Protestant clergyman, and two government officials: Msgr. Gabriel Grison, apostolic vicar of the Falls; Father Cambier, apostolic prefect of the Haut Kasai; Father De Cleene, Congregation of Scheut; Father Bankaert, apostolic prefect of the Kwango; Ross Philipp, BMS; E. J. M. Henri, royal high commissioner; and H. Weber, chief prosecutor of the Congo (L. Guebels, "Rélation complète des travaux de la Commission Premanente pour la Protection des Indigènes," p. 32).

vicar of Katanga. In 1920 de Hemptinne suggested that the Colonial Administration be unified in Brussels, in other words, that the Government-General
be moved from Boma to Brussels. His ostensible aim was to gain a greater
voice for Katangan interests in the métropole and, in his words, to "modify
the autocratic nature of the colonial government."[4] The bishop thus expressed the opinion of those who felt they had a personal stake in the colony—concessionary companies, colons, and missionaries—and those who wished
for a greater voice in the making of colonial policy and for less interference and regulation by the Colonial Administration. In this case de
Hemptinne was speaking more for a particular sectional interest than for the
Catholic missions as a whole.* There were, however, other missionaries who
felt that less interference from Boma would give them a freer hand in evangelization.

The following year de Hemptinne was to find increasing support among
Catholic missionaries due to a significant change in the administration. On
January 30, 1921, Maurice Lippens, a member of the aristocracy, a Liberal,
and a staunch anticlerical, became governor-general.

Ever since the 1910 decree there had been a constant trend toward the
establishment of larger, more integrated chefferies. In order to facilitate
administration, villages were often consolidated and moved to points along
the major arteries of communication. After the war Franck encouraged this
development. He was especially interested in the economic development of
the Congo, and saw in this method a means of increasing both administrative
control and economic benefits.[5] While paying proforma homage to the role
played by the missions, Franck was far from being pro-missionary. He was,
however, far off in Brussels; on the spot in the Congo the missionaries and
others were able to soften the impact of his attitudes and policies. With
Lippens' arrival on the scene the situation changed radically. In the domination by two Liberals of both the Colonial Administration and the Ministry
of Colonies the Catholic missions saw a threat to their interests.

Both during and after the war the Catholic missions had continued their
policy of establishing villages chrétiens which remained outside the jurisdiction of the customary chiefs in whose districts they were located (see
above, p. 14). Lippens, an admirer of Lord Lugard's concept of indirect
rule,[6] found the special status of these villages in conflict with his idea
of colonial administration. He therefore planned to bring them under the
control of the customary chiefs. At one point he even indicated that he
wished to maintain tribal government rather than Christian communities
which, in his view, tended to be a disintegrative social force.[7] He formalized his policy in two circulars, issued on January 25, 1922, and September
30, 1922, respectively.[8] The circulars ordered all native villages (this
included the Christian villages) to be placed under the authority of local
African chiefs. This was in line with his desire to institute a system of
indirect rule in the Congo. But to the Catholic missionaries it was a sign
of his anticlericalism. Lippens' suspiciousness and resentment of the

----

*The movement for Katangese autonomy, supported by colons, business in-
terests, missions, and members of the administration, had a long history.
Anyone studying the Katangese secession would do well to look back to the
colonial period in the Congo to find some of the roots of the problem.

missions was increased by what he considered to be their usurpation of civil authority and their interference in administrative matters. In his circular of January 25 he lashed out against them:

> I am sorry to note that some missionaries have the tendency to intervene in disputes between natives, or between Europeans and natives, disputes which are within the competence of the Administration or of the courts.
>
> I cannot tolerate any such deviations. Not only are they harmful to the prestige and authority of the European in general, but they are in flagrant contradiction to the role of the missionary....Furthermore, I have learned that certain missionaries have forced some village chiefs to accept the authority of catechists who, without any legal power, exert pressure on them by abusing the prestige of the missions; sometimes the catechists carry off children or adults despite the protests of chiefs and parents. They conduct them to the mission or else they transfer them, according to their interest or whim, to such and such a village, without bothering about parental ties or local customs.[9]

His second circular reemphasized his determination to place the Christian villages under the customary authority of the chief. The government, he stressed, would not allow another authority, in the form of the missions and their clients, to rival that of the state.[10] Lippens stated his case against the Catholic missions bluntly and openly. He was no doubt aware of the political strength and influence that the missions wielded both in the Congo and the metropole. Yet his circulars amounted to a declaration of war.

In the summer of 1922, he seized another opportunity to take a slap at the Catholic missions. In an interview given to the Protestants for publication in the Congo Mission News he said:

> Leaving out the religious question, I repeat that certain missions are good and well organized, and that others are less so, or are not at all well organized. We must make it our business to see that the members of the missions may be Belgian because up to the present the greater part of them are foreigners, chiefly Dutch.[11]

This last remark appears to have been a direct attack on the large Flemish contingent among the Catholic missionaries. There was in fact only a handful of Dutch missionaries among the Catholics (some were attached to the Mill Hill mission) and few, if any, among the Protestants. The term Dutch, however, is often used to describe literary or high Flemish. If the governor-general was using the term in this manner, nothing could have been better calculated to anger many Catholic missionaries. To call Flemish missionaries foreigners was to arouse all the bitterness and hatred that permeated the cultural-linguistic conflict of the metropole. To the missionaries Lippens was not only anticlerical but a fransquillon, an adamant supporter of the French language and culture and therefore antagonistic to Flemish. This attitude no doubt heightened the antagonism that already existed between the governor-general and the Catholic missions.

To the Catholics Lippens' attack on the Christian villages seemed to be in reality an attack on the position and function of the missions themselves and to threaten erosion of the power and prestige the missions had built on the foundation of mission-state cooperation. The missionaries interpreted the administration's actions as interference and responded quickly:

Now, as before, the organization of the missions cannot be subordinated to any restriction or impediment. If, therefore, they judge it advantageous to create fermes chapelles, écoles chapelles, and Christian villages, which the missions have the legal right to establish, [then] there is no one who can prevent them from doing so.[12]

The Catholic missions also defended their position in the Congo and their right to evangelize by pointing to the relevant articles of the Treaty of Berlin. Some missionaries must have been shocked to find that their position vis-à-vis the administration had changed so radically that they were now seeking support by appeal to a treaty. One Catholic bishop wrote that they were "painfully surprised" by Lippens' action, and warned that the policy of indirect rule that the governor-general had initiated would leave the Africans uncivilized and might even encourage a sense of nationalism among them.[13]

Other Catholic missionaries accused the administration of weakening the attack on polygamy by according it respect as an important customary institution, vital to the cohesion of the social structure of the tribe. One important member of the Catholic clergy in the Congo believed, however, that it was not the attack on polygamy that was weakening Congolese social institutions, but rather the forced labor that the Africans had to contribute away from their villages.[14]

Another accusation made by the missionaries was that the administration did not take sufficient account of the ways and customs of the Congolese when drafting new laws. According to Msgr. Roelens these were simply drawn up "a priori in some offices" without ever having been studied in the Congo. Not only did he regard the laws as unrealistic, that is, drawn up by an administration that was out of touch with the real problems in the bush, but he deemed the territorial administrators and the chiefs incapable of implementing the regulations originating in Brussels or Boma.[15] The clear implication was that the Catholic missionaries were far more capable than the administration of judging the needs of the Congolese, and that the policy of indirect rule rested on theories that were inapplicable to the Congo.*

The Catholics sought to weaken and isolate Lippens and Franck by opposing the latter's plan to give the governor-general greater power by further decentralization of the administration. They demanded that the Belgian parliament exercise tighter control over colonial affairs in the hope that this would limit and control the personal policies of the minister of colonies and the governor-general and neutralize the anticlerical element in the government. The campaign for decentralization failed in most of its objectives because those in Belgium who were interested in colonial affairs feared that such a policy might weaken the métropole's control over the Congo, and that

---

*A comparison of the number of administrative personnel as compared to Catholic missionary personnel in the Congo at this time attests to the deeper penetration of the missions. In 1921 there were 120 administrators in the Congo (45 more being on leave or in transit) and 315 territorial agents; this averaged out to 3 territorial agents for every 2 territories ("Centralisation et décentralisation," p. 727). The missions on the other hand had, in 1920, 791 missionaries and 8,000 catechists (Henri Anet, "Debate on the Congo Administration in the Belgian Senate," p. 12).

it endangered the cohesiveness they had been trying to establish in the colony.

In Belgium support for and opposition to Lippens' circulars followed party and proclerical or anticlerical lines. Lippens' opponents reiterated the charges made by the Catholic missionaries, while his supporters expressed suspicion of missionary power in the Congo. In a Senate debate on his policies the Socialist and Liberal points of view were clearly expressed:

> The Socialist Party has never said anything against the missions, but it will back up the Governor-General when it comes to secure the respect of the civil power against the enterprises of the religious power. [Senator Volckaert, Socialist]

> Are not the measures taken by Mr. Lippens justified by the plans of encroachment of the Roman Catholic missions on the authority of the State? ...The Congo Free State also had to resist the Roman Catholic missionaries. It could not grant them all that they demanded for what they wished to obtain was, as today, supremacy, a power outside any intervention of the civil authorities. [Senator De Bast, Liberal][16]

Meantime Franck sought to assuage the missions by falling back on a traditional approach to mission-state relations. He told the Belgian parliament: "If Europe has perhaps surpassed the era of religions by the immense progress of science, certainly Africa is still in the age of religions, and it is impossible to imagine a more efficient and powerful factor for the moral uplifting of the native than religious influence."[17] Franck held his portfolio as a member of a coalition government that included both Catholics and Liberals. It is, therefore, highly likely that he was willing to make concessions to the Catholic missions in order to prevent the issues at stake from developing into cause célèbre which might destroy the coalition and his ministry with it.

The major concession came in the form of Lippens' resignation early in 1923. There are indications that Franck, responding to Catholic pressure, withdrew his support from Lippens and passed over him when making decisions on colonial matters normally submitted to the governor-general for his comments and recommendations. An article in L'Avenir Colonial Belge (February 22, 1923) stated the writer's opinion that Lippens' resignation was due to the fact that Franck submitted recommendations direct to the Colonial Council, without the prior reference to the governor-general that had been agreed.

Catholic opposition to the administration had been centered for the most part on Lippens, although his policies appear to have had the support of the minister of colonies. Franck initiated an education commission to develop a new educational program for the Congo and named a number of Catholic clergy to it in order to deflect the attack from himself. The Catholics saw great possibilities for gaining almost complete control of education in the Congo and large government subsidies to boot. To have alienated Franck and the Liberal party at such a time would have been folly indeed. An article published in the Benedictine-controlled journal Bulletin des Missions seemed to point in this direction. The author denied that there was any concerted policy of hostility toward Catholic missions on the part of the Franck ministry. Such as did exist, he contended, were caused by the hostile attitude adopted by individual functionaries and agents.[18] Once Lippens was out of the way, it was no longer worthwhile to carry on the fight against Franck, especially in view of the Catholic missions' possible future role in a new educational scheme. The aim now was to convince the government that it was in its best interests to support the missions.

The Lippens administration was to prove only an interlude in the policy of administration-missionary cooperation. Other differences would arise later, but it was not until the 1950s that they again took on the deep antagonism that had been apparent in the years 1921-1923.

Debate Over Native Policy

Although Lippens' attempt to weaken missionary influence had failed and was followed by his resignation, the concept of indirect rule which he had fostered continued to find adherents in the Colonial Administration. Rutten, who succeeded him as governor-general,* speedily issued orders which either modified or reversed Lippens' controversial circulars: "The noncustomary villages [i.e., the Christian villages] established on government lands can be organized in autonomous groupings."[19] The order applied also to villages established around or near a mission station. If, however, such villages were established on the territory of a chefferie, they had to submit to the customary authority of the chief; they could continue to exist but could not claim exemption.[20]

Rutten's circular indicated other concessions to the missions. It ordered that the wife of a polygamous marriage could not be forced to return to her husband if she had run away and entered into a monogamous marriage (this often occurred in the case of wives converted to Christianity), but that she or her family would have to return the bride price. In addition, a chief could not prevent the erection of a mission or school unless the local administrator concurred. Rutten also rebuked those civil servants who did not allow missions to lodge children at their schools without the permission of their parents.[21] And he noted cases where catechists in charge of bush schools had been arrested without any information being given to the missionary to whom they were responsible, so that schools had been left unattended. This item was a warning to administrators that catechists should receive special treatment: if they were guilty of some dereliction, they should be allowed to continue their work until they could be replaced.

Rutten's circular restored the mission-state entente. But while it changed the policy of the administration in regard to the status of the Christian villages (about which the missions had been most concerned), it did not do away with the concept of indirect rule. Debate was to rage around this question for the remainder of the 1920s.

---

*Rutten had been a vice-governor-general when Lippens came to office. Late in 1921 he asked to be transferred from the central administration. Lippens complied, and he was named vice-governor-general of Katang ("Arrête Royal du 5 décembre 1921," in Belgian Congo, Gouvernement Général, Recueil mensuel des circulaires, instructions et ordres de service [Boma, 1922], p. 15).

CHAPTER 5

CATHOLIC AND PROTESTANT RIVALRY

Catholic Expansionism

The fierce rivalry that developed between Catholic and Protestant missionaries was almost inevitable in view of their militant characters and of the close cooperation that existed between the Catholic missions and the colonial government. The Catholics were at a decided advantage and tended toward aggressive methods and policies. The Protestants, especially sensitive to Belgian opinion after their role in the anti-Léopoldian campaign, were almost constantly seeking to reassure the authorities that they posed no threat to Belgian rule in the Congo and at times even became public defenders of certain Belgian colonial policies. Being for the most part dependent on the good graces of the colonial government and unable to apply much pressure to achieve their aims, they played a comparatively passive role in colonial politics.

After Belgium's annexation of the Congo in 1908 government pressure on the Protestants appeared to relax. The Protestant missionaries were impressed by Belgian efforts to correct many of the policies of Léopold II that had excited public criticism. In many areas, however, tensions between Catholic and Protestant missions continued. In 1912 the American Baptist Foreign Missionary Society (ABFMS) protested against Catholic attempts to keep them out of the Kwilu district, then part of the Kasai: "They claim the entire Kwilu as theirs, and are doing their best to bring influence to bear upon the authorities that permission for the [ABFMS] site may be refused."[1] The Disciples of Christ Mission in Equator Province complained in 1913 that the Catholic missionaries in its area were causing "many difficulties...continually taking boys by force in all the villages."[2] In 1915 the Baptist Missionary Society claimed that its steamer, the Grenfell, had been attacked by Catholic Africans at the instigation of a Roman Catholic priest.[3] Such reports of Catholic hostility toward Protestants were numerous, and in many cases the authorities were informed of them.

By the early 1930s the Protestants began to feel that Catholic pressure against them was mounting to such a degree that some feared their work might be undone or, at best, severely circumscribed. Their leaders decided to take action. The Congo Protestant Council (CPC) voted to appoint a committee "to investigate as fully as possible and record in written form, legally attested, if possible, as to content and signature, all evidence covering the troubles with Roman Catholics which recently have been experienced by the Protestants."[4] By October 1930 a dossier of twenty-six allegedly aggressive acts committed by Catholic missionaries was in the hands of this committee of inquiry.[5]

While the Protestants greeted the end of the Léopoldian epoch as an opportunity to gain fairer treatment from the government, the Catholics were intent on keeping alive Belgian suspicion of Protestant motives. The Protestant missionaries were portrayed as a threat not only to Catholic evangelization but to the entire Belgian colonial system. They were said to be jealous of Catholic success and determined to destroy "the colossal work of a small people."[6] Catholic critics believed that the Protestants encouraged a sense of independence and rebellion against authority that was a direct outcome of libre examen (individual interpretation of the scriptures). "Protestantism," wrote one Catholic prelate, "ordinarily has the effect of introducing a spirit of pride and independence, which renders access to grace extremely difficult. And, as one has seen in many countries, this spirit of independence, born of libre examen, has rapidly led primitive peoples to adopt a mentality of revolt against all authority, whether religious or political."[7]

Convinced of their right to spiritual hegemony in the Congo, the Catholics were increasingly annoyed by the mere presence, to say nothing of the expansion, of the Protestant missions. They looked upon them as intruders, usurpers, and corrupters of the African. The philosophical basis of Protestantism was regarded as a threat to the authority at once of the state and of the Catholic missions. The eruption of the prophet movements in the Congo during the 1920s and later (see below, chapter 13) tended to strengthen this point of view:

> Nobody will...conclude that the Protestant missionary deliberately incites the natives towards nationalist agitation, but it is evident to everybody that the thriving of Protestantism in mission countries is always accompanied by rising desires toward liberating independence. Whosoever exercises the...principle of private judgment, whosoever reads the history of all that was caused by the rejection in theory and practice of the doctrinal authority of the Church, is no longer astonished when he sees that weak-headed natives interpret Scriptures and traditions to fit in with their actual needs....Is it not characteristic that at the time of Kimbangu's arrest a Negro prophetess should have opened her Bible and shown a picture representing little David slaying the giant Goliath?[8]

The final objective of the Protestant missions in the Congo appeared to some Belgians to be the elimination of Belgian rule. An almost hysterical pitch was reached when one critic accused the Protestant missionaries of spreading the rumor that "the Americans are going to replace the Belgians" (a rumor which was current in the Congo, especially during World War II).[9]

Whether religious or nationalist in origin, the pressure on the Protestants was designed either to limit their expansion or to force them out of the colony. This was particularly true during the 1920s and 1930s. The pride of the Belgians was deeply hurt by the restraints placed upon them by the international treaties concerning the Congo. These treaties, although protecting the position of the Protestant missions, tended to give some Belgians the impression that the Protestants had forced their way into the Congo with the aid of Britain and the United States. As a result support for the Catholic missions grew stronger, even among many Belgians who were under most circumstances anticlerical. During the interwar period relations between the Catholic missions and the colonial authorities grew closer.

In recognition of the importance of the work of Catholic missions in the Congo the Sacred Congregation for the Propagation of the Faith in 1929 appointed Msgr. Giovanni Dellepiane apostolic delegate to the Congo (a post in which he was to serve from April 27, 1930, to February 21, 1949). Prior to his departure, Dellepiane sojourned in Belgium to hold meetings and discussions with church and government officials, finally arriving in Léopold-ville in April 1930. Although his office was exclusively religious in character and, unlike that of a papal nuncio, carried with it no diplomatic accreditation to the government, it was inevitable that the apostolic delegate to the Congo should become involved in questions of mission-state relations. His mere presence added weight and prestige to the position of the Catholic missions by affording them a better means of coordinating and centralizing their relations with the Colonial Administration. Over and above this, Dellepiane proved to be a skilled and vigorous advocate of the Catholic cause.

In 1951 the Comité Permanent des Ordinaires du Congo Belge et du Ruanda-Urundi was established. Prior to that, coordinated action by the Catholic missions had been limited to the plenary conferences of the Catholic bishops and the efforts of the apostolic delegate. Now this function was performed by the apostolic vicars, who were equivalent to bishops.*

The Protestants came to resent what they saw as the growing cooperation between the Catholics and the administration. They felt that many Catholic missionaries enjoyed more power and prestige than government officials. They noted that in one instance "a Belgian steamer docked at Matadi to be met by a military guard. Aboard the boat were the newly appointed Bishop, Albert Verwimp (Jesuit), and the Vice Governor-General and the Governor of the Province of Congo-Kasai. It was the Bishop who descended and reviewed the honor guard. The Vice Governor-General and Provincial Governor discreetly left the boat after the Bishop and the honor guard had departed."[10]

From the late 1920s onward the Protestants complained increasingly of unfair treatment by local administrators and other officials. In 1928 the colonial authorities "in various circulars...cautioned administrators about following a policy of religious neutrality. At times, a Catholic administrator has been known to exempt Catholic villagers from obligations to furnish laborers, and has punished native employees for following one religion and not another—practices warned against by the administration."[11] Despite these warnings administrators and others continued their acts of favoritism toward the Catholic missions, often to the detriment of the Protestants. The Belgian government contended that it was within its rights in

---

*"On questions of general interest it [i.e., the Permanent Committee] will have the responsibility of dealing with the government and its services" (Comité Permanent des Ordinaires du Congo Belge et du Ruanda-Urundi, "Statuts, 1951," article 3 [Archives of the Agence DIA (Documentation et Information Africaine)—hereafter cited as DIA]. The Permanent Committee was to be composed of nine members, including the apostolic delegate (president), the apostolic vicar of Ruanda-Urundi, and seven other members, representing other vicariates, elected by the plenary conference (Ibid.). It was to meet once a year in July; during the interim the president and the secretary would function as executives.

giving special attention to "national" (Catholic) missions in the Congo.*

The inequities that the Protestants experienced in consequence of the aggressiveness and power of the Catholic missions were not confined to one field. They underlay three other problems that tended to exacerbate relations between the Protestant missions and the government: the question of land grants and concessions to missions; the attitude of the large companies toward the Protestant missions; and the controversy surrounding medical subsidies.

Land Grants and Concessions

Protestant and Catholic missions in the Congo generally obtained land in one of three ways: (a) by outright purchase or lease from the Congolese—a procedure often followed in the days of the Independent State—or from the state; (b) by free grants from the government; or (c) through government concessions. The latter were usually of limited duration and sometimes entailed a small yearly rent. Under the Concordat of 1906 each Roman Catholic mission station was eligible for a grant of up to 200 hectares (494 acres). In 1942 Rev. H. Wakelin Coxill, who had succeeded Ross as secretary-general of the CPC, could rarely obtain from the authorities more than 25 hectares at any one time.[12] The Protestants also protested against the "thousands of hectares of land given [the Catholic missions] for diverse purposes, including the prospecting for minerals. Land was given to individuals who could then turn it over to the missions, circumventing the law."[13]

Most land grants and concessions had to be submitted for approval to the Colonial Council. Few, if any, requests for land, whether made by Catholic or Protestant missions, met with disapproval.** Almost invariably they had the support and vote of the missionary (Catholic) members of the council. It was in the interest of the Catholic missions to maintain a consistent policy in regard to land grants and concessions. To have adopted a hostile attitude toward the Protestants on this issue would have given those on the Colonial Council who opposed the Catholic missions a weapon which could be turned against Catholic requests for land. In 1948 Father Van Wing, the missionary representative on the Colonial Council, spoke out in support of a request by the American Presbyterian Congo Mission for a concession of 10 hectares in the territory of Luluabourg. Others on the council had raised doubts about the

---

*"The title national missions is accorded to those [missions] that have their central offices in Belgium, that are directed by Belgians and which have a certain number of Belgians among their missionaries in the Congo" (Oswald Liesenborghs, "L'Instruction publique des indigènes du Congo Belge," p. 248). The Belgians claimed the right to make the distinction between "national" (Catholic) and "foreign" (Protestant) missions by virtue of their interpretation of the various laws and treaties relating to the treatment of Christian missions in the Congo (see appendix A).

**This does not contradict Coxill's claim of discrimination against the Protestants (see above); the land grants approved by the Colonial Council had not been approved by the Government General and the Ministry of Colonies. Land grants to the Protestants could best be disapproved at that level and never reach the Colonial Council.

41

grant because it was from lands owned by Africans. Van Wing's support for the Protestant claim, which was finally granted, was significant, since he was a firm advocate of African land rights, especially when colonial or commercial interests tried to encroach upon them.[14] On another occasion Van Wing registered concern over a concession of land to the African Inland Mission (Protestant) because the mission was to pay for the deed rather than receive it gratis from the government. He expressed his fear that this might set a precedent and told the council "that similar grants had always been free. Is the case before us exceptional or is it an indication of a new policy?"[15]

Opposition to requests for land grants for the missions usually emanated from those members of the Colonial Council who represented Liberal, anticlerical, and colon factions; in the postwar era Senator Van der Linden was a council spokesman for these interests. He based his opposition to a request by the Scheutist Fathers for a grant of 100 hectares of free land on the fact that the Scheutists already possessed large tracts of land, having received 41,000 hectares of pasture lands by a convention signed on June 1, 1942. He decried the tendency of religious missions to enter the economic field in competition with private individuals or businesses, and observed that, given the advantages of free land, tax exemption, and so on available to the missions, individual businessmen found it hard to compete.[16] In the face of attacks of this kind in the Colonial Council, the Catholic missions were understandably more concerned to protect the basic principle of free land grants and concessions to the missions than to weaken the Protestants.

In general, both in number and size, government grants and concessions of land to the Catholic missions far exceeded those to the Protestants. The disparity is well illustrated by comparison of grants and concessions to two Catholic missions and two Protestant missions in the Lower Congo (see table 6). All four missions were important, but the Catholic missions were larger in terms of personnel and extent of penetration. Even so, the totals show a grossly disproportionate allotment of land to the Catholics. A similar disparity prevailed throughout the entire colony (see table 7).

The Large Companies

Protestant resentment was not confined to questions of equity in land grants but extended to the limitations and restrictions placed on their missions by the large concessionary companies in the colony. They believed that the Colonial Administration approved or acquiesced in these limitations, and concluded that the collaboration between the Catholic missions and the big companies, especially the Société Générale de Belgique, formed a "complete economic-religious monopoly over the whole of Congo, to which the nominal government of the Colony is humiliatingly subordinate instead of standing aloof as the impartial arbitrator in matters temporal and religious as it should."[17] Though perhaps exaggerated, this charge did contain a grain of truth. There can be no doubt that the large companies did collaborate with the Catholic missions and that the government acquiesced in this policy, to the detriment of the Protestants.

Msgr. de Hemptinne's view of the reason for the favoritism shown by the big firms toward the Catholics was bluntly stated in a newspaper interview:

TABLE 6

LAND GRANTS AND CONCESSIONS TO FOUR MISSIONS
IN THE LOWER CONGO, TO 1932
(in hectares*)

Catholic Missions		Protestant Missions	
	Grants and Concessions		Grants and Concessions
Jesuit[1]	37,208.18	ABFMS[3]	209.5
Scheutist[2]	16,066.00	BMS[4]	226.5
Total	53,274.18	Total	436.0

SOURCES: [1]T. Heyse, "Cessions et concessions foncières du Congo," Congo, June 1931, p. 523.

[2]T. Heyse, "Concessions du Mayumbe," Congo, May 1928, pp. 676-677 and 686.

[3]T. Heyse, "Cessions et concessions foncières," Congo, June 1932, pp. 500 and 504.

[44]Ibid., July 1933, pp. 183-188.

*One hectare = 2.47 acres.

TABLE 7

LAND GRANTS AND CONCESSIONS TO PROTESTANT AND
CATHOLIC MISSIONS, TO JANUARY 1937
(in hectares*)

Missions	Under Congo Independent State			Under Belgian Congo			
	Free Grants	Grants with Payment	Concessions	Free Grants	Grants with Payment	Concessions	Grand Totals
Catholic	14,425.44	–	3.00	33,716.46	7,997.00	61,380.00	117,521.90
Protestant	–	526.31	35.37	3,700.47	455.29	10.00	4,727.44
Totals	14,425.44	526.31	38.37	37,416.93	8,452.29	61,390.00	122,249.34

SOURCE: "Noted Without Comment," CMN, July 1939.

*One hectare = 2.47 acres.

NOTE: By 1958 Catholic and Protestant missions together owned 227,409 acres of land and held concessions on 267,614 acres, for a total of 495,023 acres under mission auspices (Inforcongo, Belgian Congo, vol. 2, p. 64).

Protestantism gnaws at the principle of authority wherever it can. With Belgian money principles are spread which will end by undermining the authority of the Belgians in the Congo. That is certainly one of the greatest mistakes which can be committed at this time. The big companies, on the other hand, understand that Catholicism represents a stable factor, and it is to us they have given the responsibility for education.[18]

The education of Congolese children residing in company compounds was for the most part put in the hands of the Catholic missions, and restrictions were placed on Protestant evangelization, worship, and meetings on company property. In 1934 the CPC voiced its "concern that some mining and agricultural companies still prohibit native Protestant evangelists and other workers from carrying on their work in the compounds of the companies."[19] Two major companies, the Union Minière du Haut Katanga (UMHK) and the Huileries du Congo Belge (Unilever) (HCB), were specifically mentioned in the charges. As far back as the late 1920s UMHK had adopted a policy of close cooperation with the Catholic missions in southern Katanga. The dynamic presence of Msgr. de Hemptinne at Elisabethville spurred this collaboration, and the schools on UMHK compounds were staffed by Catholic missionaries. In 1930 the Protestants in Elisabethville protested that "the regulations of the Union Minière governing their compounds and camps for Natives likewise exclude either [Protestant] missionaries or Natives from holding any public meetings within the same. Likewise, there was a previous ruling which forbade...[the Protestants from] having schools and chapels in their compounds which are really Native cities."[20] This policy seems to have been implemented with the knowledge and approval of the administration. At one point the Protestants received a communication from the Governor of Katanga stating "that new regulations had been agreed upon by the Union Minière and the Government...to the effect that chapels could not be built within the 500 meter limits" of UMHK compounds.[21]

For the Protestant missions the policy of the HCB in granting Catholic control of education within its compounds while excluding Protestant missionaries and their catechists from working in them was an even greater blow than the action of UMHK. The Protestants had hoped that Lever, being a British firm, would adopt a more favorable policy toward them. Disappointed in this hope, they objected to their treatment by the HCB, stigmatizing its policy as "one of the most flagrant and clear-cut denials of religious liberty."[22] They rejected the idea of a complaint to the Commission for the Protection of the Natives because it was dominated by Catholic missionaries, and decided to "make as strong a representation as possible to the directorship of the HCB...in order that at their posts Protestant missions may not hereafter be denied permission to build chapels and place pastors for shepherding of the Protestant adherents and inquirers laboring at such posts."[23] Emory Ross met with the British (Protestant) vice-chairman of Lever Brothers in London, who told him that "he and his directors were satisfied with the situation as it is and that therefore it seemed to him we [the Protestants] might have the grace not to trouble them further about the matter."[24]

The collaboration of the large mining and agricultural companies in the Congo with the Roman Catholic missions merely signified their recognition of the special position and power that these missions enjoyed. The companies well knew that the Catholics had close communication and influence with the governments in Brussels and Léopoldville and were generally favored by them; from their point of view, it would have been foolish and possibly disruptive to their operations to provoke the ire of the Catholics. Some large firms were known to be sympathetic to the Catholics in principle, but the companies' primary concern was not a religious one. They were, for the most part, simply yielding to the facts of life in the Belgian Congo.

Medical Subsidies

The early missionary, whether Catholic or Protestant, tended to have a limited conception of his role: he had come to preach and convert. But experience and force of circumstance were to make him realize that his involvement with the African and his world went farther and deeper than the single dimension of religion. To reach the African, the missionary found that he had to be concerned with his entire life experience, both secular and divine. Unlike the missionary, the African did not make a neat dichotomy between the two. He expected, indeed demanded, that the missionary be concerned with his earthly as well as his spiritual needs. Although some missionaries deplored it, the missions almost inevitably were drawn into providing social services, especially medical care, for the African population.

The missionaries who came to the Congo in the latter half of the nineteenth century carried with them a pharmacopoeia which, though limited, was far more effective than that available to the Africans. Consequently they were sought out to treat the many physical ills that plagued the local population. The saving of souls would have to be accompanied by the saving of bodies. Although initially unprepared for and in some cases reluctant to deal with these demands, they quickly recognized the need for establishing some ongoing medical care for the Africans. Essentially, the motivating factors behind this undertaking were: the humanitarian spirit of the West which placed a high value on the preservation of human life, and the efficacy of medical and social services as an aid to evangelization. An added stimulus was provided by missionary involvement in the antislavery campaign.

The Protestants were the first to recognize the need for medical missionaries to carry out this work. At the First World Missionary Conference, held in Edinburgh in 1910, the medical missionaries' importance for evangelization was explicitly stated: "They break down barriers; they attract reluctant and suspicious populations; they open whole regions; they capture entire villages and tribes; they give a practical demonstration of the spirit of Christianity."[25]

The Catholic missions in the Congo became increasingly uneasy about the success of Protestant medical work. A Jesuit missionary suggested that the Catholics establish an "institut missionnaire universitaire international" to turn out Roman Catholic missionaries with medical training, to counterbalance the large number of Protestant medical missionaries whom he regarded as the most effective tool of Protestant evangelization.[26]

The realization that it would be many years before the Congo would have enough doctors and other trained medical personnel to take care of its needs led the government and the missions to the conclusion that adequate medical services could only be provided with the help of trained Congolese. As early as 1917 the governor-general had issued an order for the establishment of a professional school for nurses at Boma; other schools were later established at Coquilhatville (1920), Stanleyville (1921), and Bata (1921).[27] In 1935 the government established a school for the training of assistants médicaux indigènes. These medical assistants were to be more than nurses: they were to act as auxiliaries to physicians and in some cases were to have full responsibility for the treatment of minor ills and the administration of vaccinations and injections.*

Until the mid-1920s the medical activities of the Catholic missions had been desultory. Then, however, the success of Protestant work in this area and the evidence of the ravages wrought by sleeping sickness and other endemic diseases impelled them to greater and more direct efforts. A leading spirit was Father Pierre Charles, a well-known Belgian Catholic theoretician on missions. Encouraged by him and supported by Msgr. Ladeuze, rector of the University of Louvain, a group of professors at the university established the Fondation Médicale de l'Université de Louvain au Congo (FOMULAC) to train Congolese nurses and medical assistants to help the doctors in the colonial service and missions. Aided by a gift of 100,000 francs, FOMULAC officially came into being on January 16, 1926.[28]

It was decided that the foundation would establish its first hospital and school at Kisantu, the important Jesuit mission in the Kwango. It was opened in 1928, and another was later built at Katana in the Kivu.[29] The founders of FOMULAC had foreseen the possibility of the eventual training of Congolese doctors in the Congo. Reaction against this idea by some Belgians in colonial circles was strong, and the foundation sought to reassure them that it envisioned no revolution in the social or political patterns of the colony. Its governing council denied charges that it intended to train Congolese doctors, although it spoke of Kisantu becoming a university for Africans "in the next century."[30] In 1935 FOMULAC decided to create a school for Congolese medical assistants at Kisantu, and the state decided to open one at Léopoldville that same year. Apart from the Catholic seminaries, these became the most advanced schools open to Africans in the Congo. In answer to criticisms directed at these schools by some colonials the directors of the foundation stated their beliefs in the necessity of advanced training for Congolese. Their objective was the formation of an indigenous Christian elite that could lead its people peacefully along the path to "civilization."[31]

Having emanated from the University of Louvain, FOMULAC was imbued with a Catholic outlook. It reflected the progressive philosophy of respected

---

*The stress in the Congo was on epidemiology and preventive medicine. At the core of the system lay the recensement (literally, census or counting). A doctor, an agent sanitaire (a European hired by the government and given some training in tropical medicine and attached to the Services d'Hygiène), or an assistant médical indigène would be given a specified geographical area to cover. He would be expected to visit every village in the area, seeing as large a number of the population as possible. Tests would be given for sleeping sickness, malaria, etc., and medication and vaccinations administered. Those in need of more extensive or continued care would be directed to the nearest hospital or dispensary. The system was quite effective, and the control of epidemic diseases striking. It was one of the greatest achievements of Belgian rule in the Congo.

Catholic laymen and was a spur to missionary thinking and policy. It warned the Catholic missions that, while an African clergy was necessary, the formation of a Congolese lay elite could not and should not be neglected: "It is not enough merely to have black priests. The ranks of the leaders of native society must be filled by the best elements. It is incumbent upon the missions to contribute to the formation of this indigenous elite."[32]

While closely tied to the Catholic missions, FOMULAC also cooperated with the state. On December 23, 1938, the government and the foundation signed a convention under which the latter undertook full responsibility for the medical organization in Kisantu and Katana, the two areas where it had established facilities. The state on its side agreed to pay the foundation an annual subsidy sufficient to cover about two-thirds of its operation expenses.[33] Following the tradition established by the Catholic missions in the Congo, FOMULAC formed an entente with the state. But it stressed the formation of an African elite, and therein lay its great significance. It represented the active participation of Catholic laymen in the Congo, and it was their actions that eventually helped to impel the missions and the administration to reconsideration of their educational and political policies.

Other quasi-missionary and quasi-governmental organizations were established to deal with social problems. As a complement to FOMULAC, a group of professors at the University of Louvain founded the Centre Agronomique de l'Université de Louvain au Congo (CADULAC). An agricultural school was established at Kisantu under the direction of the Brothers of Our Lady of Lourdes-Oostacker. While agricultural training was stressed, the school also offered postprimary education (école moyenne).[34] CADULAC opened additional centers at Dibaya (Haut Kasai) and Bunia (Lac Albert). Two other organizations aided Catholic medical and social work in the Congo: L'Aide Médicale aux Missions Catholiques and the Association Universitaire Catholique d'Aide aux Missions. The first was mainly concerned with the recruitment of doctors and auxiliary personnel, and the equipping of hospitals and other medical installations; the second was a general fund-raising and lobbying organization, interested in aiding all aspects of missionary work in the Congo.

The missions, both Catholic and Protestant, were also supported by two quasi-governmental organizations: the Fonds Reine Elisabeth pour l'Assistance Médicale aux Indigènes (FOREAMI) and the Fonds du Bien-Etre Indigène (FBEI). FOREAMI, founded in 1931 by the state and aided by a large gift from Queen Elisabeth, was intended to aid the regions most ravaged by disease. The FBEI, established in 1947, in effect made restitution to the Congolese for the funds contributed by the Congo to the Allied war effort and for the expenses of the Belgian Government-in-exile.* Part of its funds went to aid Catholic and Protestant hospitals and dispensaries; organizations such as FOREAMI and FOMULAC also benefited.[35]

---

*The Belgian Treasury allocated 1,780 million francs; in addition, 100 million francs was given as a gift by the prince regent, and 220 million francs was contributed by the Colonial Lottery. From its gross capital of 2,100 million francs, the FBEI derived an annual revenue of about 320 million francs per annum, to be used in its various philanthropic works; of this, about one-third was allocated for medical work (Inforcongo, Belgian Congo, vol. 1, p. 429).

The FBEI was criticized for being used in such a way as to be of special benefit to the Catholic missions. In a speech in the Belgian House of Representatives M. Janssens was critical of the way in which the FBEI was being handled; he noted that some in the Congo called it Le Fonds du Bien-Etre des Missions.[36] The Protestant missions would no doubt have concurred in this appelation, since they felt that they were not receiving a fair share of the money allocated to the missions by the FBEI—or indeed from any governmental source insofar as medical work was concerned.

In 1931 a medical missionary of the BMS complained that, in spite of the pioneering medical work done by Protestant missions in the Congo, Catholic medical efforts organized in the mid-1920s were receiving far more aid from the government:

> Public money is now used to pay twelve...[civil] doctors attached to the Catholic missions [at] a salary of frs. 95,000 each per annum, plus passages for wife and family, and they are furnished with the same camping and medical equipment as a state doctor and allowed generous credits at the provincial pharmacies.[37]

He noted that many of the medical personnel hired by the Catholic missions were not "nationals," (see above, p. 41 fn.) but either French or Italian.[38] At a meeting of the Commission for the Protection of the Natives, of which he was a member, he again complained of the inequitable treatment of Protestant medical work by the government. The commission, which included five Roman Catholic bishops, declared itself "incompetent to intervene."[39]

In a memorandum addressed to the minister of colonies in 1933, Emory Ross, secretary general of the CPC, attacked the government's policy of favoring Catholic medical work in the Congo, often to the detriment of the Protestant missions and their Congolese adherents. He accused the Catholic missions of being more strongly motivated by a desire to check "Protestant medical work [than] caring for the Natives."[40] He felt that the government was abdicating its responsibility by subsidizing Catholic medical work while exerting little or no control over it. He implied that those in the Belgian Colonial Office who made and carried out policy were pro-Catholic and thus only too willing to let the missions have their way, and suggested that this attitude had been instrumental in getting the state to assume the financial responsibility for doctors sent to the Congo by the Aide Médicale aux Missions Catholiques.* He complained that while the Protestants provided 50 out of a total 250 doctors in the Congo (165 were in the service of the state, 15 belonged to the Catholic missions, and 20 were otherwise employed or in private practice), they received only about 1 percent of the total medical budget (between 600,000 and 700,000 francs out of a total of 76,000,000 francs).

Ross also attacked the Catholic missions on the grounds that their planning of medical facilities was "guided more by confessional considerations

---

*He believed that the Catholic missions "did not even go to the Vatican; they went no farther than Place Royale [Belgian Colonial Office], where they found friendly ears. These listened so well that the plan presented by Bishop Devos was adopted by the Colonial Department." On May 28, 1925, was founded the society L'Aide Médicale aux Missions Catholiques in the Belgian Congo (Memo. to minister of colonies, Léopoldville, Feb. 14, 1933, p. 3 [Archives of the Congo Protestant Council, Kinshasa—hereafter cited as CPC-KIN]).

than by the medical needs of the Colony." In particular, he accused FOMULAC of being guilty on this score. The Bas Congo, he pointed out, was medically "well provided for" by comparison with other regions of the Congo. Four Protestant medical centers were located there in addition to the medical facilities of various companies in the area; there were also twenty doctors in Léopoldville. Why then had this region been chosen instead of the Kwango, for example, which suffered from a lack of medical facilities? He found the answer in the wish of the Jesuits "to combat the influence acquired in this region...by the Protestant medical work."[41] It seemed to Ross that the government by favoring the Catholics was subordinating the welfare of the Congolese to sectarian concerns.* He demanded that the Ministry of Colonies revert to an impartial policy that would take into account the welfare of the Africans and the treaties to which Belgium was a party.[42]

The Catholic and Protestant missions were attracted to medical work by reason of the demands of the Africans, their own humanitarianism, and the realization that it provided one of the most effective and unobtrusive methods of evangelization. The government was more than willing to encourage and aid the missions in their efforts to provide the Congolese with the more adequate medical care that accorded with both its paternalistic and its economic aims.

Cooperation between the Catholic missions and the government was characteristic of Belgian colonial policy and was advantageous to both parties. Catholic domination of the Colonial Administration was no doubt a primary factor in the state's decision to favor the Catholic missions with regard to grants of land, support of evangelization, establishment of medical missions, and the encouragement of the large companies to exclude the Protestants from their compounds. But other factors, too, underlay this decision. Chief among these were a strong feeling of national pride and an almost phobic fear of foreign designs on the Congo. The American and British Protestant missionaries seemed to them to represent such designs, while the "national" (Catholic) missions could be counted on to aid and re-enforce Belgian Colonial policies. Catholic missions were considered a reliable instrument of social control. No such confidence could be placed in the Protestant missions. The medical commitment of the missions also afforded the government some welcome relief from its financial burden and forged another link in the entente between the state and the Catholic missions. During the thirty-year period 1924-1954 the bonds forged by mutual interest remained strong. During

---

*"Medicine and hygiene constitute a public service. As such, they ought to be at the disposition of the public without religious distinctions. To act otherwise is an injustice toward the Natives, all of whom being under the guardianship of Belgium, have the right to an equal participation in the benefits provided by the Government in the field of public welfare and hygiene in the Colony. Now, we know that often the Catholic missions, even with their subsidies provided by the State, refuse to receive Protestant patients on account of their faith" (Ibid., p. 7). Unfortunately, some of this attitude can still be found in the Congo. The author was told in 1964 by one physician, working for a large mission in the Lower Congo, that serious cases were often brought long distances from areas where mission hospitals of another faith were close at hand. In many such cases the life of the patient was jeopardized.

these years the Catholics were for the most part among the staunchest defenders of the colonial system. They were, indeed, in a very active sense
an integral part of that system. At the local level they sometimes appeared
to exert more administrative authority than did official members of the administration.

The power the Catholic missions wielded and their close collaboration
with the state continued to exacerbate their relations with the Protestant
missions. The latter felt that, in view of their commitment and efforts,
they had been shabbily treated. Moreover they firmly believed that the
state had consciously adopted a discriminatory policy toward them, and that
the favoritism shown Catholic medical undertakings was only one facet of a
conspiracy to force the Protestant missions out of the Congo. Thus the
Catholic-Protestant conflict grew keener.

CHAPTER 6

THE MISSIONS AND EDUCATIONAL POLICY, 1908-1925

Until 1954 the Catholic and Protestant missions between them exercised a virtual monopoly over education in the Congo. The reasons for that monopoly and the way in which it was obtained indicate the power of the Catholic missions over certain aspects of Belgian colonial policy.

Early Mission-State Cooperation

It was natural for the Catholic and Protestant missions to establish schools for the Congolese. Reading and writing were considered necessary to enable potential converts and catechists to learn the basic tenets of the faith. The Bible and the catechism had to be taught in some organized fashion. In addition, the Léopoldian regime had encouraged the missions to establish schools that would train Congolese in basic skills, so that they could replace Senegalese and other non-Congolese Africans who were employed by the Independent State and various commercial firms. In some cases the fermes chapelles became the training ground for recruits for the Force Publique.* The missions' emphasis on education and their involvement with the state in this field were to have profound effects both on the Congolese and on mission-state relations throughout the colonial period and beyond.

The Concordat of 1906 between the Independent State and the Vatican had provided that the Catholic missions would set up schools for the Congolese, called for small subsidies to the missions for education, and granted land for school buildings. As the period of exploration and pioneering drew to a close and the missions began to devote more attention to education, they became increasingly aware that, if they were to establish a viable system of education, they needed greater government support.

The Protestants were ambivalent on the whole question of government-mission cooperation in education. The separation of church and state was a cardinal principle for their missionaries, especially those from Great

---

*"It had been agreed between the Independent State and the Jesuits that four-fifths of the young blacks brought up at Kimuenza (a Jesuit mission near Léopoldville) would later be incorporated into the native army; the other one-fifth would serve the Fathers as catechists, and, following a Christian marriage, would form the core of the mission" (E. Laveille, L'Evangile au centre de l'Afrique, p. 121).

Britain (who were all from nonconformist churches) and the United States; and it was with some difficulty that they readjusted their ideas when it came to education in a colonial setting. At their World Missionary Conference in 1910, however, the Protestants recognized the need to reassess basic principles: "It is the manifest course of wisdom for the Christian forces of any country to enter into cooperation with the Government system of education, in so far as such cooperation does not involve sacrifice of Christian principle, or the end for which Christian education is carried on."[1]

The "ends" of Christian education also were in process of reinterpretation. Early missionaries had confined themselves almost entirely to basic literacy and Bible training, but those who came later began to recognize the need for a broader approach that would encompass the needs of the larger community and "not merely...the Church."[2] This recognition brought with it the realization that while the missions were the gainers from the government presence in such matters as security, economic benefits, and improved communications, the government on its side derived certain benefits from the missions, for example, the promotion of industries, establishment of schools, literacy and scientific activity and philanthropy."[3]

The Baptist Missionary Society at Bololo, the American Presbyterians at Luebo, and some other Protestant missions established industrial training programs at an early date.* But a number of missionaries remained unconvinced of the need for training Africans beyond an elementary level. When the establishment of a United Training College for the Upper Congo was proposed,** one missionary attacked it on the grounds "that for the most part even our best and most advanced native teachers and evangelists could not fully appreciate and digest the subjects dealt with in a college curriculum... Why then cast our pearls of knowledge and instruction away in sheer wastage?"[4] Some missionaries feared that education without conversion would result in the "ruination" of the African: "the effect of advanced education beyond the normal mental development of the people without conversion to steady it, is entirely to upset the balance."[5]

For the Catholic missions in the Congo the question of the separation of church and state had little relevance. To them the function of education was a duty and responsibility of the Church. Father Charles noted that "the Church will teach in mission lands, just as she will administer the sacraments, because it is her proper function, and, in the strict sense of the word, her monopoly."[6] And in view of the considerable Protestant presence in the Congo, schools became more important to the Catholic missions and played a more vital role than normally in proselytization.[7] The result was a drive, soon after World War I, for a state-supported school system, to be operated

---

*During 1920 the Protestant-sponsored Phelps-Stokes commission carried out an extensive study of education in Africa, including the Congo. It called for reforms in order to bring better education to larger numbers of Africans. Its findings appear to have influenced those who drafted the new educational program for the Congo during 1922-1924 (Thomas Jesse Jones, ed., Education in Africa, p. xvi).

**This was not to be a college in the American sense, but rather an advanced training center for African pastors and teachers.

and largely controlled by the Catholic missions.*

It was at this juncture that Pius XI, "the Missionary Pope," ascended the papal throne in 1922. As indicated in his Encyclical Reppresentanti in Terra, issued on December 31, 1929, Pius XI realized the importance of education in the fulfillment of the Church's mission and expected the state to assist.**

Agitation for State-Subsidized Education

Concomitantly with the renewed missionary militancy of the Vatican Belgium experienced a resurgence of nationalism which tended, at least for a few years, to mute the deep dissensions inherent in Belgian society. At the same time there was a growing recognition of the need for an expanded and "national" educational policy for the Congo. It was during this period of national reconciliation that the Catholic missionaries and their supporters

---

*During the period 1922-1923 there were approximately 1,771 Protestant primary schools, with a student population of 50,860. This was with only 9 out of 18 of the missions reporting, but it included the largest and the most important missionary societies ("Enquiry on the Missionary Education System in Congo Belge," p. 20). During 1921 the Catholic missions in Congo reported 1,806 primary schools, with a student population of 45,656. Also reported, but unclassified, were 279 schools, with a student population of 13,898. It was noted that in reality the number of students was much greater than the 59,554 reported (Alfred Corman, ed., Annuaire des missions catholiques au Congo Belge, p. 199).

**"And first of all education belongs pre-eminently to the Church, by reason of a double title in the supernatural order, conferred exclusively upon her by God Himself; absolutely superior therefore to any other title in the natural order....

Again it is the inalienable right as well as the indispensable duty of the Church to watch over the entire education of her children, in all institutions, public or private, not merely in regard to the religious instruction there given, but in regard to every other branch of learning and every regulation in so far as religion and morality are concerned....

In general, then, it is the right and duty of the State to protect, according to the rules of right reason and faith, the moral and religious education of youth, by removing public impediments that stand in the way.

In the first place it pertains to the State, in view of the common good, to promote in various ways the education and instruction of youth. It should begin by encouraging and assisting of its own accord, the initiative and activity of the Church and the family, whose successes in this field have been clearly demonstrated by history and experience. It should, moreover, supplement their souls whenever this falls short of what is necessary, even by means of its own schools and institutions. For the State more than any other society is provided with the means put at its disposal for the needs of all, and it is only right that it use these means to the advantage of those who have contributed them" (Anne Fremantle, ed., The Papal Encyclicals in Their Historical Context, pp. 225-227).

led the drive for a new educational program that would tie the state to the Catholic mission schools. In their fight for state subsidization of their schools in the Congo they utilized arguments that appealed to both the fears and the national pride of the Belgians.

Writing in the semi-official journal *Congo*, Edmond De Jonghe, a militant Catholic layman who was later to become chief of the education section of the Ministry of Colonies, called upon the Belgians at home to take their colonial responsibilities seriously: "A *métropole* that would not, to some degree, have the ambition to impart to its colony her national imprint, to lead it toward participation in the benefits of its civilization would not be worthy to have colonies." In order to give the Congo this "national imprint" it was necessary to institute an educational system that would be truly national in character, and this, he contended, could best be done by the Catholic missions in collaboration with the state.[8] In the same vein Paul Coppens, a leading political figure in Belgium, argued that the philosophical and religious differences prevalent in Belgium should not be transferred to the Congo in the guise of a struggle between advocates of religious and secular education. By giving the Catholic missions control of education the missionaries could "render precious services to the territorial authorities."[9]

The appeal to national pride and responsibility was often of a negative character. Spokesmen for the Catholic missions realized that interest in the colony did not run high in Belgium, and that appeals to the nation's obligations and duties to the Congolese would fall on deaf ears if pitched solely on the level of national glorification. Accordingly, they played on the fears and anxieties of the people and the political leaders. They resuscitated the bogey of foreign designs on the Congo; they appealed to religious prejudice; they portrayed the attack on Belgian sovereignty in the Congo as not only antigovernment but anti-Catholic as well: "The adversaries of Catholic evangelization are...at the same time the opponents of the Belgian Government and of Belgium; they are the Protestant missions and schools."[10]

While granting that the Protestant missions may have had good intentions, Catholic mission spokesmen pointed out that their efforts would have ethical, economic, and political effects that would be difficult to control. Here was a conscious attempt to identify the Catholic missions with the government and to make a neat dichotomy between Catholic-Belgian and Protestant-foreign. The Protestant missions were pictured as the agents of rich foreign powers with whose unlimited resources the Catholic missions found it difficult to compete. Meanwhile the Catholics, it was claimed, had prepared the groundwork "by the sweat of their brows and at the price of their blood," only to see it fall into the hands of foreigners.[11] In the Belgian Senate, Msgr. Keesen intimated that the Protestant missions in Africa received large subsidies from their governments in order to gain political influence for their own countries.[12] There was, however, no evidence to sustain the charges that Protestant missions in the Congo were receiving such subsidies, nor is it likely that they were. In view of the relations between American and British nonconformist religious organizations and their respective governments, such support would have been surprising and contrary to general policy.

The allegation that the Catholic missions were hard pressed by Protestant competition is difficult to believe in light of the figures available for missionary activity during that period. By 1920, the Catholic missions were beginning to outstrip the Protestant by a wide margin. They had more than twice the number of Protestant missionaries in the field, and more than 375,000 converts—more than seven times the reported Protestant total. In addition, they had approximately 25 percent more central mission posts (see table 8). In the area of education, however, Catholics and Protestants seemed about equal. In general, the charge of Catholic polemicists that the Catholic missions in the Congo were being overwhelmed by the Protestants seems to have been purposely exaggerated and distorted in order to gain support in Belgium for the idea of state subsidies for Catholic mission schools.

A major plank in this campaign against the Protestant missions was the suggestion that collaboration between the Catholic missions and the government would be to the advantage of both and generally in the national interest. This position was clearly taken by De Jonghe. In outlining how such an educational program might function he urged that subsidies be given to the Catholic missions for running the schools and for inspecting them. The inspection service should be organized in accordance with ecclesiastical boundaries and be staffed by missionary-inspectors. In addition, he demanded that only schools that used the national languages (French and Flemish) be allowed to open.[13] Thus, while promoting a subsidized school system as being in the national interest, his proposals were so designed as to give the Catholic missions the maximum possible benefit: the missions were to run the program and at the same time be self-policing; and, since few Protestant missionaries at that time could have taught in French, the government was to prevent the opening and, perhaps, force the closing of Protestant mission schools.

In 1923 the Katangan subcommission of the Permanent Commission for the Protection of the Natives came out in support of De Jonghe. Noting the vast differences in instruction and quality of education, it called for a uniform program of education, under government control and inspection, and conducted with the collaboration of the Catholic missions.[14] The missions, it was implied, could do the job better and more cheaply. The question of costs was an important consideration for the Belgian Government. The métropole did not contribute to the colonial budget, and the establishment of an entirely secular system of education would have put an unbearable strain on colonial finances. Moreover it would have been difficult for the government at that time to find a sufficient number of secular European teachers to staff state schools. A government-subsidized, mission-run educational system was therefore appealing. It offered a ready-made system, with established physical plants and trained staffs, which was also willing to bear a substantial percentage of the costs. The inability or unwillingness of the Belgian Government to pay for a secular school system, combined with the knowledge that public opinion would not have supported such an investment, gave the Catholic missions an advantage which they clearly recognized.

The Catholic missions succeeded in their campaign. By exploiting feelings of pride, fear, and hostility they gained the support or acquiescence of many who might otherwise have opposed them. Their understanding of the sociopolitical tensions and pressures within Belgium contributed considerably to the success of their campaign.

New Educational Policy: Catholic Domination

Action on the establishment of an official educational program for the

TABLE 8

CATHOLIC AND PROTESTANT MISSIONS, CIRCA 1920

	Catholic	Protestant
Missionary Societies	24[1]	18[2]
Missionary Personnel	857[3]	392[3]
Mission Stations	125[3]	96[3]
Converts	376,980[4]	50,604[2]

SOURCES: [1]Alfred Corman, ed., _Annuaire des missions catholiques au Congo Belge_, pp. 7-8.

[2]"Protestant Missions in the Congo: Summary of Statistics for 1919."

[3]"Le rapport annuel pour 1920," _Congo_, April 1922, p. 568.

[4]Corman, _Annuaire des missions catholiques_, chart between pp. 200 and 201.

Congo finally came on July 10, 1922, when Louis Franck, then minister of colonies, appointed a commission, presided over by himself, to work out a plan. The commission consisted of eleven men representing various governmental and colonial interests. Among the appointees were two Catholic priests and two Brothers. No Protestant missionaries were included.[15] This loading of the commission almost guaranteed a report partial to the Catholic missions. This favoring of the Catholic missions on the question of education was largely attributable to the facts that Franck was a Liberal minister in a Catholic-Liberal coalition, and that his ministry was then under attack by many Catholic missionaries and their supporters because of what they felt to be the anticlerical policies of Governor-General Lippens.

In 1924 the Commission on Education reported its proposed program: Projet d'organisation de l'enseignement libre au Congo Belge avec le concours des sociétés des missions nationales. During 1925 and 1926 individual "national" missions and the Belgian Government signed conventions (known as the Conventions De Jonghe) under which the missions accepted the government program, thus obtaining the right to educational subsidies provided under the plan. But the government published no clear and official elaboration of the program until 1929, when the famous brochure jaune appeared.[16] The official publication clearly stated that "the schools organized in the Congo in accordance with the prescribed program...and serviced by the national Missionary Societies [would] have the right to subsidies."[17] Only subsidized schools could award diplomas and certificates that would be recognized by the government. The inspection of these schools was to be carried out by missionary inspectors: "The subsidized schools will be the direct responsibility of the missionary-inspector and the deputy inspectors named by the missionary societies."* What this amounted to was a system of self-policing; the missions would run and inspect their own schools.[18] Under the cloak of an unenforceable control the government had abdicated its power to the missions. It was extremely doubtful that a missionary-inspector would report a mission-subsidized school as not fulfilling the requirements of the program. The most that could be hoped for was that he would bring pressure on the mission to correct any fault.

After the initiation of the state program the educational subsidies paid to the missions grew, both absolutely and proportionally (see table 9). During 1925, the first year of the program, they were almost five times greater than during 1924. Subsidies grew rapidly until 1928, after which they increased only gradually, except during the depression years of the mid-thirties. Under the state program the missions received a much higher proportion of the total educational budget than previously: in 1924 approximately 7 percent, in 1925 approximately 21 percent, and in 1929 approximately 47 percent.** The Catholic missions were also the direct beneficiaries of that

----

*If the missionary-inspector and his deputies were not priests (which was seldom, if ever, the case), they had to have "a diploma of normal or higher education" (Ministères des Colonies, Organisation de l'enseignement libre au Congo Belge et au Ruanda-Urundi avec le concours des sociétés des missions nationales, p. 45) not required of missionaries. Missionaries directing or teaching in a subsidized school were also not required to have special training or degrees. As late as 1940 one observer noted that most of the Roman

TABLE 9

"ORDINARY" BUDGET EXPENSES FOR EDUCATION, 1912-1939
(in Belgian francs)

	Total Budget	Cultes[a]	Education Budget	Educational Subsidies to Missions	Per-cent-age[b]
1912	47,104,785	600,000	402,300	50,000	0.85
1914	51,936,000	783,860	593,750	31,000	1.14
1915	51,936,000	783,860	593,750	31,000	1.14
1916	54,755,912	783,860	562,770	31,000	1.03
1917	59,570,727	780,555	594,201	31,000	0.99
1918	64,988,327	793,600	848,500	31,000	1.30
1919	48,838,350	867,100	996,570	72,150	2.05
1920	60,553,874	887,100	1,297,880	72,500	2.12
1921	82,118,525	1,071,100	1,729,680	115,000	2.11
1922	83,365,935	2,063,800	1,925,213	115,000	2.30
1923	88,011,250	2,083,600	2,144,513	145,000	2.44
1924	166,234,290	2,117,000	3,432,700	220,000	2.05
1925	212,361,502	2,477,000	4,957,100	1,052,300	2.33
1926	273,294,990	2,127,192	8,597,798	3,843,508	3.10
1928	521,241,955	2,198,692	17,002,509	7,285,908	3.22
1929	574,810,492	2,622,942	18,949,881	8,963,166	3.29
1930	690,383,121	3,962,692	25,024,802	9,463,166	3.62
1931	704,640,078	3,962,692	23,879,043	9,663,166	3.36
1932	624,113,303	3,555,500	21,248,794	9,184,500	3.40
1933	725,757,940	3,555,500	19,431,493	9,184,500	2.67
1934	723,428,763	2,547,400	16,889,281	8,392,998	2.36
1935	685,503,116	2,862,000	15,971,635	8,488,375	2.33
1936	677,729,364	3,239,500	16,698,092	9,354,700	2.47
1937	665,487,207	3,474,500	18,847,722	10,268,700	2.83
1938	766,981,000	3,767,500	20,410,200	12,244,400	2.70
1939	729,364,500	3,798,500	22,310,300	13,200,000	3.06

SOURCE: Oswald Liesenborghs, "L'Instruction publique des indigènes du Congo Belge," p. 266.

[a]Subsidies to missions for activities other than education.

[b]Education expenses as compared to total expenses.

Catholic missionaries who taught in mission schools had no prior training in pedagogy (Oswald Liesenborghs, "L'Instruction publique des indigènes du Congo Belge," pp. 254-255).

**Between 1928 and 1934 it was slightly less than 50 percent; between 1935 and 1939 it climbed above 50 percent.

portion of the educational budget that was not earmarked for subsidies. A part of the budget went to finance the écoles congréganistes. These were state rather than mission schools and thus were entirely financed by the government. Practically all were run by Catholic orders under contract with the state. From this arrangement the Catholics derived minimal financial return, but de facto control over these institutions. State schools for European children in the colony were also controlled and staffed by the Catholic missions.

Thus under the expanded program of education during the interwar years the Catholic missions obtained almost exclusive control of official (state) education in the Congo. At the same time they became more closely linked than ever to the state through the system of subsidies (see table 9).*

Responsible as they now were for the education of the Congolese attending state-authorized schools, the Catholic missions were faced with the need to reconcile their obligations to the state and to the Church. They solved this dilemma by denying its existence; for them there were no conflicts. The primacy of religious and spiritual training was accepted almost without question. The object of education was to turn out Christian Africans. Success or failure was to be judged in those terms. In his report to the first plenary conference of Catholic bishops Msgr. Auguste De Clerq, apostolic vicar of Haut Kasai, speaking of directives issued for the organization of normal schools, stated: "The aim of this school is to form apostle-teachers, fellow-workers of the priest."[19] The Catholic missionaries hoped to recapture the ideal which they felt had become all but impossible of achievement in the Western world. The materialistic and rationalist values that dominated Western civilization, though not entirely rejected, were to be subordinated to spiritual values.

Education was to conform to the view of society held by the missions. The quality of instruction, though not deemed unimportant, was not the primary concern. One Catholic bishop directed teaching Sisters in the Congo "never to sacrifice moral and religious training in order to obtain good results in terms of instruction in their schools."[20] Religious and spiritual training, it was implied, would of itself make the Congolese productive members of a Christian society. This philosophy now applied in a wide range of schools, from bush schools, where religion often dominated the curriculum, to the official technical schools, where it constituted only a small part of the program. But in all schools run by missionaries, whether Catholic or Protestant, religion could not but permeate the atmosphere; by their very presence and example the missionaries taught religion, and it would have been impossible to separate their religious function from their teaching function.

Catholic Control of Non-State Schools

It was natural for the Catholic missions, with their view of the

------

*Not all schools, however, run by the Catholic missions were subsidized. Many of the rural bush schools could not meet the demands of the prescribed program and thus received no state aid. It was reported that in 1938 there were 18,110 such schools (Catholic and Protestant) with 498,832 students (Liesenborghs, "L'Instruction publique," p. 250).

paramount necessity of religious training, to seek monopolistic control of education. This of course included control of schools erected by industrial concerns.

The Decree of May 2, 1910, permitted the chefferies to erect schools and either to ask the missionaries to service them or to employ teachers appointed by themselves. In the latter case they were free to choose whomever they wished. The Catholics, as well as the Protestants, sought to gain control over the écoles de chefferies (which were at the primary or preprimary level). That the Catholics waged an active campaign here is obvious from the report of the apostolic delegate, Msgr. Dellepiane, that a convention had been concluded between himself and the governor of Oriental Province by which Catholic missionaries would take over the schools of the "chefferies and of the sectors."[21]

The schools operated by the large industrial and agricultural firms active in the Congo had a small attendance when compared with the mission-run schools,* but they were nonetheless important. Their students were drawn from the most modernized section of the population. The Congolese who worked for the large companies, especially those centered in or near urban areas, were most susceptible to change. As a potential elite, they attracted the special interest of the missions. The companies in their turn wished to establish schools that would train Congolese to meet the needs of industry. For economic as well as political reasons they tended to ask the Catholic missions to educate the Congolese within the company compounds. Their schools did not receive state subsidies, and they recognized that it would be uneconomical to undertake the operation themselves. To do so would have involved hiring European teachers and the problems and costs of such things as recruitment, transportation, family allotments, and housing, to say nothing of the uncertainty of contract renewal. The missions, on the other hand, would be faced with few of these costs and problems and would thus be able to provide staff and administrators for the company schools at much less expense.

The missions took over responsibility for running the company schools and received subsidies from the companies for their services. This arrangement satisfied both parties—the Catholic missions because it further extended their control over education, and the companies because it made it possible for them to achieve their educational goals economically. Political considerations also played their part in the companies' decision to seek aid from the Catholic missions. They were not unaware of the favored position the Catholics enjoyed vis-à-vis the administration in the Congo and the government in the métropole. They were doubtless also influenced by the institution in 1925-1926 of the government educational program in which only the missions nationales were eligible to participate.

The Union Minière du Haut Katanga (UMHK) affords an excellent example of this arrangement. The Union's educational aim was clear and definite: "the development of advanced technical training."[22] Schools financed by the company were expected to turn out technicians. A close relationship had early been established between UMHK and the Benedictine Mission in Katanga. In 1920

---

*In 1958 there were 410 "private schools" (most of which were company schools) as compared to 20,580 mission schools, subsidized and unsubsidized (Inforcongo, Belgian Congo, vol. 2, p. 147).

UMHK built a brick chapel for the Benedictines at Panda. At the same time it ceded to the government land for a school for the children of its white employees. The government gave the school to the Benedictines to run.[23] The mission was quite aware of the company's educational desires and was prepared to fulfill them, as is apparent from a statement by Msgr. de Hemptinne: "A well-chosen elite will be drawn from among the young workers for a more complete education, primary training [and] vocational training which will place useful elements at the disposal of the various divisions of Union Minière."[24] It is apparent that de Hemptinne also recognized the company's desire for social control that would make for labor peace and block agitation among the African workers. He assured the company that "this elite would in no way be oriented in a Utopian direction, toward an objective which surpasses its capabilities."[25]

Companies in other parts of the Congo adopted similar policies. In the Kwango region Lever Brothers called upon the Jesuits to establish schools on their plantations, and in the Kivu Symetain turned their schools over to the Marist Brothers and the Chanoines du Latran.[26] By the early 1930s the Catholic missions were well on their way toward a monopoly of education in the Congo, except for one major roadblock—the Protestant missions.

CHAPTER 7

THE PROTESTANT FIGHT FOR EDUCATIONAL SUBSIDIES

Rationale and Effects of Exclusion

From the time the educational policy of the government was instituted in 1925-1926 the Protestant schools began to decline in importance both in substance and in the eyes of the Congolese. This indeed was one of the aims of that policy; the administration and the Catholic missions alike were determined to limit the influence of the Protestant missions. Why allow foreigners to inculcate their nefarious doctrines into the minds of the Congolese? The Belgians considered the mere presence of the Protestant missions proof of a tolerant and magnanimous policy, since the colony was courting danger from their "subversive" activities. It was on occasion freely admitted that "our educational policy limits foreign influence—that is clear and desired. It must be unambiguously stated. If the foreigners intend to benefit from the toleration accorded them, then that's fine, but on condition that they respect the rules of the game."[1]

The Protestants, however, chose not to play the game by the rules. They recognized that acceptance of or acquiescence in the government's policy would at once weaken their position vis-à-vis the Catholics and relegate graduates of Protestant schools to an inferior status and restrict their opportunities.[2] Because, aside from the few state schools, only the Catholic schools could issue certificates officially sanctioned by the colonial government, it was often difficult for graduates of Protestant schools to get employment, despite the fact that their education might have been in no way inferior.*

The Congolese were quick to become aware of the advantages of attending the state-recognized Catholic schools. The facilities and standards of these subsidized schools were usually superior to those of the Protestant schools, and the pupils they trained had far better prospects for economic and social advancement. The favored position enjoyed by subsidized Catholic schools no doubt led to an increase in the number of converts to Catholicism. Although

---

*"Pupils from Catholic schools secure the vast bulk of government positions and are given preferment in advancement. It is frequently made plain to Protestant employees that their temporal interests lie in changing to Catholicism. A case has just been reported where the government official involved is said to have actually threatened to discharge a Protestant employee unless he became a Catholic" (Emory Ross, "The Roman Catholic Situation in Congo Belge," Léopoldville, Apr. 21, 1931, p. 14 [CPC-KIN]).

many children who entered Catholic schools were pagan and a few were Protestant, the constant religious indoctrination and social pressures to which they were subjected often resulted in their conversion. The Catholic missions exploited their advantage by frequently capitalizing on the prevailing impression that all Roman Catholic schools were state schools (in fact, many did not qualify for subsidies) and by implying that therefore all children must attend them (which was not true). In some instances, it was charged, there was collusion between the Catholics and officials who fostered this illusion. Speaking of this, Emory Ross noted:

> Not infrequently the statement is made [that Congolese children must attend Catholic schools] to assemblies of Natives in the very presence of officials, when uncontradicted, it naturally goes as any official pronouncement; and sometimes government officials themselves are so worked upon by the Catholic priests that they personally make such lawless statements, both verbally and in writing, to Natives under their rule.[3]

Thus in the minds of the Congolese the Roman Catholic missions came to be increasingly identified with the Colonial Administration.

Children beginning their education were not the only ones attracted to Catholic schools. The opportunity for secondary or technical training in a Protestant school being almost nil, many graduates from Protestant primary institutions who were interested in further education were forced to turn to Catholic-operated schools. The Protestant missionaries strongly resented the fact that nearly all state vocational institutions were in the hands of the Catholics, and believed that this often resulted in the coercive conversion of Congolese Protestants attending these schools.*

To the Protestants the almost exclusive Catholic control of official education in the Congo seemed to threaten the erosion of their work and position. They recognized that the fight to obtain educational subsidies from the government would be long and perhaps even unsuccessful, but they were determined to make the attempt. At various times they suggested the establishment of secular schools in the Congo as an alternative to government-subsidized education. Convinced that it was unfair that no public provision had been made for the education of Protestants outside the Roman Catholic system, they suggested that "a neutral national system as obtained in Belgium and the French colonies would go far to remove this disability."[4] And being in principle in favor of the separation of church and state, they would have preferred a secular system of education. It was also apparent that adoption of a secular system would have broken the monopoly of the Catholic missions. To the Catholics and to their political supporters in the Ministry of Colonies such a solution was abhorrent and counter to their basic principles.

------

*In 1928 a missionary, writing in the Congo Mission News, complained of this: "Wherever representatives of the Government have gone into the village schools, and practically insisted on taking some of our brightest pupils to attend the industrial schools in Elisabethville, the boys have been refused the privilege of attending services at our church or of coming into contact with our missionaries, with the result that after some years of rigid exclusive Roman Catholic environment they have eventually joined the Church. Several of the government officials have spoken of this with regret, but are unable to change the situation" ("Notes and Comments," p. 3).

Protests to the Colonial Government

As the problems and consequences arising from the colonial government's policy of favoring the "national" missions' monopoly of education became more apparent, the Protestants were moved to seek redress. By the early 1930s they were evincing a growing interest in obtaining government educational subsidies. The difficulties that they were experiencing as a result of the severe economic depression then prevailing provided an additional incentive. Dr. J. H. Oldham, who was negotiating with the Ministry of Colonies on their behalf, believed that educational subsidies were the key to equitable treatment of the Protestant missions.[5] The Protestants contended that they should have been eligible for the same benefits as the Catholics under the various international treaties which obliged Belgium to "protect and favor all Christian missions without distinction of nationality." They also charged that the granting of school subsidies had been so handled by the pro-Catholic Ministry of Colonies as to prevent any parliamentary discussion of the matter.[6]

Protestant missionaries were convinced that both legally and morally the colonial government's educational policy was wrong. It was, in their opinion, prejudicial to the interests not only of the Protestant missions but also of the Protestant and non-Catholic Congolese. A respected and well-known Belgian who agreed with them was Anton Marzorati (see above, p. 19). Noting that the government's policies tended to benefit "the Catholic native," he questioned the honesty of the government's claim of secularity and impartiality.[7] Maurice Lippens, the anticlerical former minister of colonies, also became an active advocate of the Protestant cause and attacked the inequity of the government's educational policies.[8]

In rejecting the Protestant protests the minister of colonies contended that the Catholic missions received subsidies as a legal right under the Concordat of 1906 between Belgium and the Holy See. He intimated that the government owed the Catholic missions subsidies as a moral obligation.[9] At the same time he informed the Protestants that they could now receive copies of the official educational program and the interpretative instructions. But while throwing crumbs to the Protestants, he conceded very little on the question of educational policy. The colonial government with its pro-Catholic orientation was not prepared to grant equality to the Protestant missions or to their followers.

Change of Official Policy

It was not until the closing years of World War II that the Belgian Government, then in exile, decided to alter its educational policies toward the Protestant missions. In May 1944 Governor-General Pierre Ryckmans called Rev. Coxill to his office and assured him "that the Prime Minister would recommend that a change be made as soon as possible after the War."[10]

The Protestants were elated about the intended change in policy but fearful about its application. In a letter to Robert Godding Emory Ross (now secretary of the African Committee of the National Council of Churches) expressed his concern whether the new policy would be implemented at every level of the Colonial Administration, especially in view of the fact that the persons responsible for its implementation had for some twenty years assiduously maintained the other policy. To avoid possible charges, especially by later Catholic governments, that the change in policy had been brought about solely as a result of Protestant, British, or American pressures, Ross urged Godding to publicly stress the fact that this was a "national decision of the Belgian Government taken on its own initiative and responsibility."[11] On February 23, 1946, the minister of colonies responded. The Belgian Government, he said, had decided "to place all the Christian missions in the colony on the same level, and with equal guarantees, regarding the granting of state subsidies in education, as well as other areas."[12]

The fight for educational and religious equality for the Protestant missions and their Congolese followers was largely won. It had been a long struggle and one to which much energy had had to be devoted. Above all it had forced the Protestants to examine, to some degree at least, the political, economic, and social problems of the Congolese. As adversaries of the government's policies, they had become advocates for the Congolese. Once the battle was won, however, they tended to withdraw from these problems and conflicts. In the crucial postwar years, when they might have provided some stimulus for social and political change, they became passive followers of Belgian colonial policies.

As for the Catholics, after nearly a quarter of a century their monopoly over educational subsidies was broken. The loss did not greatly diminish their political power and importance. It did, however, indicate to some of them that they could not always rely on their influence with the authorities to determine the course of events, and that in the future they might have to stake out a course independent of the government.

CHAPTER 8

THE MISSIONS AND HIGHER EDUCATION

The Belgians made education the key to advancement for Congolese in the
colonial system. Yet until the end of World War II they restricted access to
advanced education to the small percentage of primary-school pupils who were
allowed to go on to technical (vocational) schools. The state, the large companies, and the missions saw little need for education beyond these schools,
which were sufficient for their purposes. In general the Belgian plan was to
develop education for the Congolese from the ground up: primary education was
stressed; only after primary education had become widespread would it be possible to develop secondary-school and, later, university education.

Looking back on the prewar era Father Guy Mosmans, one of the more astute
and insightful Catholic missionaries in the Congo, noted that the general
tendency among missionaries was to regard the lay elite with great reserve:
"Let us proceed slowly; without a sudden evolution that would result in an
elite out of contact with the masses."[1] Prior to World War II the only ave-
nues to secondary and higher education open to Congolese were the technical
schools and the petits and grands séminaires operated by the Catholic missions
for the formation of an African clergy.

Pressure for Reform

This narrow, utilitarian view of education dominated missionary and
colonial thinking between the two wars. Even so, a few voices were raised to
express the hope and desire that higher academic education would be opened to
the Congolese. In 1928 a Jesuit priest called for the establishment of secondary schools which would lead to university education for Congolese.[2] Noting that the only secondary schools for Africans were the petits séminaires,
he observed that too many Congolese children who had little or no knowledge
of what the priesthood entailed were pushed into these schools. As a result
many withdrew or were expelled, with consequent loss of face; others who went
through seminary education but did not go on to become priests often became
déclassés, embittered because they found closed to them many positions calling
for the training which they had acquired. In this way much talent that could
have been directed to other vocations and areas was wasted. When establishing
their schools for nurses and agricultural assistants at Kisantu, the promoters
of FOMULAC and CADULAC (see above, pp. 46-51) seem to have had in mind the
provision of secondary and university education for the Congolese. But before
World War II the administrators of these foundations, fearing that the hostility of the colons and the administration would force the curtailment of their

efforts, soft-pedalled the idea that they might be aiming at higher education for the Congolese.[3]

The effects of the war on the Congo and the Congolese shook colonial society to its roots and put to a test the widely held preconception of the infinite patience and docility of the African. The pressures and demands made on the Congolese as a result of the war, added to the increased migration from rural to urban areas, had culminated in a Congolese prise de conscience. This new awareness elevated the goals of the people and led the évolués* to make two basic demands: recognition of their special status; and better educational and employment opportunities. By the end of the war the demand for better educational opportunities was attracting attention. The administration and the colons were, however, still reluctant to incorporate in the educational program the important changes needed to equip it for university training. This attitude was shared by many missionaries who found the Congolese demands excessive and too radical for their liking. Their failure to give support lost them the confidence of the évolués, who looked upon them with suspicion.[4]

In Belgium Father Van Wing became a leading advocate on the Colonial Council of the extension of secondary and university education to Congolese. He spoke of the discontent to be found among the évolués, of their inferior status vis-à-vis the whites, and of the abuses that they had to suffer. He cited the need for schools of higher education for Congolese outside the seminaries. In an attempt to make his readers aware of the strength and depth of these feelings among the Congolese, he asserted that the war and the rise of Congolese to the priesthood had made the évolués conscious of their own capabilities and strengths.[5] Pierre Ryckmans, writing in the Catholic journal L'Aucam soon after he stepped down from the post of governor-general, concurred with Van Wing and urged that, especially in view of the wartime sacrifices of the Congolese, the time had come to open the doors of secondary and higher education to them.[6]

At the third plenary conference of Catholic bishops, held in 1945—the last one had been in 1936—one bishop expressed dissatisfaction with the educational system then in effect on the ground that it allowed and even promoted waste of talent. He observed that many of the young people graduated from mission primary schools "were dissatisfied because they were blocked in an impasse." Only between 5 and 10 percent could hope to get into middle schools, while the remaining 90 percent languished.[7]

The growth of urban areas sparked by wartime conditions continued in the postwar era. The flow of population from rural areas caused consternation among both administration officials and missionaries. Many of those who migrated from the bush were young people who had been given a schooling oriented toward producing an enlightened peasantry. Equipped with a primary education which included agricultural training, they were to have formed the framework for a new, rurally based Congolese society. Contrary to expectations but understandably, a large percentage of these people were drawn to urban centers. One Catholic bishop, citing the school statistics for the missions in his

---

*Clerks in government service or commercial firms, nurses and medical assistants, teachers, priests, seminarians and former seminarians, businessmen, and others. In general, white-collar or semiprofessional status was the mark of this new elite; manual laborers and houseboys, although part of the new urban proletariat, tended to be excluded.

jurisdiction, noted that "of 500 children who finished primary school, about 100 are admitted to middle school, about 50 find employment in the region, [and] a number return to their villages, but at least 250 go to the large [urban] centers."[8] Once settled in the urban centers, these half-educated people who had little but muscle power to contribute to the labor market aggravated unemployment and the other problems that followed on the heels of the war.

Msgr. Dellepiane, aware of the growing pressures, spoke of the need to press for the establishment of secondary and superior education for the Congolese: "If the Catholic missions hesitated then they would destroy any possibility that the Catholic religion and Church might have had, to act upon and to influence the elite of African society."[9] If the missions did not meet the aspirations of the people, he implied, they were bound to lose ground.

It was against this background of change and conflict that the plans for the establishment of a university in the Congo were laid.

The Founding of Lovanium University

In 1948 the colonial government instituted a reorganization of the educational program in the Congo, directed toward the opening of higher education to the Congolese. The two principal innovations were: a distinction between education for the mass and education for the elite; and, in education for the elite, a distinction between technical training and higher, or academic, education. To launch its new program the state decided to subsidize five Catholic secondary schools (or colleges) in the humanities: Mbanza-Boma in the Bas Congo and Kiniati in the Kwango (both run by the Jesuits), Kamponde in the Kasai (run by the Scheutists), Dungu in Uele (run by the Dominicans), and Mugeri in the Kivu (run by the White Fathers). The most important of these was that of Mbanza-Boma, which had originally been located at Lemfu near Kisantu.

In 1947 Paul Brasseur, provincial commissioner at Bukavu and an alumnus of the University of Louvain, had pointed to the need for a university in the Congo. He had proposed that the advanced educational program already in existence at Kisantu be expanded into a university for Congolese.[10] The idea of creating the prototype of a university in the form of an école supérieure des sciences administratives had been the brainchild of Professor Guy Malengreau of the University of Louvain. The project was promoted by FOMULAC and the Jesuits, Kisantu being chosen as the site for the school. Subsidies were sought from the state, but the very idea of such a school was greeted with hostility by government officials,[11] and the request was turned down. Consequently funds were drawn from FOMULAC and CADULAC to finance it. The École des Sciences Administratives à Kisantu (EAK) became a reality in 1947. Its program was somewhat comparable to that of the colonial school at Antwerp which trained lesser Belgian colonial administrators.* Its aim was also similar: to train a cadre of persons—in this case of Congolese—who would be

---

*It was of four years' duration and included courses in law, economics, sociology, administrative techniques, etc. (The author is grateful to Father W. De Craemer, S J, director, Centre des Recherches Sociologiques in Kinshasa, for this information.)

69

qualified to take up posts in the Colonial Administration.

FOMULAC and the Jesuits succeeded in establishing EAK despite opposition from the administration and the Ministry of Colonies. But they failed to achieve their final goal. Owing to administration hostility EAK graduates were given only minor posts which were in no way commensurate with the level of training they had received. They were not allowed to exercise any authority over whites.[12] In 1956 Minister of Colonies Auguste Buisseret forced the closing of EAK on the grounds that the training of Congolese for administrative positions should be a state monopoly. Rather than reduce the level of the EAK program to that of a secondary school, the Jesuits chose to shut down the institution.*

During its short existence (1947-1956) EAK left an indelible mark on the future of Congolese politics. Among the thirty-four students that it graduated (seven of whom were from Ruanda-Urundi) between 1951 and 1956 were Justin Bomboko, Joseph Nzeza, Godefroid Munongo, and Theodore Idzumbuir.** Most of its graduates have at one time or another held positions of importance in the Congolese government.

Opposition to Lovanium

EAK and the schools at Kisantu for agricultural assistants and medical assistants were regarded by the directors of FOMULAC as the embryo of a future university for Congolese. In 1947 it was decided to name the Kisantu complex incorporating these three schools the Centre Universitaire Congolais Lovanium (CUCL).

The administration greeted this move toward the establishment of a university in the Congo with hostility. It refused to permit distribution of a circular produced by FOMULAC in 1947 on the subject of the creation of a Congolese university and signed by such notables as Msgr. Honoré Van Waeyenbergh, rector magnifique of the University of Louvain, Pierre Ryckmans, and F. Malengreau, father of Professor Guy Malengreau.[13] Nor were the leaders of the Parti Social Chrétien (PSC)—the new name adopted by the Catholic party at the close of World War II—prepared to give public support to the idea of a university; they feared that to do so might arouse the ire of the opposition. In January 1948, when Guy Malengreau, the secretary treasurer of the new CUCL, met with Pierre Wigny, the Catholic minister of colonies, to discuss the question of government support, he was angered by what he considered to be the minister's lack of understanding. He even went so far "as to threaten the

---

*EAK, by 1956, had been weakened by the split between the Jesuits and FOMULAC over the question of Lovanium University. The Ministry of Colonies, aware of the conflict, had used it as a lever to reduce the level of the EAK program (Report on talks held in Brussels July 4-12 and 23-24 between minister of colonies and representative of Permanent Committee, Léopoldville, n.d. [Archives of the Bureau de l'Enseignement Catholique, Kinshasa—hereafter cited as BEC]).

**Later to be, respectively, a minister of foreign affairs; a chargé d'affaires, a minister plenipotentiary, Washington, D.C.; a minister in Tshombe's cabinet; and an ambassador to the United Nations.

minister that he would appeal to international authorities if the Colonial Government remained obstinate in refusing to promote education in the Congo up to the university level."[14]*

The whites in the colony were also strongly against the FOMULAC proposals. They feared that a Congolese university would place the system of colonial domination in jeopardy. They were willing to see Congolese trained as agronomists or doctors, but were "strongly against the idea of training Congolese to assume political responsibilities."[15] Thus they were greatly disturbed by the establishment of the administrative school at Kisantu.

Despite strong opposition pressure the directors of CUCL pressed on with their determination to build a university of high standards in the Congo. At the same time they tried to allay the fears of those who saw in it a seedbed of revolutionaries. A CUCL brochure noted that such agitators tended to be semi-intellectuals whose superficial training led them to engage in political action. "Only a university [trained] elite," it claimed, "...could check and suppress the prestige that has been usurped by certain évolués."[16]

When it became evident to the opponents of a university for the Congolese that the démarche of CUCL had set a firm course, the Liberal and anticlerical press launched a campaign in the Congo and Belgium against the idea of establishing a university under Catholic auspices. The Catholics were accused of hypocrisy in their attitude toward higher education for the Congolese, of wishing to extend this education only to those able to attend a Catholic-dominated institution in the Congo. In Léopoldville, the newspaper L'Avenir fired a broadside at the Catholic missions for their opposition to sending Congolese to study at metropolitan universities. This reluctance, it was said, was due mainly to the missionaries' fears that the students would escape from their influence and authority, to be contaminated by the secular and humanistic doctrines prevalent in Belgium and thus lost to the Church.[17]

These fears were acknowledged in the Catholic press. In Brussels La Métropole declared that throwing open the doors of "Godless schools" to Congolese would lead them to radicalism, which would endanger the position not only of the missions in the Congo but of the Belgians as well.[18] This view was supported by La Libre Belgique which warned "that one should keep in mind the secular education given in Indo-China and Indonesia, an education not tempered by a religion that has respect for the principle of hierarchical authority."[19] On the other hand some Catholics deplored the tendency among many missionaries to keep tight rein on African converts by quarantining them from the pernicious influences of the métropole. Father Mosmans warned them that, while "one can understand why the missions sometimes hesitate to send their students to the métropole, where they risk being lost, these are the risks to run. Yet it is understandable that the missionary should seek first...to protect his Christians from external contamination and to keep them in a vase clos, in a kind of Catholic ghetto."[20] Such an attitude, he noted, would in the long run work against the success of the missions.

The missions were not, however, entirely free to send their students to study abroad, even if they so desired. Many in the Colonial Administration

---

*Father Van Wing was also present.

and the Ministry of Colonies opposed such a policy and generally refused to issue visas to such students. It was only with difficulty that a handful of Congolese were allowed to go to Belgian universities during the late 1950s. In one instance Father Van Wing, while on a visit to the Congo in 1957, obtained a promise from Governor-General Léon Pétillon that ten Congolese students would be allowed to attend the Ecole Sociale at the University of Louvain. The Ministry of Colonies, on hearing of the arrangement, balked at the idea and refused to issue the necessary visas; under pressure, however, the ministry relented, and the visas were forthcoming.[21]*

Once it was clear that the establishment of Lovanium was moving inexorably forward,** the colonial critics returned to the old arguments. The Congo, they maintained, was not yet ready for a university. As late as 1952 an editorialist for L'Avenir wrote that "one should first seriously consider the reform of primary and middle-school education, which is lamentably lacking, before promoting solutions of this kind" (the establishment of a university for Congolese).[22]

Although the PSC had a safe majority in the Belgian parliament, it was still sensitive to the criticisms of the Liberals and Socialists to whom it would have to look for support in any future coalition. Aware of the opposition of many Liberals and Socialists to large-scale aid to Lovanium, they were not prepared to exert maximum pressure on the issue of subsidies for the university. Thus, when in 1952 Governor-General Pétillon objected to the amount of the subsidies promised by André Dequae, minister of colonies, it was reduced without any great resistance on the part of the minister.[23]

Pétillon's action illustrated the continued opposition of the administration to higher education for the Congolese. Malengreau, speaking of the administration's unreconciled and unenthusiastic attitude toward Lovanium, noted that the colonial authorities found it "premature to open the door of the University to Africans, and considered such an initiative liable to accelerate the process of decolonization."[24] Pétillon even vetoed the establishment of a faculty of law at the University of Lovanium which, he feared, would produce agitators and revolutionaries. For much the same reasons he also opposed a faculty of philosophy and letters. Since resistance would probably have led to further blocking of subsidies by Pétillon, the

---

*While Congolese members of the clergy had been allowed to go abroad (especially to Belgium and Rome) to pursue their studies, the first layman to attend a foreign university was Thomas Kanza. He received his degree from the University of Louvain in 1956, thus becoming the first Congolese university graduate (Pierre Artigue, Qui sont les leaders congolais?, p. 128). The idea of sending Congolese students to Belgian universities was subsequently rejected by the administration.

**In 1950 a convention was signed between the directors of Louvain and the government, which provided for a subsidy of 70 percent (to be increased to 80 percent in 1952) for the building of the university. Thereafter, a 50 percent subsidy for expansion and maintenance and a 100 percent subsidy for professors' salaries would be paid. Subsidies never reached these proportions, because of opposition within the administration. For the years 1950, 1951, and 1952, 12,600,000 francs were allocated by the government for Lovanium (Guy Malengreau, untitled paper, unpublished, typewritten, n.d., p. 48 [private papers of G. Malengreau]).

Administrative Council of Lovanium accepted these limitations.[25]

Original plans had been for Lovanium to be ready to receive the first secondary-school graduates late in 1953, and to be located at Kisantu. In 1949, however, Msgr. Georges Six, apostolic vicar of Léopoldville, suggested that the university choose a site near Léopoldville in order to prevent the establishment of a state university in the capital. The site was accordingly changed to Kimuenza, on the outskirts of Léopoldville. The shift to Kimuenza was not effected without opposition. Those who were against the very idea of a university for the Congo saw a further danger in the proximity of such an institution to the large and restless African population of the colony's administrative center. To them it was like planting dangerous bacilli in the heart of the colonial system, with a strong likelihood of infection. Defenders of Lovanium sought to quiet such fears by noting that Kimuenza was "sufficiently far from the center of the city to assure the students a peaceful and wholesome residence."[26] Others opposed the move to Kimuenza on the ground that it would prevent the establishment of a lay university there. Pressure was put on the provincial authorities to withhold land from Lovanium, and the project was delayed. But by 1952 it was clear that Lovanium would be established at Kimuenza.*

The foundation of Lovanium University had been initiated by a group of professors at the University of Louvain with the support of the Jesuits in the Congo. In 1952, however, this partnership between Louvain and the Jesuits began to run into rough waters. In that year Father G. Van Bulck, S J, interim rector of Lovanium, submitted a plan to the Administrative Council of Lovanium for the establishment of two types of programs—one a regular university curriculum, the other an advanced technical training program. In addition, he called for a university specially adapted to the Congolese and suggested that manual labor and the use of Congolese languages be part of the program. A committee of professors, appointed by the council to consider Van Bulck's suggestions, rejected them. Lovanium, it was decided, should be a true university, with no technical schools attached.[27]

Increasing friction developed between the University of Louvain and the Jesuits as a result of this controversy and of differences with regard to the management and direction of the university. The Provincial Father of the Jesuits intimated to Msgr. Van Waeyenbergh that it would be desirable to end the relationship between Lovanium and Kisantu.[28] In 1954, Msgr. Luc Gillon, a secular priest, was appointed rector of the University of Louvanium. By 1958 all connection between Lovanium and Kisantu had been severed.

A New Threat

Lovanium was officially scheduled to open in 1954. In that year a new Socialist-Liberal government, headed by Achille Van Acker, came to power in Belgium. Its minister of colonies was Auguste Buisseret, an anticlerical

---

*The request of land from the Province of Léopoldville had been for 199 hectares. This was to avoid submission of the decree to the Colonial Council which had to approve all grants of 200 hectares and above of public lands outside the circonscriptions urbanes.

Liberal from Liège. Responding to the opposition to Lovanium among anticlericals at home and in the colony, Buisseret launched an attack shortly after he took office. Before a meeting of the Colonial Committee of the Chambre des Représentants, he expressed his belief that the establishment of Lovanium had been premature and stated that its diplomas would not be valid without his approval.

In face of this seeming threat to the very existence of Lovanium, a group of its supporters met at Louvain on June 1, 1954. Attending were Msgr. Van Waeyenbergh, the former ministers Dequae, Pierre Harmel, and Gaston Eyskens (all PSC), Senator de Smedt, and Professor Guy Malengreau. It was decided to send a delegation of the PSC to Buisseret to elicit a clear picture of his aims and policies. If the minister of colonies intended to carry out his threat, the PSC would launch a campaign against him, including interpellation on the floor of parliament. They believed that the Socialists would not back Buisseret in the face of strong PSC opposition. A few days later a PSC delegation including Eyskens, Dequae, Wigny, and De Vleeschauwer met with Prime Minister Van Acker. He promised that Lovanium diplomas would be recognized as long as student selection and degree requirements were rigorous.[29]

Shortly after this meeting, Buisseret invited Van Waeyenbergh and Guy Malengreau to his office to discuss their differences with him. Only later did they find out that representatives of the three other Belgian universities had also been asked to attend. The meeting took place on June 11, 1954. Buisseret told the representatives of Lovanium that he had been poorly informed, and that there was no question of the value or validity of degrees issued by the university. He went on, however, to question the value of the secondary training given the students, and suggested that Lovanium become a state university, run cooperatively by the four Belgian universities.[30] It would seem that the representatives of the Universities of Ghent, Liège, and Brussels were no less surprised by this proposal than were Van Waeyenbergh and Malengreau. They asked Buisseret why they had been drawn in, since Louvain had proceeded on its own in establishing Lovanium and they had no wish to intervene. Buisseret, they observed, was obligated by an agreement of the former government, which he could not abrogate.[31] Faced with this debacle, Buisseret announced that he would be left with little choice but to establish a state university in the eastern part of the Congo.*

The minister of colonies' final capitulation came during a meeting with Van Waeyenbergh, Malengreau, and Van Acker on June 15, 1954. The prime minister declared that the incident was closed, and that the government had no intention to destroy Lovanium, but merely to obtain guarantees for its diplomas. He promised that all subsidies already granted would be paid.[32]

---

*During January 1955 Buisseret created a Conseil Supérieur de l'Enseignement to make recommendations on the establishment of a state university in the Congo. The council finally recommended Elisabethville as the location for that university. The University of Elisabethville was opened in November 1956. Few Congolese were attracted to Elisabethville, especially since the limited number of graduates from secondary programs were at that time all from Catholic schools. Thus in December 1958 there were 116 non-Africans and 248 Congolese at Lovanium, and 144 non-Africans and 42 Congolese at Elisabethville (Inforcongo, Belgian Congo, vol. 2, p. 147).

After the question of government representation on the new university's selection committee had been cleared up, relations between the minister of colonies and the directors of Lovanium were correct, at times even friendly. During his stay in the Congo in 1954 Buisseret laid the cornerstone of the faculty of science building at Lovanium. Thereafter the only trouble Lovanium encountered with the government was with the Service de l'Enseignement (Bureau of Education) at Léopoldville, headed by Jean Ney, a fierce anticlerical.[33] Although not all the problems faced by the fledgling university were solved, the crumbling of government opposition meant the clearing of a major obstacle from its path. When it officially opened in April 1954, it could proceed without the fear that its existence was in jeopardy.

Protestant Reaction

The Protestants meanwhile had deeply resented the PSC government's attitude of favoring the Catholics. Coxill claimed that the "Roman Catholic government has let the Roman Catholics push in and obtain the monopoly of higher and university education for the whole of the Belgian Congo proper. The government has no other plans for a university for Congo. Whether we could have stopped this, or modified it, had we protested with sufficient vigor at the right time I do not know, but it is taking shape before our eyes."[34]

The establishment of the state university at Elisabethville only partially satisfied the Protestant missions. They certainly preferred it to a Catholic university, but they were also wary of what they considered the areligious, even antireligious, orientation of some of its faculty. Other reasons for their hesitancy were: the desire to avoid the academic disputes of the Belgian universities involved; and a belief that Elisabethville was not a truly African university, because of its preponderant white enrollment and because, as in the case of Lovanium, its program was felt to be too rigidly Belgian in orientation.[35] Under the weight of these fears and doubts the Protestants finally resolved to build their own university at Stanleyville. It was to open late in 1964 but the rebel seizure of Stanleyville shortly before that date prevented its inauguration.

Much of the credit for the establishment of academic secondary and university education for the Congolese must go to a small group of Catholic missionaries, led by Father Van Wing and the promoters and administrators of FOMULAC and, later, of CUCL. These missionaries and professors pushed, prodded, cajoled, and threatened a formidable opposition consisting of a coterie of colonial interests in Belgium and the Congo. Despite their sometimes parochial concerns, their efforts reflected their belief in the social need for education and the value of the Congolese as human beings and individuals.

CHAPTER 9

THE EROSION OF THE MISSION-STATE ENTENTE

In April 1954 the PSC lost its majority in the Belgian parliament. A new Socialist-Liberal coalition government was installed, bringing to an end seven years (1947-1954) of uninterrupted Catholic control of the Colonial Ministry. The new minister of colonies, Auguste Buisseret, was a Liberal and an anticlerical. Soon after taking office he adopted policies which were to radically alter the relationship between the Catholic missions and the state—and thereby the political character of the Belgian Congo. This shift in policy had been foreshadowed by some previous events.

The last non-Catholic minister of colonies had been Robert Godding (1946-1947), also a Liberal anticlerical. In 1946 he had instituted a policy of secular schools for white children in the Congo, in spite of the opposition of the Catholics who until then had monopolized this area of education. The Catholic missions took Godding's action as a danger signal of what might happen in the future; looking back on that period, one Catholic critic saw in it the seeds of the later breakdown of mission-state relations: "The first check to total collaboration occurred under Minister Godding. Official lay schools were begun for European children....The measures taken by M. Godding were a warning. They indicated that collaboration might shortly cease."[1] Godding's term of office, though short, was significant. A thread of continuity is discernible between his policies and those later introduced by Buisseret.

During the period of Catholic control over colonial matters which followed Godding's ministry the Liberals and Socialists continued their opposition to the educational policy followed in the Congo. After a government decision in 1948 to subsidize five Catholic secondary schools for Congolese, Godding and his followers sounded the tocsin against Catholic domination of education in the colony. Anticlerical forces in Belgium and the Congo were especially irked by what they considered to be an attempt to force white parents in the colony to send their children to Catholic schools despite the reforms initiated under Godding. They accused the PSC government of stifling the growth of lay schools for whites.[2] As an example of the concerted Catholic effort to destroy the lay school movement, they pointed to a circular issued by Governor-General Eugène Jungers in 1950. In it he had ordered officials of the administration to refrain from "participation in scholastic committees having as the objective the institution of an official lay school in a particular locale."[3]

A great deal of the concern the Liberals and Socialists exhibited on the score of secular education in the Congo was a reflection and extension of domestic political conflicts. The guerre scolaire waged over the extent of state aid to parochial schools in the métropole was a hot issue during the 1950s. The bitterness of the dispute had a centrifugal effect on Belgian politics, widening the gap between the PSC on the one hand and the Socialists and Liberals on the other. The two last-named favored official state institutions and wished to limit aid to Catholic schools; the former demanded complete equality between the two. The conflict spread, with little hindrance, to the Congo. Increased Belgian emigration after World War II had brought to the Congo a number of colons and administrators with Liberal and Socialist affiliations and heightened the interest of these two political parties in colonial matters. The new immigrants were often seen by the Catholic missionaires and their allies as agents provocateurs. One missionary critic noted that it was the européens de gauche and certains fonctionnaires who promoted the idea of lay education among the Congolese in an attempt to undermine the position of the missions.[4]

In the early 1950s the anticlerical press in the Congo and Belgium began a campaign against Catholic domination of education. In Elisabethville L'Echo du Katanga charged that "the PSC Government has shown its partiality for the Catholic establishments at the expense of all other schools."[5] L'Avenir in Léopoldville went further and called for the establishment of lay schools for Congolese.[6]

At the administrative level in the Congo demands were made in the Provincial and Government Councils* for the creation of official (lay) schools for Congolese. These recommendations were sponsored by African council members at the urging of anticlerical European members, who then gave them their support;[7] in general, however, the colonial authorities tended to ignore them. In 1951 an article in L'Avenir attacked Governor-General Jungers for rejecting the recommendations of certain members of the Government Council that secular professional schools be established in order to allow the Catholics to go ahead with plans to develop their own.[8]

As long as the PSC enjoyed a clear majority in the Belgian parliament and held firm sway over the Ministry of Colonies and the Colonial Administration the anticlericals in Belgium and the Congo had little hope that they could force a change in policy. They looked, rather, to the coming general elections to put it in their power to destroy the Catholic hegemony over colonial affairs. Toward the end of its tenure of office the PSC government initiated a policy which was to lend fire and increased public support to this desire of the anticlericals. If it had not been for the proposed concordat of 1953 and the vigor with which it was pressed, the later antimissionary policies of the Buisseret minority might have been more tempered by political compromise.

The Abortive Concordat of 1953

The convention between the Belgian Government and the Holy See, signed December 8, 1953 (see appendix B), was designed to supersede the Concordat of

---

*These were strictly advisory bodies and could only recommend to the colonial authorities. From 1947 on, Congolese were admitted as members, and Congolese membership gradually increased over the years. These bodies, however, remained under European domination. (See Crawford Young, Politics in the Congo, pp. 28-30; and Inforcongo, Belgian Congo, vol. 2, pp. 147-148.)

1906 and to formally establish the Catholic Church in the Congo with full ecclesiastical authority. This would have meant that the Catholic effort there
would be no longer a missionary enterprise, tied to and dependent on the Belgian hierarchy, but a national church in its own right, directly responsible
to the Vatican through the Holy Office rather than the Propaganda. The announcement of the signing of this convention raised a storm of protest in
Belgium, especially among Liberals and Socialists.

Once the convention was introduced to the Belgian parliament, Liberal
and Socialist reaction was swift. Debate on the convention in the Chambre
des Représentants did not begin, however, until March 1954, one month before
the scheduled national elections. A Socialist deputy, Henri Fayat, noted:
"The government is striving to ratify this treaty at the end of this legisla-
ture's existence, while relying on a majority that [will soon be] dissolved."[9]
Opposition pique at the way the convention had been handled was high. There
had been no public pronouncements by the PSC government that it was being
either considered or negotiated. The convention was, in effect, sprung on
the opposition as a fait accompli; only limited public debate at the eleventh
hour was possible. Paul-Henri Spaak accused the PSC of preparing the treaty
clandestinely, without informing members of the opposition: "This is the
first time that an international treaty of this importance has been discussed
with such secrecy." From its inception in 1952 "no one knew of it." He
noted that "there was not even one leak by the press, and that is without
precedent [especially in Belgium],...it is truly extraordinary."[10] Fayat accused the PSC, and the foreign minister in particular, of undertaking negotiations for the treaty without having consulted with the opposition parties.
A concordat negotiated in secrecy by a Catholic government, he observed,
arouses all kinds of suspicions and doubts.[11]

At the time of the sudden introduction of the treaty in the parliament
there had been an agreement between the PSC and the Liberals to confine debate during that period to such pressing and important pending legislation as
the bill on the European Defense Community. The Liberals felt that the PSC
had abrogated that agreement by inserting the convention in the legislative
calendar.[12]

Opposition and suspicion were also aroused by the manner in which the
negotiations for the convention had been handled. It had been the minister
of foreign affairs rather than the minister of colonies who had carried out
the negotiations with Archbishop Fernand Cento, the papal nuncio in Belgium.
This maneuver was apparently designed to enable the PSC to avoid as much controversy as possible, by presenting the convention as a foreign policy rather
than a colonial question which, had it become known in the early stages, undoubtedly would have drawn fire. Even more important was the emphasis the
PSC placed on the treaty nature of the convention. Its hope in so doing was
doubtless to ensure the convention's integrity after the party was out of office. When Foreign Minister Paul Van Zeeland presented the treaty to parliament, he scrupulously avoided the term concordat,* knowing full well that it
was poison to most Socialists and Liberals. Despite this, the opposition
seized on the word convention and noted that in reality the treaty amounted
to a concordat. There was also substantive opposition to the convention. It

---

*The Petit Larousse (Paris, 1964) defines a concordat as a "treaty be-
tween the Pope and a government concerning religious affairs."

78

was Deputy Fayat's contention that the treaty would give the Church a specially protected position in the Congo, beyond the control of the civil authority;
that the state would not be able to interfere with the rights given under the
convention which would supersede internal legislation. The treaty, he noted,
was not signed for a specific period but for perpetuity. He pointed out that
religious liberty and the right to teach religion were already sufficiently
guaranteed under law, without the convention. In the absence of guarantees to
other religions, it seemed to him dangerous and suspicious.[13]

Why, Socialists and Liberals asked, was the convention needed at all,
since one objective—the establishment of a national church—could be unilaterally achieved by the Vatican, and another—protection under the law—was already guaranteed under existing laws and treaties, including the Concordat of
1906. They therefore concluded that the real purpose of the treaty was to
grant the Catholic Church a privileged status and special concessions beyond
those that it already enjoyed.

Foreign Minister Van Zeeland contended that the treaty remained within
the limitations of the Colonial Charter and the Treaty of St. Germain-en-Laye.
The purpose of the convention, he said, was to continue the cooperation of the
Church and the administration in working for the "uplifting of the black population....The Church gives us the aid of her missions and her varied works in
the Congo, her unlimited devotion; we in turn contribute to her work our protection and our subsidies." This did not mean, however, that the administration was going to allow the Church to encroach on the civil sphere. It was
important that the Congo should have a Church of its own. He saw the convention merely as a continuation of long-established policies: "We believe that
in acting as we have done, we have remained within the path mapped out by
Léopold II himself." He believed those policies to be sound and saw little
need to change or deviate from the traditional Belgian colonial policy of
close cooperation between the colonial government and the missions. Minister
of Colonies Dequae, echoing De Vleeschauwer, insisted that the convention did
not mean higher subsidies.[14]

More specifically, the opposition took exception to certain articles of
the convention. Article 11 was attacked on the ground that the government's
obligation to support "Catholic marriage" might be intended to make it the
only legal form in the Congo. This was seen as an attempt to give special
sanctions to the Catholics, to the detriment of other religions.[15] Danger
was also seen in article 15. Some believed that it granted the Catholics independent control over their schools, while according them treatment (for example, the payment of salaries for teaching personnel) equal to that enjoyed
by state-run schools.[16] This, to the Socialist and Liberal opposition, clearly meant that the Catholic missions would get larger subsidies. Given the
fact that, in general, the compensation received by missionary and lay teachers in mission schools was less than that in state-run schools, opposition
concern on this point appears to have been valid.

Article 19, which had to do with land grants to Catholic missions and
facilities, was considered by the opposition to be aimed at making it easier
for the Church to obtain free land. One deputy believed that it contradicted
existing colonial legislation because, in his opinion, it violated the law
regarding land grants by eliminating the limits placed on free grants and
concessions.[17] Deputy Georges Housiaux, a leading Socialist spokesman on
colonial matters, contended that article 19 was in specific violation of a
1934 circular of Governor-General Auguste Tilkens that placed limits on land

grants to the missions.[18] The wording of article 19 could be interpreted as obliging the government to make gratuitous land grants to the Catholic Church, beyond what had been legally possible up to that time. Article 20, which provided that the state should pay what amounted to an annual salary to secular priests and missionaries of Belgian nationality and, in addition, obliged the government to partially finance church construction, met bitter opposition from the anticlericals.[19]

Interestingly, one of the most contentious points was article 21 concerning the naming of Catholic chaplains to the Force Publique. The chief chaplain was to be appointed by the Holy See, with the approval of the government. He in turn would select, again with government concurrence, other chaplains. This arrangement did not satisfy the critics of the convention. Their reaction was particularly strong on this point, since they felt that the government was abrogating some of its responsibility by leaving to Rome a decision concerning a secular institution of the state. This above all raised traditional doubts and fears among the anticlericals. Article 23 exempting the clergy and Church property from taxes seemed to some a device to give the Church special status and further weaken the sovereignty of the state over civil matters.[20] To others, including many colons, it seemed to allow the missions to engage in commerce, industry, and agriculture, while remaining exempt from taxes and duties.

The opposition to the convention in the Belgian parliament was echoed and supported by the Protestants. They were fearful that, through the convention, the Catholic Church would be transformed into a Congo state church. In the words of the President of the Federation of Protestant Churches in Belgium, Rev. H. de Worm: "The recognition by the Belgian State of the [Roman Catholic] Church in the Congo makes it an official Church, thus assuring it State protection and support, both morally and materially." To him it seemed obvious that the convention would result in the limitation or curtailment of the work of the Protestant missions, to the advantage of the Catholics.[21]

For reasons apparent to all, the Protestants were uneasy about the articles of the treaty concerning land grants to Catholic facilities (article 19), salaries for (Belgian) Catholic clergy (article 20), the legality of Christian marriage (article 11), and the prospects of increased subsidies to Catholic schools (article 15). One of the most disturbing clauses of the convention was article 26 that laid it down that difficulties arising between Church personnel and local authorities were to be settled amicably or submitted to ecclesiastical authorities for settlement. In light of their experience of Catholic attacks on their missions and adherents during the 1930s, the Protestants feared that the treaty "effectively [exempted] the Roman Catholic clergy of all ranks from the operation of civil laws and even from criminal prosecution....Only the Church itself can discipline or punish the offenders: civil jurisdiction stops at the door of any church."[22]

Despite these forebodings, as late as February 18, 1954, the director of the Brussels Bureau of the Congo Protestant Council felt that the convention was no great threat to the Protestant missions in the Congo. He believed that if the Protestants were treated on an equal footing with the Catholics in regard to the convention then they had "more to gain than to lose," since on the basis of the convention they could make demands for increased subsidies and privileges. "I think," he said, "that we have less to fear from this convention than Belgium and the Socialist and Liberal Parties....Some of the Articles will certainly mean that Belgium will be paying out huge sums of money."[23]

One day later, February 19, 1954, Coxill wrote to the minister of colonies requesting reassurance that the proposed convention would not affect the rights and position of the Protestant missions vis-à-vis the government and the Catholics. He noted that differential treatment of the Catholics "would be...contrary to the assurances given to us by the late Mr. Godding, when he was Minister of Colonies, that the Catholics and Protestants would be placed on a basis of equality."[24] To this attempt to extract a guarantee which would, after the passage of the convention, give the Protestants a basis for demanding equal treatment with the Catholics the minister replied in rather ambiguous terms: "I can assure you that this new treaty implies absolutely no change in policy regarding the Protestants and will neither modify nor weaken the good relations that exist between them and the Government."[25]

In general, however, the Protestants were against the passage of the convention, and as time advanced their opposition grew. Coxill reported that he had supplied information to Liberal and Socialist deputies for use on the floor of the parliament to argue against ratification, and established a close association with J. Rey, a deputy from Liège who became the chief defender of the Protestant missions during the debates on the treaty in the chamber.[26] In response to Rey's statements about the Protestant position, the foreign minister expressed his willingness to sign similar conventions with other religious groups in the Congo, namely the Protestants. Though somewhat interested, the Protestants never accepted this offer.

In the end, the convention never became law. Although passed by the chamber in a vote strictly along party lines, it failed to be ratified by the senate before the general elections of April 1954. The establishment of a Liberal-Socialist coalition government after the elections was its death knell.

It is difficult to imagine how the leaders of the PSC could have bungled so badly in their handling of the convention. They acted like fish out of water, yet they should have known the shoals of Belgian politics perfectly well. Thus, the minister of colonies could say at one point that "the only error, perhaps, committed by us is not to have given sufficient explanations regarding this treaty, but we did not foresee that it would provoke such a reaction."[27] This last statement is indeed startling, given the well-known anticlericalism of many Liberals and Socialists and its exacerbation by the guerre scolaire. It was predictable that they would see the convention as a device to establish the hegemony of the Church in the Congo and an attempt to encroach upon the sovereignty of the state. The increased costs that would have resulted from the convention were also a point of contention.

The apprehension of the Liberals and Socialists increased because of the treaty aspect of the convention. The fact that it could not be altered unilaterally and so would effectively bind succeeding governments did not go unnoticed. One Liberal deputy went so far as to declare that his party was not against the missions in the Congo or a modification of the laws and decrees in regard to church-state relations but was opposed to it in the form of a treaty.[28] The PSC's insistence on the word convention rather than concordat merely served to increase suspicion.

Judging from the evidence available, the initiative for the convention seems to have come from the Church. Van Zeeland admitted as much before the chamber. It was probably the apostolic delegate in the Congo, Msgr. Sigismundi, who was behind the pressure for the convention.[29] Apparently he took this initiative against the advice of some Belgian missionaries in the Congo, who were aware of the reaction that could be expected from the Liberals and Socialists.

When the PSC yielded to Vatican pressure, it committed a strategic error in introducing the convention to parliament during its last weeks of tenure. This action contravened an agreement with the Liberals that limited debate to issues already on the legislative calendar. In addition, it had been sprung on the Liberals and Socialists without their prior knowledge, or so they contended. The entire procedure was calculated to antagonize the opposition, who felt that the convention was being rammed down their throats. The substance and handling of the convention became one of the issues of the 1954 electoral campaign and probably helped defeat the PSC. The debate over the convention had in fact been less a colonial issue than a reflection of domestic concerns and conflicts, mainly between clerical and anticlerical elements and involving the question of the guerre scolaire.

The Convention of 1953 was basically an extension of the Concordat of 1906 and other legislation. It also formalized some practices, for example, the referral of differences between missionaries and administrative officials to ecclesiastical authorities, that had been practiced informally for quite some considerable time. The gains that would have been made were trifling, but the exacerbation of the Liberal and Socialist opposition was considerable and may well have increased support for anticlerical policies adopted by the new regime in 1954.

CHAPTER 10

BUISSERET: THE POLITICS OF SECULARIZATION

Soon after coming to office in April 1954 Buisseret instituted policies generally aimed at weakening the position and power of the Catholic missions in the Congo by introducing secular schools for Congolese at all levels of education; by increasing the influence of anticlericals within both the Ministry of Colonies and the Colonial Administration in the hope of breaking a long-standing Catholic monopoly; and by supporting the aims and desires of the colons in the Congo whose cause the Liberals had championed after World War II.[1]

Secularization of Education

The tempestuous fight between proclerical and anticlerical forces, which erupted shortly after Buisseret's installation, centered on the secularization of education. In a speech delivered early in 1954 the colonial minister attacked the missions for their failure to educate the Congolese, and clearly set forth his objectives:

> Education must benefit the Congo; the missionaries are incapable of providing such benefit; few among them are teachers,...few hold degrees in the arts or the sciences, few are carpenters, metal workers, mechanics, electricians or agronomists; they must rely more and more upon lay personnel; they have scant competence to organize and teach all that the Congolese want to learn.

> Instruction is a duty of the state; to create a system of lay education would be to fulfill one of the state's most eminent and most altruistic obligations.[2]

In the course of a speech at the laying of the cornerstone of the science building of Lovanium University, he said that six state-financed and state-operated schools would be established in the Congo, one in each province. It was implied that this would be on an experimental basis. So rapidly was this policy put into effect that by October 1954 new government primary schools for Congolese were opened in Léopoldville, Stanleyville, and Luluabourg, and new normal schools were operating in these cites and in Elisabethville.[3] It soon became apparent that this program was meant to be more than experimental.

83

The Coulon Commission

To build a sound foundation for his program of laicization, Buisseret sent a commission of inquiry to the colony to study the functioning of the educational system and to submit recommendations for educational reform. The Coulon Commission, as it came to be called, was in the Congo from October 15 to December 11, 1954.

The commission's observations and conclusions show that its members viewed the missions, especially the Catholic missions, and their role in education with contempt and hostility. Early in their report they recommended that the government not limit its policy of establishing lay primary schools to the important urban centers but extend it to the rural areas as well.[4] It was precisely in the bush that the missions had made their greatest physical and emotional investment. By recommending that the state build schools in the bush the commission was touching a very sensitive spot, knowing that this would produce cries of pain and anguish from the missionaries and their supporters.

The report went on to criticize the caliber of the secondary education offered by the missions. Its recommendation here was similar to that made for the primary schools: that the government increase secondary education by building numerous middle schools.[5] Harking back to Buisseret's criticism of the missionaries' ability to run secondary schools, the commission noted the lack of trained missionary personnel and suggested that the state erect and run technical schools, hitherto almost entirely in the hands of the missions.[6]* It complained that the missions which ran these schools, although subsidized by the state, often made a profit from the sale of the products turned out by the students. The commission suggested that the schools discontinue this practice, and that the subsidy of any school continuing it be proportionately reduced.[7] This proposal in part reflected the complaints of some colons who felt that the sale on the open market of goods so produced was cutting into their own sales.

Missionary control of education was also criticized on the ground that it oriented students toward seminaries and academic secondary schools rather than technical schools.[8] Especially in regard to seminary training there was some truth in this allegation. But the popularity of these schools was due even more to the career opportunities that such an education might offer to aspiring Congolese youth; these schools were the main road to social and economic success in the colonial setting. Though technical training may have seemed to the commission the way to "civilization," it was not so viewed by the Congolese themselves. Guy Malengreau, in his critique of the Coulon report, felt that the commission had given undue stress to this aspect of education: "We are convinced, for our part, that the weaknesses of our Congolese education are to be found in the academic rather than the professional schools. There are, in the Congo, more excellent engineers, capable carpenters or competent mechanics than humanists."[9] The members of the commission seemed less concerned with Congolese desires and aspirations than with the

---

*Many of the technical schools in the Congo were écoles congreganistes, i.e., state schools run and staffed by Catholic missionaries on a contractual basis.

wishes of the colons, the large companies, and many in the administration to impede Congolese political development and to satisfy the need for skilled labor.

A major attraction of missionary control of education was that it would cost much less than any secular system, thus saving the state a large sum of money. This fact had been stressed in the Ten-Year Plan for the Economic and Social Development of the Belgian Congo, the colonial government's master plan for the 1950s: "If the missionaries, whose cost to the government is now estimated to be 450,000 frs. per annum, were civil servants, then the total expense would be in the order of 750 million francs."[10] The Coulon Commission disputed this, claiming that, since the missions had been allowed to hire two-thirds of the teaching staff from among the laity and at higher salaries costs had greatly increased.[11] The system of subsidies was, it observed, often complex and almost, if not quite, as costly as a system of secular schools.[12] But for the commission it was a question not of cost but of honor: "The traditional argument, favorable to the missionaries, of low-cost education is at once subject to question,...in any case, it is unworthy of a great civilizing nation, guardian of a rich colony."[13]

The report insisted that, as proselytization would always be the main aim of the missions, it was incumbent upon the state to assume the mantle of responsibility "in matters of public instruction and explicitly abandon the notion that this rests...with the missions. In this sense, official sanction must be reserved for...lay schools that are open to all."[14] Article 22 of the Colonial Charter, it was noted, forbade the state to delegate its powers to private individuals or groups.[15] Here the commission went beyond the experimental program outlined in Buisseret's speech at Lovanium and looked forward to the construction of a secular system of education that would significantly reduce the role of the missions.

For Coulon and his collaborators the tenor of church-state relations in the Congo was reminiscent of the Middle Ages:

It is not without reason that since the disappearance of old Paraguay, some consider the Congo to be the one remaining theocratic state. Incontestably, on both the religious and political level at least, the missionary deals with people as a sovereign with his vassals; respected by some, feared by others, but always obeyed, always making the rules and in a way that brings to mind...his own narrow self-interest [rather] than the greater interests of the population as a whole.[16]

Their report was aimed not merely at educational reform but at weakening the very foundations of missionary power in the Congo.

The tone of the report and the charges it contained stirred up a tempest in Belgium and the Congo. The report itself and the members of the commission came under heavy attack by the proclericals. To Guy Malengreau, the report reflected a gross distortion and misunderstanding of colonial realities by men who had little knowledge of the Congo. He described it as filled with "exaggerations, falsities, and calumnies."[17]* He criticized the depth and method of the commission's investigation. The time it had spent in the Congo had been too brief to enable it to get a clear and comprehensive

---

*In an interview with the author Father Van Wing pointed out that only one member of the three-man commission had ever been to the Congo previously, while another member, Renson, had no experience in education.

picture of the problems and prospects of the situation. And the sources of the data utilized in the report were deemed to be far from the best.[18] Commission members were accused of being unduly influenced by testimony given by individuals hostile to the Catholic missions, while assiduously avoiding clarification or cooperation by the missionaries themselves.[19] The Catholics were willing to admit that weaknesses existed in the educational system as it then operated in the Congo, and that reform was desirable. But instead of conducting an objective investigation the Coulon Commission had carried on an inquisition and had produced a polemic against them. The supporters of the Catholic missions proposed that another investigation be made to determine the educational weaknesses and needs of the Congo,[20] Father Van Wing suggesting a new inquiry by a group of educators drawn from the Service de l'Enseignement of the Ministry of Colonies.[21]

The Coulon Commission had written its report in fifteen days, while aboard the S.S. Boudoinville en route from Matadi to Antwerp. The document was submitted to Buisseret soon after the commission arrived in Belgium; a short time later educational subsidies to the missions were cut back. Catholics saw the work of the commission and its final report as part of a carefully preconceived plot by the minister of colonies to deprive them of state aid, while giving him an excuse to promote secular education.[22]

In Belgium the report became a domestic issue on a par with the guerre scolaire. It was presented in a manner that seemed calculated to set the secular schools up as rivals to those of the missions rather than to offer a policy of building these schools as an alternative for those who did not want to attend confessional schools. A wall of suspicion and hostility arose between the Parti Social Chrétien (PSC) and the Catholic missions on one side and the Parti Socialiste Belge-Parti Libéral Belge coalition on the other. Built on a foundation of mutual distrust, it made any reconciliation difficult and potentially unstable.

Meantime Buisseret, on his return from a short tour of the Congo during 1954, had sought to calm Catholic apprehension regarding his plans for lay schools by holding out an olive branch. He stated that both lay and mission-sponsored education could exist side by side in an atmosphere of good will and fair play. "There is," he said, "no question of creating an antireligious lay education."[23] A few weeks later, while the Coulon Commission was still en route to Belgium, Buisseret announced on December 14, 1954, that he had ordered nine new secular schools opened in the Congo as an experiment. Though religious instruction was to be offered on an optional basis to students attending these schools, Catholic discontent was not assuaged.

Among the protagonists of the Catholic missions in the Congo were some who were not opposed to the introduction of secular schools as such, but feared that Buisseret's aim was to destroy the substance and structure of Catholic accomplishments in education and other spheres, and thereby much of the influence of the missions. Msgr. Felix Scalais, apostolic vicar of Léopoldville, in a speech to the Government Council stated: "I am not in principle opposed to state education,...[but] the rights of the Church must be safeguarded."[24] Some supporters of the missions went so far as to concede the need for secular middle and secondary schools, but insisted that primary education should be left in missionary hands.[25]

During the months that followed Buisseret's tour of the Congo and the publication of the Coulon report the Catholic missionaries became increasingly apprehensive about and opposed to the accelerated laicization of education. The Catholic hierarchy deemed lay schools and the policies which accompanied their introduction antireligious.[26] In the eyes of the missionaries, therefore, the aim of the colonial minister was to turn the Congolese not merely away from their schools but—more importantly—away from and against the Church. The missionaries and their supporters could hardly be expected to tolerate such a situation.

In the Belgian parliament the PSC took up the cudgels to protect the interests of the missions. Admonishing Buisseret, former Minister of Colonies Albert De Vleeshauwer said: "You have fashioned [the lay schools] into a weapon to be used against all other schools."[27] Buisseret denied that his plans for secular schools were in any way antimissionary,[28] but the opposition greeted his denial with incredulity. If this were so, it asked, then why, only eighteen months after he had announced that his program was experimental, were there now sixty-four lay schools of different types already in existence?[29] Wigny demanded a guarantee that the missions would be allowed to continue to function freely in education and would continue to receive subsidies in accordance with previous agreements.[30]

It was this last point especially that irked the Catholic opposition in parliament. De Vleeschauwer, Dequae, and Wigny, the major PSC spokesmen on colonial questions, submitted a bill calling upon Buisseret to present his "educational experiments" to the chamber for review and approval.[31] Dequae accused him of having deliberately bypassed the usual channels in order to implement his policies: "Neither the parliament, nor the advisory bodies of the colony, nor the new body, the Conseil Supérieur de l'Enseignement au Congo Belge,* has been consulted."[32] Buisseret was regarded as having attempted to present the missions with a fait accompli, probably in the hope of avoiding voluble opposition that might have prevented the implementation of his program. Instead, his action had provoked the wrath of the missions and clerical forces and had deepened their suspicion of his policies.

The Coulon Commission had based its recommendations for the establishment of secularized education partly on what it considered the mediocre quality of missionary schools and partly on the needs and desires of the Congolese. It noted that the existing system gave non-Catholics practically no choice but to send their children to schools where they would be subject to pressures to convert. Entrance to mission schools was itself a problem; the commission claimed that the missions limited the number of entrants and diplomas to the minimum required for the award of subsidies and usually gave preference to adherents.[33] The missions were also indicted for "brutally smashing" the societal structure of the Africans while offering them no adequate substitutes.[34] Only through secular education, it was claimed, could the Congolese find his true identity.

While criticism of the Catholic missions and their schools was to a degree justified, it did not necessarily follow that the solution lay in a system of lay education. To give the évolué the identity and satisfaction he sought would require more than a change in the structure and philosophy

----

*Instituted by Buisseret in December 1954 as a consultative body on questions dealing with education in the Congo. Of its sixteen members only three were missionaries (one Protestant and two Catholics). Set up by Buisseret in the hope that it would aid his policies, the council balked; it refused to give its imprimatur to the Coulon report, although the colonial minister had requested it. (Interview with Father Van Wing.)

of education; it would require a change in the entire Belgian colonial system. Lay education, though desirable, was no panacea for the ills afflicting the Congolese. This, however, did not prevent Buisseret from presenting it as such.

During the parliamentary debate on the colonial budget in 1954 Buisseret declared that he had initiated his policy of secular education only under great Congolese pressure.[35] He said that he had received many letters and petitions from Congolese demanding secular education. One letter—signed by Anatole Kalombo (a teacher in a Catholic school), Rodolphe Yava (a bank employee), Remy Mwamba (a former student of the Institut Saint-Boniface at Elisabethville), and Victor Lundula (former first sergeant in the Force Publique)*—gave two major reasons for the writers' support of lay education: too many children were excluded or expelled from mission schools for such trifling reasons as absence from mass or because their parents lived in supposed "unregulated union" (this usually meant polygamy); and many children were turned away from mission schools because their parents were non-Catholic or Protestant.[36]

The Catholics vehemently denied these charges, claiming that their schools were open to all without distinction: "A pupil will never be expelled from school or refused admission because he is a pagan or does not wish to convert."[37] Statistics of the composition of central primary schools in the Vicariat de Luluabourg (Kasai) were cited to give validity to this point (see table 10). While denying many of the accusations made by Congolese évolués and the Liberal-Socialist opposition, the Catholic missions acknowledged that dissatisfaction with their schools did indeed exist in certain of the Congolese population. Among the reasons for this dissatisfaction they listed: the desire to throw off the morality imposed by the missionaries; the failure of some of their children in mission schools; and the hope of better training in the French language;** anger with missionaries for personal reasons; and the belief that secular education would be superior.[38] In parliament De Vleeschauwer, focusing on this last point, urged that the reason why many Congolese favored lay schools was their desire for an education equivalent to that received by Europeans; it was not, he insisted, because these schools were antireligious.[39]

Buisseret was assailed for attempting to woo Congolese students to the new secular schools by underhanded and devious methods: "Certainly you will have an abundance of pupils in your lay schools. The hunting methods used by

---

*Yava later became a prominent member of the Confédération des Associations Tribales du Katanga and a senator in the National Parliament; Mwamba was at one time minister of justice in Adoula's government; Lundula was appointed commander-in-chief of the ANC and was later instrumental in bringing about the fall of the Gizenga regime in Stanleyville (Pierre Artigue, Qui sont les leaders Congolais?, pp. 184-185, 246-247, and 315).

**The Coulon report had been particularly critical of the limited French-language training given to Congolese in missions schools, especially those run by Flemish congrégations. The authors of the report felt that the Congolese were handicapped by this deficiency (Belgium, Ministère des Colonies, Mission pédagogique Coulon-Deheyn-Renson, p. 123).

TABLE 10

FAMILY ORIGINS OF PUPILS IN CENTRAL PRIMARY SCHOOLS
IN VICARIATE OF LULUABOURG, 1954

	Number	Percent- age of Total
Children of pagan parents	15,024	58
Children of Christian parents	10,894	42
Total	25,918	100
Children of monogamous marriages	18,440	71
Children of polygamous marriages	7,382	28.8
Unclassified	96	.2
Total	25,918	100

SOURCE: "Rapport sur la question scolaire au Congo Belge et Ruanda-Urundi depuis l'avènement de M. Buisseret, avril, 1954, jusqu'au 25 janvier, 1955," Brussels, 1955, typewritten (in author's possession).

NOTE: One factor of significance not indicated in the above figures was the number and percentage of those who entered as pagans as compared with the number and percentage of those who had been converted to Christianity by the time they left the mission schools. From all indications the conversion rate was high. It should also be kept in mind that children of pagan parents who entered mission schools were not necessarily pagan themselves, while the children of Christian parents had almost invariably been baptized. As of 1952, it was said that between 75 percent and 80 percent of the pupils attending primary schools run by Catholic missions were pagan, and that many who graduated remained pagan ("Rapport sur la question scolaire," p. 33).

your agents betray the spirit of your war machine."[40] The administration was
also charged with sending letters to African chiefs urging them to send the
children of their villages or sectors to official schools.[41] In his reply
Buisseret stated that his policies had the support of "the majority of the
blacks"; that, so far from being seduced into sending their children to secular schools, they had demanded such schools from the government.[42]

The Catholics were fearful that it was the government's intention to
create within the administration a Congolese cadre drawn only from graduates
of official schools, thereby "seizing the future elite for themselves, while
leaving the inferior echelons to the missions."[43] This would have made the
mission schools less attractive to the Congolese and would have eroded support for the missions among the évolués who were to be the future leaders of
the Congo.

Buisseret and the Protestants

Anathema though it was to the Catholics, Buisseret's laicization of education tended to be welcomed by the Protestants. During the postwar years
the latter had found themselves under mounting pressure by their adherents to
provide better schooling beyond the primary level; it was in this area that
they were found especially wanting. And now the Coulon report had criticized
Protestant missions for "miserable facilities, ignorance of French, [and]
seemingly rudimentary teaching methods."[44] Many Protestant missionaries felt
that they could provide neither the funds nor personnel necessary to build or
staff an adequate secondary-school system. To look to the government for aid
was not incompatible with their philosophical position on the separation of
church and state; in fact, as early as 1950 the Congo Protestant Council (CPC)
had passed a resolution encouraging the establishment of lay schools at the
secondary and technical levels.[45]

Protestant desire for a state system of secular education was reinforced
by the fear that Protestant children allowed to enter Catholic secondary institutions would be subjected to pressure to convert to Catholicism. Such a
draught would be extremely bitter to swallow. But even without this, there
remained the question whether the Catholics would allow the Protestant students to freely enter their schools in preference to students from their own
primary schools.[46] The Catholics denied that they excluded Protestants merely because they were non-Catholic, but granted that many who attended Catholic schools did convert; at the same time they denied any pressure on them to
do so.[47]

Initially, therefore, the Protestants were more than willing to take a
favorable view of Buisseret's policy. They saw it as relieving them of a
burden and fulfilling a long-sought desire. They were ready to comply with
an administration request to purchase Protestant school buildings for conversion into official schools, their only proviso being that religious instruction by teachers of their choice be allowed in such schools.[48] But this
early good will toward Buisseret and his policies was soon to be dissipated.

During September 1954 the minister of colonies ordered that the words
national and foreign, used to describe missions, be dropped from official
documents.[49] Yet one year later Coxill, now director of the CPC's Brussels
Bureau, was told by a member of Buisseret's office that the Colonial Ministry
had decided to maintain the distinction between foreign and national missions
for fear the Catholics would introduce foreign missionary orders.[50] It was

pointed out that this was contrary to promises made by Godding in 1946 and by Buisseret himself. The ministry's action was a major blow to the aspirations of the Protestants, who considered these designations one of the last barriers to their achievement of full equality of status with the Catholics.

The Protestants then tried another course. In the hope of winning recognition for Protestantism as a national church, the CPC asked Coxill to explore the possibilities of establishing a "maison mère" (headquarters) in Belgium. It was proposed that the Brussels Bureau become the "Secrétaire Général en Belgique des Missions Protestantes au Congo."[51] Acceptance of this proposal by the Brussels authorities would have meant the eligibility of Protestant missions to receive state subsidies for their religious activities. George Carpenter, director of the Africa Committee, and others rejected this on the ground that it would embroil the Protestants in Belgian political issues irrelevant to their own objectives.[52] The Protestants, however, were not to be given the opportunity of exercising an option in regard to the establishment of a maison mère. Buisseret effectively squelched the idea. Replying to Coxill, he said that he would consider granting the Protestant missions a maison mère in Belgium if they "first recognized respectively the ecclesiastical and academic authority of the Synod of the Union des Eglises" (of Belgium).[53] This was one maneuver in a concerted effort by the Synod to gain control of the Protestant missions in the Congo and especially of the Brussels Bureau of the CPC—an effort marked by undertones of conspiracy between the Synod and the Ministry of Colonies.

A Belgian Protestant missionary who had spoken with Buisseret during the latter's tour of the Congo and Ruanda-Urundi reported that the minister considered that a representative of the Belgian Protestant churches should aid Coxill in representing Protestant missionary interests in Brussels.[54] The minister seems to have ignored the fact that activity by Belgian Protestant missions in the Congo was almost nil, most of their efforts being centered in Ruanda-Urundi. In February 1955 Coxill informed Joseph Ohrneman, secretary of the CPC, that the Reverends De Worm and Pishal of the Synod had gone to the Congo with the support of the Ministry of Colonies, but without following the normal procedure of informing the Brussels Bureau. Their mission was to persuade the directors of the CPC to allow the Synod to represent them in Brussels; on their return to Belgium they were to report to the Ministry of Colonies.[55]

While attending a conference in Paris an official of the London office of the International Missionary Council (IMC) met with Guy Smet, advisor to the minister of colonies on Protestant mission matters. Smet told him that the Belgian government was prepared to offer larger subsidies to the Protestant missions if it could deal with one agency (that is, the Synod), as it did in the case of the Catholics, and urged the IMC representative to inform the Protestants in the Congo of this offer, which he did.[56] At the time Carpenter and Coxill were strenuously endeavoring to convince Ohrneman and the CPC that the proposals of Smet and the Ministry of Colonies were a danger to the status and future of the Protestant missions.* If Ohrneman and the

_____

*"The proposals outlined by Mr. Smet were motivated less by desire to aid Protestant missions than by anxiety to prevent the return of the Catholic missions in the Congo to their former dominance. The real motive is anticlericalism. I am convinced that under no circumstances should we permit

CPC were at first not aware of the underlying objectives of the Synod and the Ministry of Colonies, they soon became so. In a letter to Buisseret dated April 11, 1956, Ohrneman rejected the suggestion that the Protestant missions accept the Synod as their legal representative to the Belgian government in exchange for the subsidization of church activities. He suggested that Coxill's office and the CPC be given the legal status required. This marked the end of the Synod-Ministry of Colonies' attempt to capture the CPC and its Brussels Bureau.

Carpenter seems to have been quite right in describing anticlericalism as the main motive of this effort. Buisseret and his advisors no doubt hoped that the Synod, if put in control of the Protestant missions, would be able to counter Catholic attacks on their policies, that, in fact, if the Protestant missions were made a national church, they could be used as a weapon in the war against the Catholics. Under the Synod, the Protestants would have become more directly and deeply involved in the guerre scolaire in both Belgium and the Congo and would have defended government policies against Catholic onslaughts. Buisseret would thus have gained support in his efforts to wrest control of education from the Catholics, while the Synod would have increased its power and influence in Belgium and the Congo.

As a result of these machinations the Protestants, who had looked forward to the end of Catholic control of the Ministry of Colonies and had welcomed the introduction of secular schools, became disillusioned. They felt that the Liberals had gone back on their promises and had ignored Protestant needs. They perceived that the colonial minister had attempted to manipulate them for his own ends, and that in the long run this might well have proven detrimental to their own needs.

Buisseret and the Colonial Administration

While in office, Godding had effected some changes within the Colonial Ministry that later became a boon to Buisseret and his program. He diminished the status of the Direction de Culte et de l'Enseignement (Department of Religion and Education) in an attempt to weaken the influence of the Catholics who had dominated that department in matters dealing with missions and education. On the other hand, he sought to strengthen the position of the anticlericals within the key Service de l'Inspection which was responsible for the inspection of mission schools and the implementation of the educational program. This was deplored by the Catholics who believed that the "Inspection Service serves as a reservoir for candidates destined for higher posts" within the Colonial Administration,[57] and to whom the thought of losing control of the Colonial Administration was odious.

Dequae, colonial minister from 1950 to 1954, strove to reverse the changes effected by Godding, especially within the Services Administratifs

---

ourselves to be used in a political maneuver dominated by this motive. If we let the present government use us against the Roman Catholics then as soon as a Roman Catholic government comes into power we could expect them to use the government against us, and we should be in no position to protest" (Carpenter to Ohrneman, N.Y., Sept. 8, 1955 [CPC-KIN]).

de l'Enseignement (Administrative Services of Education [ASE]). His main objective was to prevent anticlericals from getting important administrative posts. The possibility that Jean Ney might be named inspector-in-chief of the educational service in particular agitated the Catholic missions. Ney was described by one missionary as "a very dangerous man because of his ultrasecular tendencies, a man who is hostile to Catholic teaching and whose conduct is deplorable."[58]

The missions convinced Dequae that something had to be done to avoid this possibility; in their words, it was necessary "to clean up the situation in the ASE."[59] Negotiations between officials of the Ministry of Colonies and the Catholic missions were conducted between July and November 1953. Dequae, Jules Van Hove (inspecteur royal and chef de cabinet of the minister of colonies), and a prominent Catholic missionary met in Brussels with the express aim of finding a man who was absolutely reliable and at the same time in line for promotion to fill the top post in the ASE. Unable to come up with anyone, they devised an alternative plan—for a structural reform of the administration. Van Hove suggested that a new department "covering education and religion be established within the Government-General, which would be autonomous of the Inspection Service." Being a new department, it could be staffed from departments other than the Inspection Service, whose members would be prevented from transferring to ASE. Thus it was hoped that "those whom the late Minister Godding had appointed would be cut off from access to key positions in the administration of education."[60]

This plan was then broached to Marcel Van den Abeele, administrator-general of the colony, and Governor-General Pétillon, both of whom opposed it. The pro-Catholics ascribed Pétillon's recalcitrance to lack of understanding of the Catholic point of view regarding education. One missionary complained that Pétillon "doesn't allow himself to be influenced easily."[61] Dequae at first refused to override Pétillon, but during Pétillon's absence on vacation in February 1954 he decided to create a new department to deal with religious matters and education. M. Bozlée, a "good Catholic," was then appointed provincial commissioner of Stanleyville, to be kept in reserve until the time was ripe for his elevation to the post of director general of the planned department.[62] The defeat of the PSC at the polls in April 1954 cut short these maneuvers.

One of Buisseret's first acts after he took office was to appoint Ney to the directorship of the new Direction Generale de l'Enseignement et de Culte (Department of Education and Religious Affairs) which had been established by Dequae. By naming the very man whom the missions had gone to great lengths to keep out of office, the colonial minister made Catholic animosity against himself inevitable.

The fact that Buisseret had claimed the colonial portfolio did not mean that he had total control of the ministry itself or of the administration in the Congo. Over the years the Catholics had come to dominate the administrative apparatus within both these organizations; they held the key posts and many of the lesser posts in nearly every department, the Direction Générale de l'Inspection being an exception. Many had civil service status and could not be fired. Coxill reported that Georges Brausch, an important member of Buisseret's cabinet, had complained to him about this problem. "He [Brausch] knows that many of the officials in the Colonial office have been there for years and are out-and-out PSC men whom he cannot trust."[63]

Faced with a staff whose interests and persuasion were often diametrically opposed to his own, Buisseret established inside the colonial ministry a _ministère gris_ from which he could claim the loyalty necessary for the implementation of his programs. This ministry within a ministry was composed in the main of the members of his cabinet. It included the following strongly anticlerical members: Breuls De Tiecken, _chef de Cabinet_; Col. Cattoor, _chef de Cabinet adjoint_; Léon Lecompte, educational affairs; Marcel Zimmer, financial affairs; Strausch, social affairs.[64] Members of the cabinet assumed direct responsibility for much of the business normally handled through regular ministry channels, especially on questions relating to missionary activity or the appointment of men to important posts within the colonial service, in particular the educational service.[65]

Leading members of the PSC, resentful of the manner in which colonial policy was being carried out, vehemently attacked Buisseret and his cabinet:

> In a honeyed tone the minister speaks of tolerance, but at the same time the representatives of the minister pursue, in the Congo, a policy which is quite the opposite of these words. Behind the back of the Governor-General of the Congo, the minister's cabinet gives instructions which turn the proper operation of the Administration upside down.[66]

They accused the colonial minister's cabinet of neither knowing nor understanding conditions in the Congo, and considered that many of its decisions were, especially from a Catholic viewpoint, in the best interests of neither Belgium nor her colony. It was felt by some highly placed Catholics, Father Van Wing among them,[67] that Buisseret's cabinet was more anticlerical than the minister himself, but that he often blindly followed their lead.

The Kasai, particularly the Apostolic Vicariates of Luluabourg and Kabinda, was a prime testing ground for Buisseret's laicization policy. Members of the minister's cabinet and anticlericals in the Colonial Administration played leading roles in the attempt to break the missions' educational monopoly in this area, where the Catholics were considered to be extremely powerful and influential.

Buisseret had not made public his decision to build a secondary school at Luluabourg when he first announced his general plan for the establishment of these schools. This particular decision was not revealed until later. The Catholics surmised that the plan had been revised on the initiative of Lecompte, Buisseret's advisor on education, who, as former préfect of the Luluabourg _athénée_, had a special interest in that area.[68] His collaborators were two officials of the Provincial Government of the Kasai: André Brasseue, director of education at Luluabourg, and Fernand Trockay, director of the Native Labor Office. Lecompte was accused of having written a Congolese member of the Kasai Provincial Council encouraging him to demand the establishment of lay schools in the Kasai. Msgr. Bernard Mels, apostolic vicar of Haut-Kasai, in a letter to Msgr. Verwimp, president of the Permanent Committee of Catholic Bishops, expressed his indignation that the director of the Native Labor Office was traveling throughout the province and meeting with évolués in order to "sing the praises of lay education."[69] The Catholic hierarchy in the Kasai had no doubt that behind these actions lay a plot, conceived and directed by the members of the colonial minister's cabinet, to expand lay education "behind the back" of the administration.[70]

The Catholics claimed that pressure was brought to bear on Congolese parents and the traditional authorities to support the laicization of education in the Kasai. The state offered to build schools within the _circonscriptions indigènes_, and, once they were built, tried to induce the "councils

of notables" to elect to have them serviced by the government as lay institutions. Father Mosmans noted that the traditional leaders "were forced to
ask for lay schools" even if they had earlier requested Catholic schools.[71]
Parents were urged to withdraw their children from Catholic schools and send
them to official schools.[72]

What happened in the Kasai, it was contended, was merely a glaring example of what was taking place throughout the Congo. For the Catholics it
was a policy of la guerre scolaire, directed from Brussels by members of
Buisseret's cabinet who, when necessary, overrode or bypassed the Colonial
Administration. In the words of one Catholic missionary it was "la politique
de cabinet ou de court-circuitage."[73]

Buisseret and Educational Subsidies

To put his program into operation, Buisseret had to find the funds for
building, staffing, and running the proposed secular schools. This was
especially difficult during his first year in office when he was still
saddled with the educational budget of the preceding government which provided for payment of large subsidies to the missions. He diverted money
originally intended for the missions to the financing of the new official
schools.[74] In so doing he blocked or restricted promised subsidies and thus
unilaterally abrogated agreements concluded between the missions and the
previous government.*

In the budgets adopted after 1954 Buisseret sought to favor the official
schools. When the educational subsidies paid to the missions during the fiscal years 1955-1957 are compared with those paid during the previous years,
their total amounts show an overall increase, but their proportions to the
amounts allocated for official schools show a decrease (see table 11). Despite the increase in subsidies, the missions were dissatisfied with the
treatment they were receiving. They considered that they were being attacked
and harassed in various ways by a government that was determined to reduce

---

*Referring to this, one writer noted that "the government had in the
meanwhile ordered restrictions of subsidies to the mission schools, unilaterally denouncing the conventions signed with the missions" (XXX, "La
politique scolaire au Congo du point de vue missionaire," p. 300). This re-
fers to those conventions signed in 1948 and 1952 between the various missionary societies and the government. These conventions established a new
basis for mission-state cooperation in the area of education, superseding
the Conventions De Jonghe which had expired in 1948 after having been in
force for twenty years. In accordance with the Dispositions Générales of
1948, which were mutually agreed to, the missions would receive educational
subsidies on the following basis: 70 percent for schools in large urban
areas (all categories), 70 percent for secondary schools, and 50 percent
for all other schools (including boarding schools—internats) that followed
the state's program (Quatrième conférence plénière des révérendissimes
ordinaires du Congo et du Ruanda-Urundi, p. 36).

TABLE 11

EDUCATIONAL ALLOCATIONS IN "ORDINARY" BUDGETS, 1950-1957
(in thousands of francs)

	Total Educational Budget	Subsidies to Missions[a]
1950	299	196
1951	358	212
1952	482	278
1953	721	450
1954	772	458
1955	911	517
1956	1151	614
1957	1420	670

SOURCE: "L'Enseignement en Afrique Belge," p. 96.

NOTE: Additional funds were allocated each year under an "extraordinary" budget.

[a]Not included are subsidies for agricultural, medical, or social schools, which came under another heading. In addition, the écoles officielles congréganistes were fully financed by the state though run by the missions.

their role and influence in the Congo.*

The Coulon report had criticized the mission schools for the poor quality of their teaching personnel. Most classes, especially at the primary
school level, were taught by Congolese teachers. Coulon and his colleagues
considered these classes substandard and attributed this situation to what
they considered to be the poor quality of the training given at Catholic
normal schools. They recommended that Congolese teachers be trained in
schools to be established by the state.[75] In the ensuing years the government built its own normal schools. But faced with the immediate problem of
staffing state schools, it found that the only source was the mission
schools which had until then monopolized primary education. It therefore
offered attractive terms in an attempt to attract Congolese instructors from
the Catholic schools, and was accused by the Catholics of raiding staff from
their schools.

The mission-state conventions of 1948 and 1952 (see above, p. 95 fn.)
accorded the missions the right to hire and receive subsidies for European
lay teachers for their schools. The Coulon report was critical of mission
hiring practices. It claimed that the Catholics limited their recruitment
of lay teachers to either Catholic schools in Belgium or the Service Inter-
fédérale Belge d'Enseignement Libre au Congo which was tied to the Confédération des Syndicats Chrétiens (which in turn was tied to the PSC) and that
those hired in this manner often lacked the necessary qualifications.[76] Taking into account their background and views, it was natural for the Catholic
missions to recruit among their own adherents; and it was just as natural
for the Coulon Commission to reject this practice. The report suggested
that the state name "the teachers and the principals, as the ecclesiastic
superiors now do."[77] In 1946 Godding had made a similar recommendation in
regard to the lay schools, calling upon the Ministère de l'Instruction Publique, which was in charge of the secular school system in Belgium, to recruit a number of teachers for them.[78]

Buisseret and his cabinet were accused of manipulating teacher recruitment for official schools in the Congo in such a way as to effectively exclude Catholics. It was charged that "the dossiers [of teachers] are
personally examined and acted upon by the office of the minister, an anticlerical selection being thereby assured."[79] Teachers holding degrees from
Catholic normal schools or universities, it was alleged, were automatically
excluded.

The Catholics also felt aggrieved in regard to disbursements from the
Fonds du Bien-Etre Indigène (FBEI). Prior to Buisseret's administration the
missions had been the major recipients, grants going mainly to build and support schools, medical facilities, and social centers, most of which were run
by the missions. The Coulon report had recommended that "the FBEI ought to

---

*In 1951 the Catholic missionary hierarchy in the Congo established an
educational commission to deal with the government. By 1955 it had become
apparent that this commission alone was not sufficient to deal with the many
problems arising in the area of education. Therefore, in April 1955 Abbé
Joseph Moermans was appointed director of the Bureau de l'Enseignement Catholique (BEC). BEC had been established by the Comité Permanent des Ordinaires
du Congo Belge in July 1954. Moermans was to be the spokesman and liaison
for the missions to the government on matters pertaining to education.

reserve its resources for the construction of secular schools or schools remaining the property of indigenous districts."[80] Buisseret's program made the state an important recipient of FBEI aid. This deprived the missions of money they had been counting on. The colonial minister indicated at one point that he wished to "dissociate" medical work and teaching, which he considered "purely governmental" in nature, from "strictly evangelistic works."[81] The channeling of FBEI funds into government projects was an attempt to translate this into action. It was noted that in the Kasai FBEI funds had been largely denied to the missions, while the state used foundation money to build a number of complexes which included social centers, medical dispensaries, and primary and secondary schools. Meanwhile the missions, it was alleged, were refused permission to build similar facilities in the same area.[82]

The missionaries were particularly enraged by government actions in the matter of the FBEI. A meeting of Catholic bishops of the Province of Kasai denounced these actions as a "true declaration of war."[83] The regulations governing the FBEI allowed grants only to projects outside the centres extra-coutumiers, i.e., in nonurban areas. Until 1954 it had been accepted that mission posts not within the urban areas were eligible to receive aid from the FBEI. Buisseret, however, gave the rules a new interpretation, designed to cut off FBEI grants to the missions. He claimed that the very nature of mission posts separated them from the customary milieu and that they were accordingly ineligible for FBEI grants. The opposition in parliament chided Buisseret for resorting to such devious means to achieve his ends.[84]* This manipulation of FBEI funds appreciably widened the gap between the missions and the state.

Land Grants and School Construction

Buisseret also sought to inhibit the expansion of the missions by denying or putting impediments in the way of their requests for land or for school buildings. De Vleeschauwer brought this problem before the parliament, charging that the missions were denied the smallest piece of land for school construction.[85] As an example of the delaying tactics employed by the government, he cited the request by a Catholic mission for a school, to be constructed at Limete (Léopoldville). In March 1954 the authorities had agreed to this request and had tentatively accepted the accompanying plans. But the government withheld final permission and required new plans from the mission; nine months later permission to go ahead had still not been granted. Similar stalling tactics were employed elsewhere.[86]

The most sensitive question between the missions and the state was that of subsidies for school construction. Money promised to the missions for school construction was blocked, and mission requests for such funds were

---

*While thus denying FBEI grants to the missions the government sought to use them to its own best advantage, sometimes playing fast and loose with the regulations. The Provincial Commission of the FBEI at Léopoldville on one occasion proposed to employ FBEI credits to construct official schools just outside the bounds of the centres extra-coutumiers ("Constructions d'écoles officielles par le FBEI," Léopoldville, 1956 [BEC]).

denied. Meanwhile the Colonial Ministry was allegedly allocating credits for the construction of official schools* for which the budget had made no specific provision.[87] The missions were forced to cut back their projected plans for school construction. De Vleeschauwer placed the blame for this squarely on the minister of colonies:

> There is no longer money for the necessary schools which we have been waiting many years to see built, because you, M. Buisseret, have appropriated 85 million in credits from the budget in order to give it to your schools, which were to function four months after your decision without any further formality. It is without precedent, even in the Congo.[88]**

In one instance, requests for subsidies for school construction submitted by the Vicariate of Luluabourg went unheeded, some for as long as two years. Msgr. Mels felt "absolutely sure [that the government] automatically slid the dossiers dealing with the demands of the Catholic missions under others."[89] He charged Buisseret and his colleagues with the deliberate sabotage of mission efforts to build new schools.

During the month of December 1954 the governor-general's office, acting on the orders of the minister of the colonies, issued two letters which escalated the already stormy conflict between the missions and the state to hurricane force. On December 8, 1954, Vice-Governor-General Hendrik Cornelis wrote to the leaders of the Catholic and Protestant missions that financial difficulties facing the government forced a reduction in the subsidies, which had been determined by the convention of 1952, for the salaries of African teachers and for the internats (boarding schools). The convention had provided for the total subsidization of the salaries of qualified Congolese teachers in mission schools approved by the state. The government now proposed to reduce salary subsidies to the level of the 1948 convention, that is, 90 percent for teachers in secondary schools and 80 percent for teachers in other schools. Subsidies to the internats were to be reduced from 80 percent to 50 percent of annual expenditures. The government also called for a reduction of the number of internats and of internat enrollment. "The missions were informed that the new subsidies for the internats would go into effect on January 1, 1955."[90] It was not clear whether Cornelis was ordering the missions to comply with this new policy or was requesting their voluntary acquiescence in it. The tone of his letter to the CPC implied the former, but the closing paragraphs read:

---

*Construction of official secondary schools took precedence. Buisseret and his cabinet were especially interested in asserting the influence of secular education in this area over that of the missions (see Moermans, "Aux révérendissimes ordinaires du Congo Belge non-membres du Comité Permanent—enseignement général pour autochtones répartition des crédits," Léopoldville, 1957 [BEC]).

**In 1956, 186 million francs were allocated for school construction (for Congolese); of this amount only 59 million were for mission schools. In 1957, 269 million francs were allocated of which less than 60 million went to mission schools (Annales parlementaires de Belgique: Chambre des Représentants, 1956, p. 489).

I would appreciate your acknowledging receipt of the above by informing me of the opinions eventually arrived at by the Protestant Council.

Upon receiving your reply, I will inform the missionary associations of the new arrangements.[91]

Two other government communications to the missions quickly followed. On December 18, 1954, the directors of écoles officielles congréganistes and subsidized schools for Europeans were informed that subsidies for the salaries of white lay teachers would be paid only in the case of those constituting less than two-thirds of the entire teaching and administrative staff.[92] Little more than a week later the governor-general let it be known that the state would no longer support the cost of first-level primary schools for boys.[93]

The missions regarded these actions as arbitrary and unilateral moves on the part of the government and raised the question of possible abrogation of the convention of 1952 which stated that "no modification will be made in the tenor of these general arrangements of 1952 without the previous agreement of the two parties."[94] The Catholic missions submitted this legal question to three well-known Belgian jurists, MM. Sohier, Struye, and Wigny. All three agreed that the government was in a weak position, and that the convention of 1952 was legally binding on both parties. Sohier's opinion stated: "To modify the subventions on the matter of treatment of the teachers, without the agreement of the missions, is legally open to attack."[95] Another Belgian lawyer, M. Moyersoen, informed Msgr. Verwimp that he had discussed the problem with Auguste De Schrijver and Wigny, and that all had agreed that the Catholic missions should not yield to the government's demands which, in their opinion, constituted a breach of contract.[96]

In Léopoldville an extraordinary meeting of the Permanent Committee of Catholic Bishops was held January 10-15, 1955, to discuss the government's letters, the convention of 1952, and possible courses of action. Four possible steps were considered: to close all the schools; to bring the question before the Conseil d'Etat; to bring a court case against the government; or to establish organizations of lawyers to fight for the cause of the missions. The committee adopted the first alternative as offering the most effective means of eliciting a positive response from the authorities. It therefore informed the governor-general:

> The carrying out of the announced measures will categorically force the missions to close the greater part of their schools and, confronted with the impossibility of determining which schools should be sacrificed, the missions will be forced, in all practicality, to close every one of them.[97]

In his reply Pétillon denied that the government meant to take unilateral action. "The minister has instructed me to tell you that his intention is not to unilaterally modify a multilateral agreement, but to begin negotiations with a view towards...amending this...agreement." He asked that the letter of December 8, 1954, be interpreted "as proposing negotiations."[98] Verwimp regarded this reply with skepticism. To him it seemed that the letter of December 8 and those which followed had been meant as orders, not proposals. If they were proposals, he informed Pétillon, then "it is absolutely impossible to accept them.[99] He demanded adherence to the convention of 1952 as an indispensable condition for the withdrawal of the decision to

close all Catholic schools.[100] The Catholic missions were not about to relinquish one of their most effective weapons in return for a mere promise to
negotiate. If they had carried out their threat to close all their schools,
the entire educational system in the Congo would have been thrown into a
state of disorganization and chaos, with which the government would have
found it difficult to cope.

The Catholics used the controversy surrounding the letter of December 8
to air all the grievances they harbored against Buisseret's methods and policies. They accused him of many violations of obligations which the government had undertaken with regard to the missions. Buisseret issued a denial
of the Catholic charges, asserting that it had never been the intention of
the government "to violate, either directly or indirectly, the conventions[101]
which had been concluded between the colony and the missionary societies."

On January 25, 1955, at Buisseret's request a meeting between himself,
Msgr. Verwimp, and Governor-General Pétillon was held in Léopoldville. The
colonial minister expressed his willingness to reconsider the points raised
in the letter of December 8.[102] Msgr. Verwimp, however, expanded the discussion to other aspects of the minister's policies which the missions felt
to be obnoxious. Among the major Catholic demands were continued subsidization of schools at the previous level; no reduction of subsidies for internats; and withdrawal of the letters of December 8, 18, and 27 of the previous year. Verwimp demanded strict equality of treatment between lay and
missionary education.[103]

Following this meeting Buisseret drafted a communiqué clearly acknowledging his about-face. The communiqué was submitted to the Permanent Committee of Catholic Bishops, which rejected it as being "too general and not
explicit enough."[104] It was the committee's intention to commit the minister as precisely as possible to a new policy in regard to the missions.
Verwimp proposed a revision of the communiqué which was more specific and
noted points of contention and concession more precisely. He called for a
clear statement asserting the government's respect for the convention of
1952, and confirming "a real equality between government and missionary education."[105] In his response to these proposals the minister clarified his
concessions in regard to strict adherence to the convention of 1952 and the
continuation of subsidies to internats, and promised "a real equality between government and missionary education."[106] This revised communiqué was
issued with the approval of the Catholic bishops, although with some reser-
vations. The missions had won a significant battle against the minister of
colonies. The result, however, was not peace but an uneasy truce.

The Buisseret-Moermans-Thompson Agreement

On June 9, 1955, Buisseret launched a new assault against the missions
by issuing a circular requiring them to solicit public bids for school construction.[107] Before this the missions had not been required to invite com-
petitive bids but had been free to choose whom they wished to construct
their schools. Especially in the bush they often constructed the schools
themselves with the help of African labor and without any recourse to private contractors. Abbé Joseph Moermans, director of the Bureau de l'Enseignement Catholique, protested the new government requirement, urging
that the missions could construct schools at less cost than could private
firms. He noted that the latter often would not or could not undertake

101

construction in the bush; some had tried to do so, he indicated, only to a-
bandon the effort before completion.[108]

In March 1956 Moermans negotiated an agreement in Brussels with the colonial minister which provided for the division of school subsidies between
the state, the Protestants, and the Catholics on the basis of 45 percent, 10
percent, and 45 percent respectively.[109] Though somewhat skeptical, the
Permanent Committee of Catholic Bishops accepted the agreement.[110] The committee's skepticism was confirmed when Buisseret informed Moermans that the
Catholic share would be 45 percent of the credits allocated for general and
technical education, not of the total allocated for education.[111] This restrictive interpretation was the work of that bête-noir of the Catholics,
Ney, the anticlerical director of education in the Government General and
one of the chief negotiators.[112]

For the Protestants the press reports of the Buisseret-Moermans agreement were a rude awakening. In spite of its intimate concern to them, they
had been neither consulted nor kept informed during the course of its formulation and approval. On May 23, 1956, Coxill, Thompson, and Ohrneman, representing the Protestant missions, met with the governor-general to protest
the government's unilateral action in this affair and to seek clarification
of the agreement.[113] The Protestants, however, did not repudiate the Buisseret-Moermans agreement but contented themselves with demanding that they
be included in future negotiations about it.

The remaining conflicts over the agreement were ironed out in a series
of meetings held in Léopoldville during late summer 1956 between Buisseret,
Moermans, and Thompson. The resulting Buisseret-Moermans-Thompson Agreement,
as it came to be called, was signed on August 28, 1956. Catholic and Protestant acquiescence was obtained at the price of increased grants to both.*

Buisseret, however, cannot be accounted the loser in this drama. He
had achieved two of his major aims: the assurance for his program of secular schools of enough funds for expansion without the risk of their being
blocked by the opposition, and the reduction of the influence of the missions in such areas of education as the schools of administration. By accepting the 45:10:45 formula the Catholic missions acquiesced in the fact
that the eventual size of the secular school system might equal or even sur-
pass their own. The conflict between the colonial minister and the Catholic
missions did not end with the Buisseret-Moermans-Thompson agreement, even
though this had more or less settled many of the points upon which they
clashed.** Tension and ill will continued between the government and

---

*The Catholics were "to manage at least half" of the écoles sociales
built by the state and their 45 percent would not include the écoles congreganistes. The Protestants were granted "16 percent of the credits affecting general education for Africans," to be included in their overall 10 percent share (Buisseret, Moermans, Thompson, "Interprétation de l'accord de
mars-avril 1956, entre le Ministre des Colonies et les missions au sujet des
constructions scolaires," Léopoldville, Aug. 28, 1956 [BEC]).

**Controversy arose over attempts by the government to narrow or evade
some of the provisions of the agreement. Soon after it had been signed the
Ministry of Colonies insisted that equipment and furnishings for the schools
to be built were not covered, since only "construction" had been mentioned in

Catholic missions throughout the remainder of Buisseret's term of office, though at a fluctuating level and without ever again rising to the heights attained during 1954-1956.

Buisseret's anticlerical policies, in particular his attempt to secularize the educational system at the price of weakening the mission-run schools, had undermined the entente between the state and the Catholic missions. Relations had in fact been so transformed during these years as to shatter the very basis for close cooperation. Before Buisseret's appearance on the scene the missions had felt that they had an investment in the continuity of a colonial system that supported their efforts and aims. The changes wrought by the Liberal minister of colonies convinced many missionaries that continued unquestioning support for the colonial system was now counter to their interests. In an article written during Buisseret's ministry Professor Van Bilsen noted that the introduction of an anticlerical policy in the Congo had opened a political Pandora's box:

> M. Buisseret has made it understood that the missionaries were not all-powerful....There is also a movement [among Congolese] to free [themselves] from the tutelage of the missionaries, sometimes felt to be tyrannical. But what M. Buisseret and his friends have not foreseen is that this black "anticlericalism" was above all [an expression of] anticolonialism, of black nationalism.[114]

The missions felt constrained to respond to this new phenomenon. Events during the period 1954-1958 had so changed the political equilibrium of the Congo as to convince the Catholics that their future survival and growth lay in an entirely different direction.

---

the accord. The Catholics also charged that the government had tried to include funds not covered by the agreement, and had diverted other credits which were supposed to be included. Finally, contrary to the understanding which had been reached, the government proceeded to establish administrative schools with six-year programs (Moermans to De Schrijver et al., Léopold-ville, Jan. 29, 1957 [BEC]).

CHAPTER 11

THE EMERGENCE OF A CONGOLESE ELITE

As far back as 1925 a commission established to study the problem of labor in the Congo had warned that the déracinés who gathered around the industrial and commercial centers could become the focal point of subversive activities.[1]* During the 1940s a new class of Congolese—the évolués (see above, p. 68 fn.)—had emerged and was coming into its own within the burgeoning urban centers. For several years after the end of World War II few évolués had more than an école moyenne (technical or middle school) education. In later years more of them achieved a secondary education, but only a handful obtained university degrees. In 1948 Father Van Wing estimated the évolué population in the Congo to be about 40,000 out of a total work force of some 750,000.[2]

Benevolent Paternalism and Educational Gradualism

Under the pretext of national development the educational system had

---

*The commission had further recommended that a maximum of 25 percent of the total work force be recruited for work in the urban centers. As of 1950, it was reported that labor recruitment in four out of six provinces had exceeded this percentage, as follows: Léopoldville 49 percent, Katanga 44 percent, Kivu 42 percent, Oriental 29 percent, Equateur 24 percent, and Kasai 20 percent (Jean Comhaire, "Evolution politique et sociale du Congo Belge en 1950-1952," p. 1045).

Attempts to control migration toward the cities proved inadequate as the demand for labor increased and the lure of urban life attracted more and mored Africans from the bush. The growth of the two largest urban areas in the Congo illustrates the size of this movement:

	Population of Léopoldville	Population of Elisabethville
1935	26,622	22,858
1940	46,884	26,780
1946	110,280	65,397
1951	221,757	95,559
1955	340,000	120,000
1958	388,961	182,638

(Compiled from Thomas Hodgkin, Nationalism in Colonial Africa, p. 67; and Inforcongo, Belgian Congo, vol. 2, p. 15).

been designed to prevent the growth of an African elite. The entire population—or at least a major part of it—was to advance at the same pace. In this way there would be no danger of the emergence of a class of embittered déracinés who might upset both Congolese society and Belgian rule. Moreover condemnation of a mainly literary or bookish education that did not meet the "real" (that is, economic) demands of the colony was general. Yet it was exactly this type of education that the évolués were demanding.

The emphasis on gradual development was not confined to education; it pervaded the attitudes of Belgians toward the Congo and the Congolese in every sphere, until it almost took on the aura of dogma. Benevolent paternalism had become the keystone of the Belgian colonial rationale. Pierre Ryckmans summed it up in a phrase: "Dominer pour servir."[3] The Belgians felt it incumbent upon themselves to carry out their civilizing mission, the needs of the indigenous population ostensibly being uppermost in their minds.* But it was also clear that this would be a process dictated from above.** At the apex were to be found the state, the large companies, and the Catholic missions. The two first-named were to concern themselves with the more mundane needs of the people, while the last-named were to look after their spiritual and moral needs. The members of this triumvirate were expected to aid and support each other; church and state were seen as inextricably linked in the drive to fulfill Belgian colonial objectives.

Because of mission monopoly of education all or nearly all of the évolués had at some point in their lives attended mission-operated schools.*** It is not surprising, therefore, that the missions became concerned with évolué hopes, strivings, and conflicts. For nearly the first time in their more than fifty years in the Congo the missionaries were forced to be responsive to a group of Congolese who could organize and articulate their demands. Throughout the years from 1945 to 1960 the missions, especially the Catholic, struggled to adjust to a new and rapidly changing situation and to the often

---

*For their attempts to introduce the carte d'immatriculation and the carte de mérite civique see appendix C.

**This policy has been described as Platonism: "Platonism is implicit in the sharp distinction, social and legal, between Belgian philosopher-kings and the mass of African producers; in the conception of education as primarily concerned with the transmission of certain unquestioned and unquestionable moral values, and intimately related to status and functions; in the belief that the thought and behavior of the mass is plastic, and can be refashioned by a benevolent, wise, and highly trained elite; that the prime intent of the mass is in welfare and consumer goods—football and bicycles—not liberty; and in the conviction that it is possible, by expert administration, to arrest social and political change," (Thomas Hodgkin, Nationalism in Colonial Africa, p. 52).

***An analysis of Pierre Artigue's Qui sont les leaders Congolais? indicates that 110 prominent Congolese listed therein had attended Catholic schools, while only 15 had gone to Protestant schools. For many others mentioned in Artigue's work data were lacking, but it is doubtful that the ratio of Protestants to Catholics would have been very different even if data had been available for all of his three hundred or so listings.

conflicting demands and expectations of the Congolese and the Belgian colonial regime.

Despite the misgivings of many of their colleagues and countrymen in the Congo, progressive Catholic missionaries and laymen fought for better educational opportunities for the Congolese. They pointed out that, unless the Church could capture the imagination and loyalty of the new elite, it would have reason to fear for its future. At the fourth plenary conference of the Catholic bishops Msgr. Guffens emphasized the necessity of promoting the formation of an educated elite, even at the price of giving up the policy of gradual development of the masses: "This task must be done, even if its accomplishment has to somewhat retard the access of part of the population to secular knowledge, [even] to a Christian life itself."[4]

But many missionaries, while welcoming the new-found prise de conscience of the Congolese elite, were anxious about its consequences. In 1946 Signum Fidei, the journal of the Association des Anciens Elèves des Frères Chrétiens, published a series of editorials and articles concerning the effects on the évolués of the libertarian and democratic ideals expounded by the Allies during the war. The editors, Belgian missionaries, feared that these ideals might be turned into weapons to be used against both the missions and colonial rule. They attempted to interpret the meaning of democracy for their readers and to explain missionary views on this subject: "To listen [to those who extol democracy] the past centuries have known nothing but oppression and servitude. This dark age has come to an end, they say! The dawn of emancipation is here, full of prosperity, of goodness....The key to earthly paradise has been rediscovered!" Those who vilified colonization were "ignorant" and "without scruples."[5] There can be little doubt that many missionaries feared that among the évolués democratic concepts might become the basis of an anticlerical lay philosophy and pit them against the missions.

Evolué Demands: Growth of Antimissionary Feeling

With their expanding social and intellectual horizons, the évolués became more vociferous in their demands for increased educational opportunities for Congolese. Here the missions offered a natural target for criticism. The évolués were especially critical of what they felt to be the mission schools' lack of interest in higher education; they believed that the missions were deliberately depriving them of advanced education. Buisseret's policies had merely exacerbated a discontent already rife among the évolués, Catholic and non-Catholic alike.*

The Catholic missions, aware of the discontent of the elite and fearful of losing its confidence and loyalty, pressed for educational reform. Indeed, it was in large part owing to their pressure that in 1948 a new educational program was adopted which provided secondary education for Congolese. This did not mean, however, that the missions had made a clear break with

------

*Marcel Lihau noted in 1958 that "the educational controversy that began four years ago revealed in a striking way, the existence of a faction of [Congolese] opinion that is unfavorable to the missionaries" ("Les aspirations nationales au Congo belge," p. 157).

the philosophy of educational gradualism they had previously endorsed and that had so far dominated the administration's policy.

The évolués grew increasingly skeptical on the question of whether the Belgians would ever extend them the respect and recognition that they believed to be their due. The reluctance of the administration and the European settlers to accept them as equals could perhaps be grudgingly understood. But their reaction to the missionaries was bitter. The missionaries had posed as the friends and protectors of the Congolese and were supposedly concerned with their interests and development first and foremost; yet in many cases their attitudes and actions toward the Congolese appeared identical with those of other Europeans.*

Among many Congolese the feeling grew that the missions were not for them, that they had actually deceived them. These rumblings of discontent had become louder during the Buisseret period, when the missions were attacked for giving the Congolese an inadequate education. During the late 1950s much of the previously latent opposition and hostility of the Congolese toward the missions burst into the open. Even those who supported the missions warned them about increasing anticlericalism among the Africans. Marcel Lihau, a Louvain graduate, one of the first Congolese to receive a higher degree from a Belgian university and later a member of Ileo's government, admonished a meeting of missionaries in these terms: "If one even finds that African Catholics criticize the missionaries...isn't it, perhaps, because they don't find in them all that they hope for: an adequate response to their most pressing and urgent anxieties and hopes?"[6] Evariste Kimba, later to become a leading member of the Confédération des Associations Tribales à Katanga and minister of foreign affairs in secessionist Katanga, painted an even blacker picture: "No one can be ignorant that at the moment the missions, and particularly the Catholics, are apparently losing their influence among the Congolese. In effect, they are represented, by certain able...propagandists, as the number one enemy of all progress for the Africans."[7]

A major criticism levelled at the Catholic missions was that of ethnocentrism and inability to deal with important African social, political, and economic problems. In Congolese eyes missionary actions and attitudes were frequently characterized by misunderstanding, excessive prudence, and timidity. Lihau informed the missions that three steps were essential if they were to halt the process of alienation among their Congolese adherents: "the clergy [should] align itself, without reservation, on the side of the Africans;...the missionaries should be among the most progressive and dynamic architects of social and political evolution in the country;...the missionary should shed [his] superiority complex and [attitude of] clerical paternalism [which would be] judged heavy-handed or authoritarian."[8] Like Lihau, other members of the Congolese Catholic elite who did not become completely disaffected also called upon the missionaries to initiate changes in policy that

_____

*One leading évolué expressed his belief that "Europeans, including the missionaries, put us all in the same sack. To them we are all ignorant children. When we dare to offer our opinion to a European, they think we are arrogant. Sometimes we ask ourselves, what good is the training that the missions have given us, has it totally failed?" (Massion, "Relations humaines entre belges and congolais," p. 16).

would transform their role and their relations with the Congolese.

The Belgians had for some time viewed Catholicism as a major factor in tying the Congolese to Belgium and as playing a key role in the establishment of the Belgo-Congolese community. Writing in 1939, Antoine Sohier, a lawyer and Liberal Catholic from Elisabethville, had noted that "Catholicism is the national religion of our nation, tomorrow it will be the national religion of the Congolese. What a powerful tie between two peoples!"[9] To realize this goal, the whites—including the missionaries—would have to allow the rising Congolese elite access to positions of responsibility and importance, and extend to them the recognition and respect reserved for equals. Otherwise the Church would become "une affaire des Blancs."[10]

Policy Reassessment by Catholic Progressives

In accepting a close relationship with the colonial authorities the Catholic missions had readily acquiesced in and indeed contributed to the administration's view of the Congolese elite. Many, if not most of them, pictured the model évolué as the product of a petit-bourgeois mold—a conception more Belgian than Catholic. Both missionaries and members of the administration envisaged a loyal elite which would be an example to the rest of the population and whose role was to be essentially passive. Thus a subtle contradiction was to be found in the attitude of the Church and administration: while ostensibly wishing the évolués to be community leaders, they constantly inveighed against the formation of an elitist attitude that would have provided the basis for active leadership. The end result of this was that the missionaries, so long accustomed to the possession of nearly unquestioned authority in ecclesiastical and other matters, now found themselves confronted by an increasingly discontented flock, led by évolués who would no longer accept the prescribed passivity and servility.

During the 1950s a number of the more astute and progressive Catholic missionaries became aware of the criticism levelled at the missions by a vociferous elite among the laity within the Church. This new awareness led to a spate of privately circulated papers and articles published in leading Belgian Catholic journals which sought to investigate prior assumptions and to reevaluate the evolving role of the Church in the Congo.* In a paper delivered to a Catholic organization in Brussels Father K. Plessers stated that

---

*The Protestant missionaries were on the whole much less astute than the Catholics in evaluating the changes that were taking place in the Congo during the 1950s. While various Catholic missionaries had begun as early as 1945 to call for changes in basic missionary policy in view of the rapidly evolving situation in the Congo, Protestant missionaries for the most part held on to the Belgian thesis that economic, social, and political peace could be maintained in the Congo by a process of insulation. Thus a Protestant missionary could write in 1952: "Governmental paternalism, a careful screening of all who enter the colony from the outside and an active endeavor to anticipate the needs and ambitions of the African population have kept nationalism, Communism and other disturbing factors without the gates. The Church is thus not as yet striving with these disrupting forces, but has a

the Church was losing its influence among the évolués. He noted that the évolués were, with some justification, highly critical of the missionaries, the major complaints being that the missionaries often called them immoral, materialistic, and arrogant; tended to accord them less respect than they accorded Europeans; could not always be trusted not to report what they heard to the administration; and tended to place themselves on pedestals.[11]

This growing distrust and alienation from the missionaries on the part of the indigenous Catholic elite was a threat to the growth, even to the survival, of a Congolese Catholic Church. As Plessers' remarks go to show, at the heart of évolué resentment against the missionaries lay the feeling that the latter were often too authoritarian and haughty in their relations with the Congolese. Missionaries no less than other whites were often con-temptuous of the ability and individual work of their adherents. Some like Father Pascal Ceuterick, superior of the Catholic mission in Kolwezi (Katanga), warned their fellow missionaries that "our latent and perhaps un-conscious racism has made us look upon the natives as inferior beings who expect everything from the Europeans."[12] Another critic, Father Placide Tempels,* was even more scathing in his admonishment:

---

clear field, with its greatest hindrance the ever rebellious heart of man and his inertia" (H. D. Brown, "The Church and Its Missionary Task in the Congo," p. 302).

The Protestants, while often consciously rejecting an identification with the Belgian Colonial Administration, nonetheless strongly identified with its goals and assumptions. This led to a degree of self-deception among Protestant missionaries. Being foreigners (i.e., non-Belgian), they could rationalize that they were free agents who were chiefly concerned with the needs and interests of the Congolese while tempering the impact of Belgian colonial rule. Certainly there was some truth in such an assumption, but it was far from the total reality. Carpenter's assertion that "Protestant mis-sionaries, being mainly foreigners were obviously not instruments of Belgian colonial controls," strikes one with the naiveté of its simple logic (George W. Carpenter, "Whose Congo?," p. 281).

It would seem that the Protestants escaped much of the criticism the évolués aimed at the missions because the Protestants were foreigners who did not have close viable ties to the Belgians, as did the Catholic missions; the Protestant members of the Congolese elite were much smaller in number and for the most part less well-trained and organized than their Catholic brethren; and the Protestants had endowed their followers with the notion of the sepa-ration of Church and state and an antipolitical or apolitical attitude. Of these three factors the second is undoubtedly of greatest importance in ex-plaining why the ferment which the Catholic missions experienced during the 1950s failed to strike the Protestants with equal force.

*His Bantu Philosophy, first published in 1945, had an important impact on missionary (and, one might add, scholarly) thinking about the African as "man." The conception of the Africans held by the Western world had for some time been dominated by the belief in the preliterate and prerational nature of the African as propounded by Levi-Bruhl. Tempels presented the African as a rational and, moreover, a philosophical being, concerned about the world he lived in and his place in it. Central to his theory is the idea of the life force or vital force (force vitale) which he claimed was the determining fac-tor in Bantu religion and, indeed, in every aspect of Bantu life.

We have had the idea that we stood before them like adults before the
newly born. In our mission to educate and to civilize, we believed
that we started with a "tabula rasa" though we also believed that we
had to clear the ground of some worthless notions, to lay the foundations in a bare soil. We were quite sure that we should give short
shrift to stupid customs, vain beliefs, as being quite ridiculous and
devoid of all sound sense.[13]

Many missionaries were perhaps less comfortable about their prejudiced
feelings toward the African than were other whites in the Congo. For Christian missionaries were committed to a Judaeo-Christian ethical system which
teaches the equality and brotherhood of all men before God. Yet what was
preached as universal truth was in practice more honored in the breach than
the observance. The missionaries had felt quite at home with a paternalistic
policy; it meshed nicely with their self-image as teachers and good parents.
Thus many were irked by évolué criticism and appeared to look on the Congolese as ungrateful children who were questioning, indeed attacking, parental
authority. And they may have felt that the Africans, by not conforming to
their expectations were threatening their conception of their role and purpose.

The rapid change in the social and political situation during the 1950s
seems to have outdistanced any corresponding adjustment in missionary attitudes. A major problem for the missions was that of educating missionaries
in the bush areas about the new forces now at work. The view such missionaries took of the Congo tended to be microscopic, to center on the limited
jurisdiction of their own mission stations rather than on the colony as a
whole. Many had difficulty in adopting new attitudes and approaches to the
Congolese. This was especially true of those who had served long in the
Congo and were deeply committed to paternalism and close mission-state cooperation. Father Mosmans cautioned his fellow-missionaries that the pace of
change in the Congo was so rapid that those out of touch with the urban centers tended to overlook the importance of the new ideas and movements fer-
menting there. This was in part due to the "backward mentality" of some
missionaries in regard to Congolese advancement. This adherence to authoritarian and paternalistic attitudes served to alienate the African population.[14]

Buisseret's policies had weakened the bonds binding the missions to the
government and the commercial firms in the colonial triumvirate. Taking advantage of the resulting shock, a number of progressive churchmen encouraged
the missionaries to give up their traditional commitment to the colonial
system and some of their prior goals. One missionary called upon his colleagues to relinquish any sentimental attachment to the past: "No longer
believe yourselves all-powerful, don't hang on to the christianitas of the
old regime; it is past and it must be forgotten."[15]

Noting that the aspirations of the Congolese would sooner or later
bring them into conflict with the established authorities, Father Mosmans
broached the question of the position the Church should take in such a conflict:

The Church must remain above these...conflicts. The pattern of cooperation [with the government] which has until now been faithfully followed
runs the risk of making the Church appear to be tied to the Government.
If this should continue, the Church will be blamed for tactical errors,

for tardiness, for mistakes, for all those things which are harmful to the African. In the end the Church would be considered as an outsider.[16]

In a similar vein Father Plessers advocated that the missions rediscover their Augustinian roots: "Political concerns...should not be confused with religious concerns, they differ from one another. This is the meaning of the words 'render unto Caesar that which is Caesar's'."[17]

The missions faced a dilemma: they had either to continue to collaborate and identify with the colonial system or to throw in their lot with the Africans and transform themselves into a truly national church. They could not successfully grasp both horns at the same time (though many tried), nor could they ride in limbo between them. Given the goals of their vocation, the missionaries seemed to be facing an easy and obvious decision. Yet some doubted whether they were capable of making it.* Some gave up their deeply ingrained and comfortable patterns of behavior with reluctance and remorse; others would never change, out of inability, choice, or both.

Realizing these difficulties, one observer of the missionary scene was led to ask two significant questions: Is the Church which has been in the Congo truly the Catholic Church? From a sociological point of view, is it truly embodied in African society?[18] Whether affirmative answers to these questions were possible or not, the missionaries in the Congo were under increasing pressure to give such answers. The African Catholic elite demanded it. "The Church will not become African without Africans. The time has arrived for us Congolese to realize that it is up to us to build a new city and a Congolese Church in the Congo."[19] And the Vatican encouraged it. In the encyclical letter Fidei Donum of April 21, 1957, which dealt almost exclusively with Catholic missions in Africa, Pope Pius XII stated "that the Church should be solidly established among other peoples, and a Hierarchy given to them chosen from among their own sons."[20]

Growth of a Congolese Clergy

The establishment of a Congolese Catholic Church necessitated the formation of an indigenous clergy to assume its responsibilities and direction.

---

*Plessers evinced such skepticism when he noted the attitude of many missionaries first toward the Africans and then toward the large commercial firms:

> Missionaries, too used to authoritarian methods, do not adjust easily to a new tenor of relations, which must be truly humane and cordial.... [While] the collaboration with the large capitalist trusts was useful, this need not have the consequence of tying us to their errors. However, the fear of irking these trusts and of losing their subsidies often makes [us] hesitate to take a position against injustices committed [by them]....

> To make them hold their tongues, it suffices to shower them [i.e., the missionaries] with money, [perhaps] a fine automobile..."

(K. Plessers, "L'Evolution religieuse au Congo belge, l'église face à ce tournant, journées d'études missionnaires Centrale Jociste, 9-12 avril, 1956," Brussels, 1956, p. 9, mimeographed [in author's possession]).

It was here that a fundamental difference was revealed between the administration and the Catholic missions in the Congo. The Church, because of its catholic character, could not isolate itself from the Congolese as the administration did. It was forced, because of its own principles and often contrary to the feelings of many missionaries, to elevate Africans to formal equality with white members of the hierarchy, and therefore to deal with the question of African development on a somewhat more realistic basis.

Much of the pressure for the formation of an indigenous clergy came directly from the Holy See. Over a span of forty years four popes issued encyclical letters* directly concerned with this question:

> Maximum Illud, 1919 (Pope Benedict XV)
> Rerum Ecclesiae, 1926 (Pope Pius XI)
> Evangeli Praecones, 1951 (Pope Pius XII)
> Fidei Donum, 1957 (Pope Pius XII)
> Princeps Pastorum, 1959 (Pope John XXIII)

In accordance with Vatican policy, pressure was brought to bear on the Catholic missions in the Congo to devote more of their energy to the training of Congolese clergy, and to give them greater responsibility. A letter addressed by the prefect of the Sacred Congregation for the Propagation of the Faith to the Third Plenary Conference of the Catholic Bishops of the Congo and Ruanda-Urundi (held in 1945) expressed restrained but clear displeasure that the question of the native clergy was not to be dealt with by the conference. It enjoined the conferees to "never fail to keep in mind questions relating to the subject of the clergé indigène et séminaire which constitutes the most important problem of the missions."[21] At the next plenary conference meeting in Léopoldville in 1951 a letter from the Sacred Congregation for the Propagation of the Faith was read which urged the missions "to entrust mission posts to the native clergy."[22]

Most missionaries at first viewed the African clergy as auxiliaries who could relieve them of some of their less appealing pastoral duties, thus allowing them freedom to concentrate their efforts on education and social problems. But, as it became necessary for the Church to affirm its supranational position in the face of rising Congolese political aspirations, the task of building an autonomous African Church became imperative. Congolese clergy

---

*Typical of the exhortations to the missions in these encyclicals were the following:

"In fact, a native priest, having a place of birth, character, mentality, and emotional make-up in common with his countrymen, is in a privileged position for sowing the seeds of the Faith in their hearts; indeed, he knows much better than a stranger the ways of persuasion with them" (Benedict XV, Maximum Illud, quoted in Anne Fremantle, ed., The Papal Encyclicals in Their Historical Context, p. 328).

"This Apostolic See, abundantly and at the opportune time, has taken measures especially in recent times, to establish or reestablish a hierarchy in those areas in which local conditions favored the foundation of Episcopal Sees, and if possible, to place locally born prelates at their head" (Pope John XXIII, Princeps Pastorum, quoted in ibid., p. 326).

would have to be trained and given the opportunity to handle the tasks and responsibilities of the Church in an independent manner.

With this in mind the Catholics, in conjunction with the PSC, had pressed in 1954 for the passage of the proposed convention between Belgium and the Holy See (see above, pp. 79-82) which would have ended the missionary status of the Church in the Congo by establishing a national, though not necessarily a wholly Congolese, hierarchy. The convention, however, failed to pass the Belgian parliament. Had the Catholics so wished, they could have established a hierarchical structure without government permission. That they chose not to do so suggests a split between the missions and Rome. Many missions appear to have been reluctant to hand over authority to the Congolese or to allow rival missionary orders into what they considered their own territory. Progressive missionaries urged the missions to change their attitude on this issue and to submit to a reform of Church structure by doing away with the existing ecclesiastical divisions.[23] It was not until early 1959 that the Vatican designated the Congo an ecclesiastical province.

The problem of establishing a Congolese church and an indigenous Congolese clergy was not the same for the Protestants as for the Catholics. Because of their heterogeneous nature and their rivalries and disputes, the Protestants evolved no clear, uniform policy, although they made attempts to agree upon common goals. Yet on the face of it, in view of the essentially congregationalist attitude of the Protestants, the transformation of Protestant missions into churches might have been expected to be both simpler and more rapid than that of the Catholics. Yet for the most part this was not the case.

Until the 1930s the Protestants had taken practically no action in the direction of African ecclesiastical autonomy. It was the economic depression of the 1930s and the resulting financial and personnel problems among their missions that led the Protestants to think along those lines. In 1934 they established the Church of Christ in the Congo which aimed at including all Protestant churches in an organization which would provide unity and common identity for all Protestant Congolese. This effort failed, according to one observer because of the "hindrance by the colonial set-up with its mind-set of authoritarian control by white leaders and its distrust of genuine autonomy; and...the divergence of views among missions as to the value of ecumenicity."[24]

During the 1940s and 1950s Protestant leaders continually impressed upon skeptical missionaries in the Congo the desirability of according greater autonomy to their African followers. Carpenter stated that "many missionaries themselves are not yet convinced that it is possible for the African church to provide its own leadership on a colony-wide basis. Many are completely unaware of the advance that is taking place elsewhere in Africa in this field."[25] And another Protestant writer noted, with a hint of exasperation with his colleages, "that no nation or grouping of peoples, however much underdeveloped and undereducated, will permanently accept dominance in their life by foreigners. This does not apply only in the political sphere—it applies equally in the spiritual."[26] The need for an autonomous church and leadership was recognized by the Protestants, but owing mainly to mental inertia action came slowly.

By 1955 there were 1,518 Protestant African pastors and 2,052 Protestant missionaries in the Congo. At first glance this might seem to be an impressive accomplishment; but only 452 of these Congolese pastors were consecrated, and of these a bare handful had received training in any way comparable to that of their missionary colleagues.[27] Many had attended Bible schools which gave only a smattering of theological training;* a smaller number had gone to pastoral institutions such as the École de Pasteurs et d'Instituteurs at Kimpese in the Lower Congo. During the 1950s a few Congolese were sent abroad, mainly to the United States, for theological training.

Not until 1950 did the Protestants consider bringing Africans into positions of leadership in the Congo Protestant Council. And even then they leaned to the idea of a separate African church council whose central consultative council would consult with the CPC on church matters on the latter's initiative. Missionary dominance over African churches would thus continue under the guise of greater autonomy.[28] In truth, it was force of circumstance rather than argument that impelled the Protestant missions to transfer responsibility to the African churches and pastors. This transfer was effected on a wide scale during the period just prior to and following independence.

Yet both Catholics and Protestants recognized the fact that an African church without an African clergy would be an anomaly. Soon after their arrival in the Congo during the Léopoldian epoch the missions had recruited catechists to aid them in the task of evangelization, and as early as 1905 the White Fathers had established a seminary at Boudouinville to train Congolese priests. In 1917 Stephano Kaoze, a graduate of Boudouinville, was ordained as the first Congolese priest in modern times.

Mainly because of policies fostered by the Vatican, the 1920s and 1930s witnessed the rapid growth of a system of clerical training for Congolese. It offered two levels of education: the petit séminaire, a six-year program in Latin and the humanities, and the grand séminaire, an eight-year program (three of philosophy and five of theology) which after a period of probation would lead to the priesthood. By 1958 there were twenty-six petits and four grands séminaires** operating in the Congo.[29] Table 12 illustrates the growth of these institutions and of the African clergy from 1938 to 1959.

Pope Benedict XV had urged in his encyclical letter Maximum Illud that the training of indigenous clergy be of the same caliber as that of European priests.*** The grands séminaires established in the Congo did not perhaps achieve standards fully equivalent to those of their European counterparts, but until the late 1940s they offered the Congolese their only available

---

*In 1956 there were 65 Bible and pastoral schools in the Congo (E. M. Braekman, Histoire du protestantisme au Congo, p. 345).

**The four grands séminaires were located at Mayidi (Léopoldville Province), Boudouinville (Kivu), Kabwe (Kasai), and Niangara (Oriental).

***"If...the indigenous clergy is to achieve the results we hope for, it is absolutely necessary that they be well trained and well prepared. We do not mean a rudimentary and slipshod preparation, the bare minimum for ordination. No, their education should be complete and finished, excellent in all its phases, the same kind of education for the priesthood that a European would receive. For the local clergy is not to be trained merely to perform the humbler duties of the ministry, acting as assistants of foreign priests. On the contrary, they must take up God's work as equals so that some day they will be able to enter upon the spiritual leadership of their people" (Thomas J. M. Burke, ed., Catholic Missions, p. 13).

TABLE 12

AFRICAN SEMINARIANS AND PRIESTS, 1938-1959

	Petit Seminarians	Grand Seminarians	Priests
1938	963	135	37
1939	1,042	157	31
1941	1,077	185	34
1943	1,061	239	66
1944	1,128	236	75
1945	1,111	221	93
1946	1,185	226	112
1947	1,298	246	122
1948	1,395	260	139
1949	1,370	251	154
1950	1,348	276	174
1951	1,712	266	198
1952	2,066	295	218
1953	2,100	333	245
1954	1,777	317	262
1955	1,951	341	283
1956	1,864	340	314
1957	1,911	369	298
1959	2,617	369	369[a]

SOURCE: Centre Interdiocésain des Recherches Socio-Religieuses, "Evolution du nombre des prêtres et séminaristes congolais," Léopoldville, n.d., typewritten (DIA).

[a]The authors noted that the figures reported for 1959 were not accurate. According to reports submitted to them there were 417 Congolese priests that year; they determined, however, that this figure was exaggerated and estimated a maximum of 369 for the whole of the Congo.

avenue to a higher education. It is therefore not surprising that many attended the seminaries who had neither the intention nor the inclination to enter the priesthood. Even among those who did quest after that vocation, many never completed the course or failed to be ordained. Crawford Young has estimated that "as of 1960 there were some 3,000 former students of the Catholic seminaries" in the Congo.[30] In company with the African clergy and the graduates of technical schools, these former seminarians dominated the upper echelons of the Congolese elite.* Many became clerks in the service of the Colonial Administration and, later, leaders in the independence movement.**

Attitudes Toward the Congolese Clergy

It was the black priests, however, whom the whites in the Congo regarded as the cream of the Congolese elite, true <u>civilisés</u> whom they considered to be paragons of virtue and achievement among the African population. It was to them that conservative whites would point as evidence of the efficacy and justice of the Belgian colonial policy of "civilizing" the African, while progressives would cite them as justifying the extension of advanced education and more responsible jobs to Congolese in general. In Nigeria the Africanization of the churches spurred the demand for Africanization in other spheres.[31] The same may be said of the Congo, although the pace there was much slower.

Not unnaturally the Congolese populace took pride in and identified with the African clergy. Their achievements were proof that Congolese too could hope to attain positions of status and respect. This pride was, as already suggested, shared by many whites, although for different reasons. But among

----

*Just prior to independence there were some 445 graduates of technical schools (Young, <u>Politics in the Congo</u>, p. 200). Thus, despite the fact that there were relatively few university graduates at the time of independence, there were nevertheless many highly trained Congolese. What lacked, however, was a fund of political and administrative experience, which the colonial administration kept them from gaining. For an interesting discussion of this point see Herbert Weiss, "Comparisons in the Evolution of Pre-Independence Elites in French-Speaking Africa and the Congo," pp. 130 ff.).

**An outstanding example is Joseph Kasavubu, leader of ABAKO and former president of the Congo, who had at one time desired to become a priest and had studied at the <u>grand séminaire</u> of Kabwe in the Kasai for three years before being asked to leave (Charles-André Gilis, <u>Kasa-Vubu</u>, <u>passim</u>).

Until 1954-1955 certificates of graduation from the <u>petits séminaires</u> were accepted by the Colonial Administration as proof of the fulfillment of the educational requirements for employment by the government as a clerk. The Buisseret regime, following its anticlerical tendencies, demanded that such candidates must pass an examination given by a central jury in order to be eligible. This was no doubt intended to lessen the attractiveness of the <u>petits séminaires</u> for Congolese (see untitled mimeographed paper issued by the Centre de Documentation and d'Information Congolaise, Léopoldville, May 14, 1955 [DIA]).

the whites, both missionaries and nonmissionaries, there existed a great deal of ambivalence toward the Congolese clergy. Father Van Wing could assert in 1959 that "it is only in the Catholic Church that black bishops and priests are superior to whites" in the Congo,[32] but this condition was of fairly recent date. Despite their alleged equality, many African priests were for years treated by the missionaries as inferiors. Addressing the Second Plenary Conference of the Catholic Bishops of the Congo and Ruanda-Urundi in 1936, Msgr. Auguste Huys made the point that the indigenous clergy "will be accepted in the community and put on an equal footing with the missionaries. They will take their place according to their rank in the priesthood; they will take precedence over the Brothers. However, they will not be given duties which will give them authority over a [white] Father or a Brother."[33] The missions adhered to the principle of equality in regard to the African clergy, but tempered it with such prejudice and mistrust as almost to negate it. True, African priests often ate the same food, shared the same quarters, and did the same work as their missionary brothers, but disdain, even contempt, was nonetheless communicated to them.* The existence of a Congolese clergy was not sufficient proof of lack of racial discrimination within the Church.**

Until the mid-1950s the Catholic missions in the Congo were more concerned with maintaining good relations with the Colonial Administration and the whites than with pressing for true equality for the Africans, whether within or without the Church. Vatican demands for equal treatment of indigenous clergy were qualified in the words of one missionary by "certain special conditions which reserve to us the maintenance of an atmosphere [agreeable] to the Europeans who govern the regions of the Belgian Congo and Ruanda-Urundi."[34] The preoccupation of the missionaries with white opinions is well illustrated in the instructions given to the African priest in the 1930s regarding his relations with whites while traveling:

> He should be sure to be well groomed, to be aware of his position and avoid anything which might be shocking. He should be polite and alert, and ready to perform small favors.

> After having greeted a White and having amiably answered his questions, withdraw. If invited to remain, do not stay too long, in order not to be bothersome.

---

*The degree of mistrust is reflected in a statement by Huys: "A [black] priest is strictly forbidden to leave the mission alone, even for a visit to a neighboring village, outside of his normal duties, without having first informed the Father Superior or his replacement about where he is going, and the purpose of this visit, and without having obtained his authorization ("Statuts du clergé indigène," p. 45).

**Msgr. Jean Jadot took note of the extent of racial discrimination within the Church: "I note the parts [of the church] reserved for blacks and for Europeans;...the benches, often broken, for the blacks, and the seats or prie-Dieu for the whites; [the fact]...that the whites go for communion first and the blacks afterward; the manner in which baptismal rites for white and black infants are carried out. Even in regard to marriages and funerals and to the hospitality offered in missions [I note] where one receives whites and where blacks are not allowed, etc." ("Exigences missionaires actuelles," n.d., pp. 5-6 [private papers of Jean Jadot]).

Above all be discreet in the double sense of the word, do not be embarrassing, and do not talk too much.[35]

It is unlikely that these humiliating restrictions endeared either missionaries or whites in general to the Congolese clergy. The frustration and resentment which many black priests must have felt in the face of such hypocrisy can easily be imagined.

But if the Congolese clergy felt bitterness toward the missionaries, they did so in the context of a confused love-hate relationship. The missionaries had enabled them to achieve a privileged position among Congolese—yet as time went by they found themselves viewed by both the European and the African communities somewhat as pariahs. They had embraced Western concepts and values—only to be rejected as equals by the whites, including many missionaries—and in the process they had become alienated from their own people; the indigenous clergy were, in the eyes of many Africans, "Europeans with black skins." With this in mind, Jacques Meert, secretary-general of the Jeunesses Ouvriers Chrétiens movement in the Congo, was led to question the hothouse approach of the missions in training a Congolese clergy that remained isolated from the struggles of its people.[36]

This state of affairs caused some missionaries to reexamine their attitudes toward the indigenous clergy and to suggest reforms. Father Mosmans noted that "at every stage in the life of a secular [African] priest the missionary plays the role of 'master' or paternal guide" and recommended that the African clergy be given greater recognition and responsibility.[37] To those who called for a change in the treatment of the African clergy the question at issue was not that of meting out justice; it was that of bowing before a rising nationalist storm. The hour was too late, they urged, to wait for the African clergy to constitute a majority of priests in the Congo* before allowing them to assume authority. Realism demanded that "a majority of missionaries...be called to 'serve' with a minority of [African] secular priests."[38] The major step to be taken was the appointment of a handful of Congolese bishops. In 1956 Msgr. Pierre Kimbondo was named auxiliary bishop of Kisantu.** By 1958 there were 366 African priests and 1,170 other African religious personnel (Brothers and Sisters) in the Congo.[39] But the appointment of a few Congolese bishops did not mean that control of the Church in the Congo had passed into their hands; on the contrary, domination by the missionaries continued right up to independence.***

---

*It was reported that in 1953 there was a total of 2,110 priests in the Congo, of whom 1,554 were Belgian, 313 were foreign, and 246 were African ("Echos et nouvelles," Revue du Clergé Africain, July 1954, p. 425).

**Beside Msgr. Kimbondo there were Msgr. Joseph Malula and Msgr. Joseph Nkongolo (both consecrated in 1959).

***The appointment of Congolese bishops did not necessarily bring about a change in attitude among missionaries toward the African clergy. Some, indeed, were irked by the very idea of being subordinate to any Congolese, bishop or not. At the grand séminaire of Mayidi a missionary professor was reported to have spoken disparagingly of Msgr. Kimbondo before his students: "Do you believe that you have raised a saviour? Do you think that your Kimbondo is as intelligent as we [whites]? The Pope has merely conferred a

During the last decade of Belgian rule in the Congo, there was some difference of opinion among missionaries concerning the role the indigenous clergy should assume in regard to the rising tide of nationalism. Some preferred to bar political participation by Congolese priests, usually on the grounds that they were not prepared for it, or that such participation would create divisions within the Church, or that it would make it a target for attack by the various political factions. The Church would then be in danger of losing its national character.

When in the early 1950s it was proposed that African priests be given seats on the government councils, some missionaries expressed doubts as to the wisdom of such a policy. But they went on to urge that, if the colonial government was really going to allow Congolese to sit on such councils, it would be preferable that they be representatives of the Church, making it clear, however, that they should be selected by the Catholic bishops.[40] The intention was that they should represent Church rather than Congolese interests.*

Other Catholic supporters warned that so short-sighted a policy would only result in increased hostility toward missions and government alike. Sohier quoted history to make this point: "How many cases are there to indicate that the black clergy, in spite of feelings of unity [with the white missionaries], take the lead in protesting for their people, as was the case with our own democratic priests, or as with the Irish parish priests, spirits of civil war?"[41] A few missionaries went so far as to express the hope that the African clergy would be in the vanguard of Congolese political and social development and eschew the passive role hitherto assigned to them.** Some heeded this call to action.

_____

simple title on him." In response the seminarians boycotted masses and courses and threatened to leave the seminary en masse, only to relent after Msgr. Verwimp gave his apologies and assurance that such an incident would not recur ("Un conflit au grand séminaire de Mayidi," n.d. [DIA]).

*Until 1954 the missions continued to follow their policy of cooperation with the Colonial Administration, and African priests were instructed to act in ways which promoted that policy: "The native priests will do what is required of them, and will not recoil from any personal sacrifice that is compatible with their conscience, in order to win over to the work of the mission the benevolence of those who represent the authority of the government" (Huys, "Statuts du clergé indigène," p. 62).

**Former seminary students complained to the author that they often felt isolated from the world around them. They tended to blame this on the missionaries who greatly restricted their contacts with the Congolese population and censored the reading matter available to them. As if to confirm this, one is struck by the scarcity, right up to independence, of articles dealing with social, economic, and especially political problems in the Revue du Clergé Africain, a journal specifically directed at Congolese seminarians and priests.

CHAPTER 12

THE VOLUNTARY ASSOCIATIONS

In the Congo, as elsewhere in Africa, voluntary associations in the form of proto- or pseudo-nationalist organizations played a significant role in political development.[1] They helped their members to adjust to their new urban environment; they allowed "an important minority valuable experience of modern forms of administration"; and they formed proto-political units from which nationalist organizations and parties later emerged.[2] The missions, especially the Catholic missions, were deeply involved in the formation and development of these voluntary associations.

Lay Organizations

By the mid-1950s the question of the laity within the Church had become an acute and central problem for the Catholics. At the same time the early missionary idea of establishing in the Congo an isolated Christian Utopia came under increasing attack by progressive Catholics who saw in it a refusal to come to grips with the colony's problems and realities. The secretary-general of the Jeunesses Ouvriers Chrétiens (JOC) warned that "the traditional approach of the missions no longer responds to the problems confronting them"; in his view the missions were engaging in "isolated actions" that evaded the general problems facing Congolese society.[3]

The hostile political atmosphere of the Buisseret period did much to convince even the more conservative members of the Catholic hierarchy of the need to change their methods. The years 1954 to 1956 saw the fading of any hopes the Catholics may have entertained of returning to their position during the pre-Buisseret era. The Catholic bishops perceived, in some cases with regret, that a new era was approaching, and that their only alternative to regression was to keep pace with it:

> Our adversaries have inaugurated a new era by appealing to the will and desires of certain Congolese, who wanted lay schools. The traditional paternalism of the missions has to give way, perhaps too soon, to modern democratic ideas. To ignore this, and hang onto the past would be a profound error that we will pay for dearly. The step has been taken, and it will continue to go forward in spite of us.[4]

In earlier decades the Catholic missions had acted as a powerful and independent mediating force between the Congolese and the administration, but Buisseret's policies and the consequent mission-state feud compelled them to seek Congolese support. The Church could no longer afford to remain aloof from its adherents. This was made clear by one Catholic bishop who stated that, even if the political picture in Belgium were to become more favorable, the missions still could not fall back upon their old association with the state. In the future the Church must seek support from "the lay associations."[5]

Vatican policy encouraged and reinforced the trend toward a greater role for the Catholic laity. In various papal encyclicals the missions had been urged to organize and give greater responsibility to laymen.* The missions in the Congo had responded to the urgings of Rome with little enthusiasm until the pressures of the government-led anticlerical campaign made them appealing, if not enticing.

Lay organizations were not entirely new in the Congo. But the idea that missions should share responsibility with the laity was novel indeed. To missionaries accustomed to almost feudal power over their mission domains the prospect of treating their vassals on terms of equality was fraught with all the difficulties that attend the change of any deeply ingrained human habit. A number of progressive Catholics, however, within and without the Church, spurred the campaign for greater lay participation in both spiritual and secular affairs. Some, like Father Mosmans, believed that the missions should no longer be active in all fields of human activity but should narrow their role to their apostolic function and leave political and social matters to laymen and the secular authorities.[6] If this were not done or if it were done too slowly, it was feared that many Catholics would become disaffected by the clericalism of the missions.**

Missionary anxieties centered on the growing populations of the urban centers. Many of those who left the bush for a new, urban way of life were Christians; the question was whether, once in the cities, they would remain Christian. Under the spell of their rural romanticism, the missionaries had been comfortable in their relationship with their African adherents while in the bush, where they had been ever-visible figures of importance and influence. Conditions in the urban areas were far different, and the effects of the new opportunities and attractions they encountered and of the loosening of traditional bonds caused many Africans to drift away from the Church. The missionaries realized the problem and were impressed by the need for organizations of laymen that would enable the Church to gather its straying sheep and keep them in the fold.

---

*One example: "We wish to have associations of Catholic men and women organized everywhere, as far as circumstances permit associations for youth engaged in literary and scientific studies; for laborers and journeymen; for athletes. Let clubs of other kinds, and pious confraternities be founded, since all such organizations may be called auxiliary troops for the missions" (Pope Pius XII, Evangeli Praecones, June 2, 1951, in Thomas J. M. Burke, ed., Catholic Missions, pp. 50-51).

**In 1955 an organization of young missionaries and laymen was founded in Louvain. Known as the Afrika Kring (African Circle), it conducted weekly discussions on questions dealing with Africa and especially the Congo. The White Fathers were active in its direction, and it tended to foster progressive views, although speakers of all political shades were invited to speak before it.

After World War II the missions joined the administration and the large companies in promoting various types of organizations for the évolués, with the aim of keeping their activities "non-political and under European control."[7] A UNESCO study reported that "no African associations in the Congo other than those formed for mutual aid are permitted to exist without official permission, and the identity cards of all would-be members are officially examined."[8] It appears that, in addition to their purely apostolic aims in promoting lay organizations, the missions also wished to exert a degree of social and political control over the emerging African elite and their proletarian brethren in the urban centers. If the whites did not provide some outlet for the social and political demands of the Congolese, they would risk grave consequences. It was hoped "to divert revolutionary ideas" by building organizations that would serve such a function.[9] As evangelists and as part of the ruling triumvirate, the missionaries had much to fear from secularized political radicalism.

The first major Catholic effort to involve laymen in a social and religious program was the establishment in 1932 of Catholic Action,* a world-wide organization especially designed to keep the urban masses within the Church while helping them to adapt to new conditions. It also aimed to give the new elite a sense of participation in the activities and responsibilities of the missionaries without interference in the question of primary control. At the Second Plenary Conference of the Bishops of the Congo and Ruanda-Urundi, Msgr. Dellepiane had listed among the conditions for membership in Catholic Action the requirement that members should be "disciplined and subject to the authority of the hierarchy."[10] Twenty years later the bishops, again meeting in plenary session, criticized the chaplains attached to the various organs of Catholic Action for their autocratic attitudes toward the laity, and placed great stress on the need for the Congolese "to learn to conduct their own affairs."[11] The reassessment of the role of Congolese within Catholic Action in 1956 was undoubtedly due in large part to the anticlerical campaign conducted by the government and the rising tide of discontent among the évolués, including the militant Catholics.

A number of organizations, established under the auspices of Catholic Action to enlist men, women, and children, attempted to encompass the entire spectrum of human activity. They dealt with the religious, social, economic, and—indirectly—with the political problems of the people. In the religious sphere such associations as the Legion of Mary, the League of the Sacred Heart, and the League of the Holy Virgin were active. Social problems were the major concern of the mutualités (mutual aid societies), the Family Movement, and the various foyers sociaux (social centers) which had been established throughout the Congo.** The last-named helped new arrivals to the

---

*Promoted by the Vatican, it aimed at drawing Catholic laymen into social and religious activities and programs under the auspices of the hierarchy. Pope Pius in his encyclical Fidei Donum emphasized that "attention must be given to the growing development of Catholic Action and to the satisfaction of religious and cultural needs of a generation which, deprived of sufficient food, might be exposed to the danger of going outside the Church to seek nourishment" (Burke, Catholic Missions, p. 69).

**In 1952 there were 31 social centers in the Congo and Ruanda-Urundi—26 in the centres extra-coutumiers, 4 in military camps, and only 1 in the bush (Miessen, "Assistance sociale indigène au Congo," p. 358).

urban areas adjust to their new environment. Staffed by Europeans and Congolese évolués, they would aid the inhabitants with such practical problems as getting a job, writing a letter, finding a house, or even how best to do one's marketing or cooking. In 1948 the missions were instrumental in establishing among the miners at the Kilo-Moto gold mines the Excelsior Society which provided a library, sports, films, and so forth. A similar cultural society, the Etoile, was established for the workers of the Lever plantations.[12]*

Youth movements were also introduced by the Catholics. The most prominent of these were the Scouts, Guides, and Xavierians.** In 1956 Msgr. Verwimp stressed the need for rapidly expanding the Catholic youth movements in response to a plan to establish a secular, government-sponsored youth organization in the major centers of Léopoldville, Elisabethville, Bakavu, and Stanleyville.[13] It was feared that a jeunesse d'état would pose a threat to Catholic youth and perhaps to the Church itself. Youth organizations of this kind do not, however, seem to have become significantly politicized in the Congo. From a political standpoint, it is the economic organizations affiliated with the Catholic missions that are most interesting.***

Trade Unions and Affiliated Organizations

From the days of the "red rubber" regime to the granting of independence in 1960 the missionaries were involved in Congo labor problems. The Protestant missions, having been instrumental in bringing an end to the atrocities of forced labor under Léopold II's rule, remained for some time sensitive to the issue. The harsh treatment of African workers was ameliorated after annexation in 1908, but forced labor did not come to an end.[14] In 1913 the Congo Mission News reported that soldiers had been used to impress workers for the copper mines at Mbembe.[15]

Quasi-legal means were also employed to recruit labor. On occasion the police would stage raids in the African quarters and round up large numbers of persons, who would then be sentenced to perform service for the state. Such raids seemed to be synchronized with the government's need for labor.[16] In 1928 a conference of Protestant missionaries meeting in Léopoldville passed resolutions warning the colonial government about labor recruitment practices then being used in the Congo; among these were the forcing of women to "carry provisions to official markets," the recruitment of workers for railways far from their villages, the employment of children, and the disregard of "forced labor for the benefit of private companies."[17] The Commission for the Protection of the Natives also put pressure on the government to suppress many of the abuses of the forced labor system.****

---

*Merlier believed that the major function of this collaboration between these companies and the missions was to avoid social and economic unrest (especially strikes) among the workers (Michel Merlier, Le Congo, p. 220).

**It was reported that the Xavierian movement had 27,535 members in the Congo in 1960 ("Echos et nouvelles," May 1960, p. 301).

***Some such organizations, e.g., the farming and marketing cooperatives and the caisses d'épargnes (savings associations), though mainly economic in nature, indicate the depth of involvement of the missions in Congolese society.

****The commission, however, compromised its position on this question. In 1923 it accepted a sixty-day maximum of forced labor for Africans (Ioan Davies, African Trade Unions, pp. 32-33).

Labor recruitment was a major problem plaguing the Congo. It became particularly acute during the colony's rapid industrial and economic growth in the 1920s.* Until then most forced labor had consisted of portage for the state and the corvées levied for the building of roads and railroads. Industries required a labor force that was more permanent in nature, but during those early days they had difficulty recruiting it. The need for large numbers of men, the sparseness of population in many areas, and the mobile character of African migratory labor led many firms to resort to illegal practices in their efforts to get a sufficient number of workers.[18]

Pressure from missionaries and others, and the realization of the disruptive social, economic, and political effects of forced labor recruitment decided the government to attempt to compel the industrial firms to cease such practices. Forced labor was considerably diminished thereafter, but it did not entirely come to a halt.[19] As late as 1951 Father Van Wing complained of the use and abuse of child labor,[20] and Msgr. Albert Brys noted that the continuation of corvées and forced cultivation of certain crops was disrupting village life and swelling migration to the urban centers.[21] Not until 1954 were the "last administrative forms [of forced labor]...abolished."[22]

Here, as in other sectors of Belgian colonial life, paternalism was the keynote of the white attitude toward the African. In 1922 a decree established the contrat du travail (c-d-t). All Congolese workers hired under a c-d-t were guaranteed a minimum salary, rations, and housing, but they were

---

*In the 1920s the Congo experienced great economic expansion. With this boom came an increased demand for African labor. At that time Africans were still loath to leave their villages and go to work for the white man on his plantations and in his mines and industries. In 1922 it was estimated that of a total male population of 3,300,000 only 155,672 were salaried workers ("Colonisation et prolétariat," Congo, January 1925, p. 123).

A debate flared in 1924-1925 over whether or not the state should force Africans to work for European-owned enterprises. Many missionaries opposed this suggestion, seeing in it nothing more than an extension of the forced-labor practices followed by the state—forced labor for state works was then still legal, but its use by private companies or individuals was illegal under the Colonial Charter ("Rapport de la commission pour l'étude du problème de la main d'oeuvre au Congo belge," Congo, January 1925, p. 695). When in 1924 the government appointed a commission to study the problem, it nominated no missionaries (Ibid., p. 693). The commission was faced with the almost insoluble problem of attempting to protect African interests while at the same time seeking to serve those of the private European enterprises. It supported government regulation of recruitment and working conditions and recommended that not more than 25 percent of the total adult male population should be recruited for work in private enterprises—10 percent for those within two days' journey from their village and 15 percent for local enterprises (Ibid., p. 700). In response the governors of Congo-Kasai and Equateur suggested that 50 percent of the native population could be recruited for local work, i.e., within a 60-km. radius (Ibid., pp. 700-701 fn.). Many of the commission's regulatory recommendations were adopted, but they were more often honored in the breach than the observance. Thus the fight against forced labor and exploitative labor practices continued from the 1920s until the 1950s. The missionaries were involved in much of this fight.

bound to their employers, and infringements of the contract (for example, repeated lateness) could entail severe penalties. Europeans, working under a contrat d'emploi, suffered no such restrictions.[23] Some employers, Union Minière de Haut Katanga (UMHK) being the foremost, practiced an even more benevolet form of paternalism than called for by the c-d-t. In order to establish a stable and permanent labor force, they provided their workers with higher wages, more benefits, and living conditions above the obligatory standard. The prohibitions and penalties which bound the African under the c-d-t were rationalized as necessary because of his essential laziness and lack of respect for work. Father Pierre Charles sought to puncture this balloon. Europeans, he noted, had attempted to sanctify work and thus justify their position in regard to the African worker, but "sacred when used in this sense meant nothing more than obligatory, inescapable, unquestionable, necessary, and therefore boring."[24]

It is doubtful whether many of Father Charles' missionary colleagues would have agreed with him before World War II. They generally supported the government's labor policies, which were in line with their own paternalistic attitude. At the second plenary conference of the Catholic bishops of the Congo, held in 1936, the leaders of the Catholic missions praised the government's pursuit of "labor legislation which draws the admiration of other colonial countries." It would be unwise, they noted, "to brusquely elevate [the African] to an economic and social level too far above his moral development." The idea of Congolese workers organizing to defend their own rights and interests struck the bishops as both ludicrous and abhorrent: "It will be a long time before we can hope that our black workers will be capable of defending and promoting their true interests in an intelligent manner, and engaging in discussions with their employers. It would even be dangerous to suggest such an idea to them."[25] Yet within a decade this attitude was to undergo a radical change.

During the period 1940-1945 the Congo experienced the beginning of an economic boom that was to last for nearly fifteen years. The war brought a rapid expansion in the number of wage earners,* and an enormous growth of the economy that brought with it increasing social and economic dislocation. Disquiet and dissatisfaction were evident among large numbers of Congolese, partly because of poor working conditions and low wages and partly because of the government's increased use of corvées and forced labor (sometimes in disguised form) in order to fulfill its wartime goals. Discontent came to the surface in a number of strikes which racked the Congo during the war years. The most notable of these were the strike of UMHK workers at Lubumbashi (Katanga) in 1941 and the dock strike at the port city of Matadi in 1945. Both strikes were broken by the use of the Force Publique,** and in both cases workmen were killed.[26] The repressive measures the administration used to break these strikes discouraged Congolese workers from joining or forming trade unions. But they neither quieted their unrest nor erased their grievances.***

---

*From 530,000 in 1939 to 768,000 in 1944 (Merlier, Le Congo, p. 166).

**It was during this period (1944) that the Force Publique mutinied at Luluabourg.

***The chief grievance had to do with salary levels. The minimum salary prescribed under the c-d-t was oftentimes more mythical than real. It was reported that during 1950 planters in the Kivu paid their workers one franc (two cents) a day (Crawford Young, Politics in the Congo, p. 208 [quoting Fernand Bézy, Problèmes structurels de l'économie congolaise, Louvain, 1957, p. 168]).

Aware of the impending social and political dangers, many missionaries implored the government and the large industrial and agricultural firms to give Congolese workers a fairer share of the economic pie. Father Van Wing warned the government that to increase salaries and lower prices "is the only effective way to render subversive propaganda inoperable, and to obtain the orderly and peaceful collaboration of the natives."[27] Msgr. Brys employed even stronger terms to condemn the economic policies being pursued by the colons: "The entire economy of the Congo, with its industry and commerce... is an economy by the whites, for the whites, and for the profit of the whites....The black people are in fact a people of servants, of dependents, of wage earners in their own country."[28] In the years following the war some progressive churchmen, aware of the growing discontent of Congolese workers, especially the elite, cried out for reform. In part they feared a radical change which might weaken the position of the Church; but they also were impelled by a belief in social justice. Many were convinced that the solution for the economic, social, and political problems which plagued the Congo lay in the establishment of a solid Congolese middle class whose prudent realism would be a brace against radical change. Many progressives supported the demands of the évolués for equal pay for equal work or, if not that, at least for salaries that were more realistic in view of the cost of living.[29] This naturally led them to attack the severe limitations placed upon Congolese workers under the c-d-t.

Progressive churchmen of this type were, however, but a handful during the years immediately following the war. Most of their missionary brethren still subscribed to the view that the Africans, by reason of their primitive and undisciplined nature, must be treated firmly; that demands for economic, not to mention political, equality were premature and merely reflected the presumptuous character of some Congolese. A report outlining conditions at the grand séminaire at Kabwe during 1945 noted that the clerks and catechists who worked for the seminary were asking why the Fathers did not pay them salaries equal to those paid to whites performing the same tasks. The answer they received was the stock reply by whites in the Congo to such demands: the Congolese had neither "the professional conscience" nor the "feelings" found among whites and therefore could not expect to be treated as equals.[30] It was not until 1956, under the pressure of the Buisseret regime, that the Catholic episcopate in the Congo laid down a general policy for the Church that "a difference in salary based uniquely on a racial difference would be unjust."[31]

There were also differences of opinion among Catholic missionaries on the question of Congolese trade unions. Those opposed to such unions pointed to the lack of training, understanding, and experience among Congolese which made them unfit for membership, let alone leadership, of such organizations. Chief among these opponents was the clerical and political conservative Msgr. de Hemptinne. Speaking at the bishops' conference in 1945, he claimed not only that the Congolese were unprepared for this step but that it would undermine their "sense of discipline" and open the door to their exploitation by professional agitators.[32]*

---

*In 1943 he had caused a stir by addressing a memorandum to the governor-general in which he denounced the war effort as such and the demands that were being placed upon Congolese workers as a consequence. He included in this

126

These sentiments no doubt found support among other members of the Catholic hierarchy, but a clear difference of opinion was also evident. Speaking before the same conference which de Hemptinne had addressed, Msgr. Dellepiane stressed the need for missionaries to concern themselves with the plight of Congolese workers and supported the formation of trade unions.[33] One of the most forthright statements in this regard was made in an article appearing in the semiofficial journal Zaire: "It is unjust to impose on workers contractual clauses which injure their rights as men and Christians," and therefore "it is unjust to prevent workers from taking part in professional associations, through which they can defend their legitimate interests."[34]

In 1946, largely in response to the demands of the évolués and their supporters, Governor-General Ryckmans issued a decree allowing the formation of Congolese trade unions. This concession was, however, so bound by qualifications as to reduce the effectiveness of any such unions.* The kind of trade unionism encouraged under the 1946 decree was more akin to that which exists in totalitarian systems than that which one finds in Western democracies, Belgium included. The state maintained strict control, while offering the Congolese a façade of free association in defense of their interests.

In 1945 the Confédération Générale des Syndicats (CGS), an all-European trade union formed in the Congo during the war, asked the major Belgian trade unions to recognize its organization as the sole legitimate spokesman for European workers in the Congo. The Confédération des Syndicats Chrétiens (CSC), which was closely identified with the Catholic party and Church in Belgium, refused. The refusal appears to have been motivated mainly by the left-wing character of the CGS.[35] But the CSC was also critical of the fact that the CGS had organized strikes in the Congo.

In 1946 two CSC agents were sent to the Congo to organize African and white sections of the CSC. They arrived only about two months after the decree legalizing the formation of Congolese labor organizations had been

---

memorandum a condemnation of the decision by the administration to allow European trade unions to organize and agitate for better conditions. This, he believed, was having a deleterious effect on Belgian rule: "Everywhere, a spirit of antipathy and defiance is gaining ground. The native is drawing away from us; more and more he escapes from our influence and prestige..., Belgium is on the way to losing her African glory" (Pierre Joye and Rosine Lewin, Les trusts au Congo, p. 194 [quoting André Corneille, "Le Syndicalisme au Katanga," Elisabethville, 1945, pp. 179-180]).

*The various ordinances which spelled out the details of Ryckmans' original decree laid down the following limitations: (1) the right to strike was only to be granted after a long period of arbitration and conciliation had proved unfruitful, or if the employer broke the agreement, and then only with government permission; (2) African trade unions could only be organized among members of one trade or enterprise, and then only on a regional or local level—no confederations were allowed; (3) membership was restricted in an attempt to eliminate the possibilities of dissident elements capturing the organizations; (4) finances were tightly controlled, and the unions were encouraged to have European advisors who would either be representatives of European trade unions or religious chaplains (Louis Ballegeer, "Syndicalisme indigène au Congo belge," pp. 101-105).

promulgated. By the end of the year they had succeeded in establishing four African Christian trade unions.[36] The CGS also made an attempt to organize African affiliates. In 1946 it gathered African workers with specialized skills into the Syndicat des Travailleurs Indigènes Congolais Spécialisés.[37] But the CGS had little enthusiasm for supporting Congolese trade unionism, and this syndicat never amounted to much. Nor were the other two major Belgian unions very interested in organizing Congolese workers in those early days. The more important of them,* the Socialist Fédération Générale des Travailleurs Belges (FGTB), disdained involvement on the ground that Ryckmans' decree would keep Congolese unions "under the yoke of the administration.**

The abdication of the field by the other labor organizations gave the CSC a dominance that it wielded for nearly a decade. In 1953, out of a total of sixty African trade unions, fifty were syndicats congolais, as CSC affiliates were called.[38] By the end of 1956 the number had reached seventy, with a membership of some eight thousand.[39] This, though obviously a small number in relation to the total labor force, is noteworthy in view of the fact that only 8,829 Congolese workers belonged to trade unions in 1956.[40]

The clerical-anticlerical disputes of the Buisseret period led the competitors to vie for the allegiance of the Congolese proletariat. The quasi-monopoly established by the Christian trade unions was soon placed in jeopardy. The year 1956 was momentous. The Catholic missions, the Congolese, and the two most important Belgian political parties, the Parti Social Chrétien and the Parti Socialiste Belge, issued major policy pronouncements on the Congo. All four statements asked for amelioration of working conditions and liberalization of the laws governing union organization.[41] The Catholics were particularly fearful of what appeared to be growing efforts on the part of the Socialist party to increase Congolese membership in the FGTB-Congo. The bishops warned Congolese adherents that "Catholics cannot affiliate themselves with associations that have a non-Christian inspiration, such as those which follow the doctrines of liberalism, socialism, or communism."[42]

Even before the 1956 bishops' declaration the Catholic missions had made a conscious and concerted effort to oppose Buisseret's policies through the medium of the trade unions. Meeting in 1955, the Permanent Committee of Catholic Bishops discussed a variety of tactics to counter the threat posed by the introduction of lay schools and the reduction of educational subsidies. Its members urged the missions to "oppose the baneful action of the present

---

*The other was the Confédération Générale des Syndicats Libéraux.

**The FGTB was almost totally inactive in the Congo until 1951, when it took over what remained of the CGS. Even after that it remained chiefly concerned with white workers. Not until the mid-1950s did it begin to make a major effort to organize Congolese affiliates (V. Charles, "Chronique sociale congolaise," p. 963).

The only nonaffiliated Congolese union until just prior to independence was the Association du Personnel Indigène de la Colonie, founded in 1946 by a group of évolués working for the administration. By far the most effective of all Congolese unions, it eventually forced the government to accord Congolese working for the administration the right to be employed under terms equal to those enjoyed by white workers under a "unified statute."

Government" by acting "through the trade unions, if their lay personnel are so affiliated."[43] The logical "lay personnel" for the missionaries to act through were the teachers in Catholic schools throughout the colony. These teachers were disgruntled because in many cases the government paid them less than it paid teachers at official lay schools.[44] And they, perhaps more than any other group of laymen in mission employ, had the sophistication requisite for such an organization.

The Fédération des Moniteurs Catholiques (FEMOCA) was founded at Mikalayi (Kasai) in December 1954, the founder and guiding spirit being Msgr. Bernard Mels. Addressing his fellow bishops, Mels made it clear that the initiative had come from the missionaries, not from the Congolese. It was his intention that the leaders of FEMOCA should be Congolese* and be "aided" by chaplains appointed by the local bishops. In addition, each local committee was to have as its director the Superior of a mission post.[45] The opening speaker (a missionary) at the Mikalayi conference, which witnessed the founding of FEMOCA-Luluabourg, informed his Congolese listeners that "whatever our enemies say, we will first follow the divine direction of our Ecclesiastical Superiors." The speaker went on to dispel any possible doubt as to who the enemy was: "If we discuss some of the actions of our rulers, if we oppose some decision, that does not in the least diminish our attachment and fidelity to Belgium, to whom we owe all."[46]

Thus, in order to protect their own interests against the government, the missions formed a company union and took the rather extraordinary step, in the light of the history of the Congo until that time, of legitimizing the Congolese right to oppose the government's authority. They had, by implication, questioned the legality of the Colonial Administration and hinted that its members did not necessarily represent the will of the Belgian nation. They had come to depend on those who had previously been dependent on them. In their hour of peril they came to look upon the laymen organized within FEMOCA as their active allies.**

While willing to organize Congolese teachers to aid them in their struggles against the anticlericals, the missionaries intended, however, to retain strict control over them. When in 1955 the CSC attempted to organize Congolese teachers into unions independent of the missions, the missions protested violently. The bishops' conference held in 1956 adopted a resolution that teachers "form a group separated in every way from the Christian trade unions."[47] But apparently CSC organizers paid little heed to this resolution, for more than a year later Catholic missionary school inspectors felt it necessary to warn them not to contact teachers directly but only through FEMOCA.[48]

---

*The president of FEMOCA-Luluabourg was Cléophas Bizala, later minister of education in the Ileo government (Pierre Artigue, Qui sont les leaders congolais?, pp. 38-39).

**At the Mikalayi conference Msgr. Mels stated: "[The authorities] no longer listen to us. Only when they see the solidarity of the monitors and missionaries, and when they hear your voice united with ours...will they give that which you and we desire" (Vicariat de Luluabourg, "Compte-rendu des journées d'étude des moniteurs catholiques," Mikalayi, Dec. 21-25, 1954, p. 2 [BEC]).

In their dealings with the CSC regarding the organization of Congolese teachers the Catholic missions were concerned with their own interests rather than those of their teachers. They were unwilling to allow their teachers to join even Christian unions that were independent of missionary control, for fear they would start to demand better pay and working conditions. The paternalistic bear-hug of the missions seems to have stifled the growth of initiative in their Congolese teachers who never used the great potential for political action that they possessed.*

On July 23, 1957, a decree was issued liberalizing the government's trade union policies: Congolese trade unions were to be allowed to federate on a colony-wide basis, and the restrictions on their organization and membership were to be eased.[49] As a direct result of this decree the hitherto all-white CSC-Congo extended to include the syndicats congolais. A little later it was reorganized** and became independent of the metropolitan CSC.[50] From a membership of some 8,000 in 1957 it grew to 38,422 by September 1958,[51] and to more than 50,000 by 1959.[52] The 1957 decree was to a great extent the product of the conflicts of the Buisseret period. One of its aims seems to have been to break the virtual Catholic monopoly over Congolese trade unionism. In this it was successful. By 1958 the Socialist FGTB-Congo had attained a membership of 40,000.[53]

Catholic efforts to involve African workers, however, were not confined to mission-inspired unions or the CSC affiliates. During the 1950s they created organizations designed to support and promote Catholic objectives in the Congo with ties to both the missions and the syndicats congolais. The largest and most effective of these was Jeunesses Ouvriers Chrétiens (JOC).

A section of JOC had been established at Léopoldville as early as 1932, but it was not until 1953 that a serious effort was made to build a colony-wide organization. In that year Msgr. Cardijn, the founder of JOC in Belgium, went to the Congo and promised aid in expanding the JOC movement there. The following year witnessed the arrival of a delegation of JOC-Belgium, headed by Jacques Meert and a Miss Pauwels.[54] The organizers of JOC were highly critical of missionary methods; themselves geared to produce a cadre of young militant Catholic workers, they believed that the missionaries' monastic and bush-oriented inclinations tended to alienate them from the needs and problems of the urban population.[55] JOC, they thought, could succeed where missionary limitations had led to failure. JOC centered its efforts on recruiting young manual and white-collar workers, and sought to aid its members in every aspect of their daily lives, whether relating to family, work, or religion. It organized its militants in the fight against the antimissionary and

---

*Herbert F. Weiss makes the point that "in French West Africa the European 'leftist' was often a teacher; in the Congo the virtual monopoly by the missions of the educational system meant that the Europeans in education were on the whole very conservative and paternalistic. This, perhaps, is the reason why African teachers were so important in the nationalist movements in French-speaking West Africa, whereas they played an essentially unimportant role in the Congo" ("Comparisons in the Evolution of Pre-Independence Elites in French Speaking Africa and the Congo," p. 134). Consideration of the action of the missions in regard to the formation of Christian trade unions for Congolese teachers leads one to agree with Weiss.

**In 1960 the CSC-Congo became the Union des Travailleurs Congolais.

anti-Church policies of the Liberal-Socialist coalition. But its most significant political contribution was its promotion of a more progressive policy among missionaries. Meert urged them to establish "an autonomous and
independent Church, oriented primarily toward supporting Congolese aspirations, a Church that would be willing to run the risk of losing European support in so doing."[56]

Two other organizations closely linked to JOC were the Ligue des Ouvriers Chrétiens (LOC) and the Mouvement Ouvrier Chrétien (MOC). LOC was an extension of JOC but was limited to adults. It had been backed by Meert and
Alphonse Sita, a prominent Congolese layman. MOC on the other hand was a
general organization whose members also belonged to other organizations, such
as trade unions, JOC, or LOC. Its aim was to promote unity among all Christian workers and to help them to organize social welfare activities. MOC was
also important in promoting political development. Its members, aided by
Europoean militants, pressed for economic and political reforms that would
grant more benefits and greater freedom to the Congolese. Among its members
could be counted Joseph Ileo, Gaston Diomi, and Joseph Ngalula, all of whom
had important roles in the struggle for independence.

In addition to their role in labor unions and affiliated organizations
the missions were instrumental in bringing into being farming and marketing
cooperatives (the best known of these was located at Kisantu) and caisses
d'épargnes (savings associations) for the benefit of the Congolese. Though
mainly economic in nature, these measures indicate the depth of missionary
involvement in Congolese society.

When viewed in the perspective of its role in certain West African and
East African nations, trade unionism as a vehicle for political action failed
in the Congo. For this the Catholic missions and the CSC were in large part
responsible. Their essentially conservative nature and their fear of radical
change did much to politically emasculate the Congolese trade-union movement.
Motivated more often by the fear of their anticlerical enemies than by a desire to improve the living conditions of African workers, they created unions
that were passive and dependent appendages. It was not, however, they alone
who were responsible for the political ineffectiveness of Congolese trade
unions. The administration's extremely restrictive policies and decrees also
did much to strangle progressivism and Congolese initiative in this area, as
did the timidity of the Socialist and Liberal trade unions. The Catholics
certainly deserve credit for committing themselves at an early date to the
cause of the Congolese worker. Had they shown greater courage, they might
have built a more viable political heritage for the Congo. As it was, their
role in other, less well-structured organizations was more significant for
the development of Congolese nationalism.

Alumni Associations

It was within the various alumni associations and évolué clubs that
many, if not most, of the future leaders of the Congo had their first significant political experience. These protopolitical organizations, as well as
the tribal associations, were in many cases initiated or supported by the
Catholic missions. They were of particular importance in the Congo where,
until 1957, almost all overt political activity by Congolese was prohibited.

131

The major alumni associations in the Congo were the Association des Anciens Elèves des Frères Chrétiens, the Union des Anciens Elèves des Frères Maristes (UNELMA), the Association des Anciens Elèves des Pères Jésuites, and the Association des Anciens Elèves des Pères de Scheut (ADAPES). These organizations had existed for some time (ADAPES for example was founded in 1925) but had remained more or less dormant until 1945 and did not become important until the early 1950s. Politically, ADAPES was the most significant of the four. The Scheutists, controlling as they did the Vicariate of Léopoldville, were most effective in guiding their alumni association toward political goals. Their situation at the political and administrative center gave them a distinct advantage over other missions.

After the war ADAPES underwent a reformation. Its membership increased to 15,000;[57] and Jean Bolikongo was elected president, a post he retained until 1959. His presidency was later to have great impact on Congolese politics. In 1945 he had helped found the Union des Intérêts Sociaux Congolais (UNISCO), an organization that attempted to bring together members of the Congolese elite who were officers of the various alumni associations. Its objectives were "the elimination of practices of racial discrimination,...the amelioration of the social conditions of Congolese" and the protection of the rights of the évolués.[58] The first president was Eugène Kabamba; he was succeeded by Bolikongo in 1946. That same year Joseph Kasavubu was named spokesman for the association. In his first address to its members, entitled "The Right of the First Occupant," he alluded to the inherent rights of the Congolese to the land occupied by the Belgians.[59] In order to qualify Kasavubu for membership in UNISCO, Bolikongo had arranged to have him elected secretary-general of ADAPES.[60] There are indications that in May 1954 Kasavubu attempted to reorganize ADAPES into a political organization with himself in a central role.* If so, he failed.[61]

That members of the Congolese political elite associated with the mission-sponsored alumni associations "tended to be of a moderate kind"[62] cannot be assumed without qualification. True, such figures as Bolikongo and Jean Pierre Dericoyard, former president of UNELMA, might be classified as moderates; but certainly Kasavubu and Patrice Lumumba, former president of the ADAPES branch at Stanleyville,[63] would not have been included in that category. It does appear, nonetheless, that the conservatism of the missions inhibited the transformation of the alumni associations into political parties, and that évolués seeking political expression directed their energies elsewhere. But, as it turned out, in this centrifugal splitting of the elite the ethnic factor was perhaps more influential than the conservatism of the missions. In any case there is no doubt that the missions wished to encourage the elite along moderate lines and paid special attention to their intellectual as well as their political development.

---

*During the same year he was elected president of the Association Bakongo (ABAKO). It is interesting to speculate whether Kasavubu would have used ABAKO as his political base if he had been able to transform ADAPES. But the composition of ADAPES almost certainly foredoomed this effort.

Evening Courses

Discussion groups, Belgo-Congolese clubs, and cercles des évolués were aided and encouraged by the Catholic missions in the hope that they would exert an influence on the growing and restless Congolese elite. The effect was negligible. But in another area, the establishment of evening courses for évolués, the impact was substantial. Cut off from further schooling by the age limits set by the administration and by the lack of educational facilities, many évolués nonetheless thirsted for higher education. Aware of this desire and of the opportunities the situation offered for increasing their own influence, various Catholic missions in the urban centers established special evening courses open to Congolese. The evening program established under the auspices of the Scheutist Fathers in Léopoldville was eventually to have great political import for the Congo.

In 1952, on the initiative of Abbé (later Bishop) Joseph Malula and Father Joseph Ceuppens,* the Conférence Sociale et Philosophique (CSP) was founded in Léopoldville. An executive committee was named which included Malula (president), Ileo (director), Jose Lobeya, and Pedro Victor; Ceuppens was appointed counselor.[64] The organization's aim, as stated in its statute, was to "develop the individual and the Christian."[65] Admission was limited to those with sufficient intellectual training—in other words, to évolués.** Reorganized in 1955 under the stewardship of Meert and Malula,*** it was renamed the Centre d'Etude et de Recherche Sociale (CERS).[66] The promoters of CERS set forth as one of its aims the development of Christian leaders and organizations able to combat what they considered to be the materialistic, antireligious, and Marxist tendencies being introduced into the Congo by the existing Socialist-Liberal coalition government. Ultimately, they hoped, Congolese lay militants would be able to establish social and, "at the opportune time, political" organizations to combat the objectives of the anticlericals.[67]

In Belgium the socialist newspaper Le Peuple attacked CERS on the ground that it wished to create "a Catholic elite and a Catholic party, which would grasp the levers of power at the opportune moment."[68] If this was indeed its goal, CERS was in large part a failure. On a political plane, however, its influence should not be underestimated for from its ranks emerged the first significant political manifesto authored by Congolese.

---

*Malula was a product of the Scheutist seminary at Kabwe and was being groomed by Msgr. Six for a high post. Ceuppens was the director of Agence DIA, the Catholic news agency in the Congo; he was at the time influential in both missionary and government circles.

**Among those enrolled in the CSP were Bolikongo, Diomi (later an important leader of ABAKO), Jacques Massa (later minister of social affairs in the second Ileo government), Ngalula (later minister of education under Adoula), and many others who played prominent roles in the political development of the Congo.

***A greater number of courses was introduced at a higher level, and Meert invited professors from Lovanium University to teach some of them. The courses offered included some in political development, comparative politics, and law (civil and international) (CSP, Projet-statuts, 1952 [DIA]).

The beginnings of political parties were discernible in the lay movements and voluntary associations fostered and aided by the missions. But it
is in the messianic and syncretistic movements which proliferated in the
Congo that the real origin of Congolese nationalism must be sought.

CHAPTER 13

THE MESSIANIC AND SYNCRETISTIC SECTS

As transmitters of both Western culture and Western religion, the missionaries often provided the models and symbols for African protest movements.
During a period when secular political expression and organization were prohibited, the Christianity introduced by the missions offered the Africans the
fantasy equivalent of a social and political revolution.

African Responses to Missionary Teachings

The missionaries' attempt to reconcile loyalty to the colonial government with loyalty to the Congolese involved more than the ambivalence and conflict it set up within themselves; it also rendered them suspect to the Africans. Brotherhood, equality, and the other promised fruits of the new religion were not forthcoming. And the Congolese tended to see the missionaries
as part of the colonial system and as destroying or weakening many such foundations of their society as bride price, polygamy, and circumcision. Yet rejection of the missionary was not necessarily accompanied by rejection of his
religious ideas and ideals, many of which had immediate relevance for them.*
The Bible with its promises of radical social and political renovation
attracted the Africans.** It was not difficult for them to draw an analogy
between the sufferings, privations, and hopes of the Old Testament Jews and
their own condition under the colonial yoke.*** Africans also found in the

---

*Georges Balandier has noted that within the Christian church the con-
tradiction between the teachings and the actions of the colonizer was pointed
out. Christian teachings were the cause of dreams that greatly helped the
black to grasp the reality of his condition ("Messianismes et nationalismes en
Afrique noire," p. 64).

**A study of independent church movements found the availability of the
Bible to be a prime cause of the demand for these movements (David B. Barrett,
"Reaction to Mission: An Analysis of Independent Church Movements Across Two
Hundred African Tribes" [Ph.D. diss., Columbia University, 1965] p. 10).

***André Ryckmans, son of the former governor-general and a territorial
administrator in the Lower Congo during the 1950s, recorded that "thousands
of verses [of the Bible] can be cited which would show the similarity of Belgian rule to the oppression of the Egyptians or Assyrians" (Jean Kestergat,
ed., André Ryckmans, p. 176).

Old Testament confirmation and affirmation of the value of certain aspects of their own culture which were under missionary attack. Ironically, the basic tenets of the new Christian culture gave them instruments to attack missionary teachings. They pointed to the apparent contradictions between missionary condemnation of polygamy, circumcision, and animal sacrifices and ancient Jewish acceptance of these practices.

For this situation the Protestant missions seem to have been more responsible than the Catholics.* The latter did not rely on the Bible as an instrument of evangelization but on a catechism that demanded memorization as opposed to individual interpretation. Many Catholic missionaries placed the blame for the outbreak of messianic movements in the Congo at the doorstep of the Protestant missionaries and their encouragement of free interpretation (libre examen).** One Belgian visiting a Protestant mission school in the Congo observed to its directors that "the children in your schools seem to dwell with particular relish on the plagues of Egypt and the crossing of the Red Sea. Could you counsel them to moderate their emphasis on these events?"[1]

The missionaries promised a new life through conversion. To many Africans this meant the opportunity to attain the material and social benefits enjoyed by the white man. More often than not, however, they found their condition little changed after conversion; the promised rebirth failed to occur. Not unnaturally, many responded with bitterness and suspicion—but not necessarily with total rejection of a Christianity whose efficacy was obvious to them from the success of the Europeans. The solution to the problem must, it seemed, be sought elsewhere. The Africans came to place the blame for their dilemma on the missionaries who, they felt, were withholding from them the total meaning of Christianity—and thus the total

---

*A study of prophet movements in the Lower Congo concedes that the Protestants give rise, more often than the Catholics, to messianic movements (Effraim Andersson, Messianic Popular Movements in the Lower Congo, p. 262). In a similar vein David Barrett cites "the strength of the Protestant missionary force" as a significant factor in determining the rate of secession from missionary churches, the possibilities being greater "when [the] ratio of ordained [Protestant] missionaries to population is high" (Barrett, "Reaction to Mission," p. 100).

**Some observers have noted that the Catholics may be less prone to encourage messianic movements because they are less disruptive of the culture. But while their less rigid morality, greater tolerance for human frailty, ability to substitute Christian for pagan symbolism (e.g., the religious medal for the fetish), and elaborate ritual were no doubt attractive to the African and may have eased the transition, the Catholics were probably no less destructive than were the Protestants of traditional social systems. Like the Protestants, they vigorously attack polygomy, fetishism, bride price, etc. The fact that they did not give rise to as many separatist and messianic movements as the Protestants is probably attributable, at least in part, to the discipline of Catholicism, which fostered greater dependence and passivity among its converts than did the various versions of Protestantism. The fact that Protestantism was itself heterogeneous and at one time heretical no doubt also encouraged African breakaways.

culture.* Behind these feelings lay the wish for magical solutions to their problems.

The African's belief that the missionaries had denied them the total truth and had corrupted Christianity formed only one part, however, of the foundation of discontent upon which the separatist and messianic movements were built. Another important part was the desire to strengthen and preserve certain elements of traditional culture which were deemed valuable.** The solution was to be found in syncretism and messianism.

Kimbanguism, Mpadism, Tonsi, and Dieudonné

Kimbanguism, the best-known prophet movement of the Congo, made its initial appearance among the Bakongo during the early 1920s. Simon Kimbangu, its founder, had been a catechist for the Baptist Missionary Society in the Lower Congo. One day in 1921 he claimed that God had come to him and commanded him to preach His word (the Bible) and to cure the sick by laying on hands.[2]***

The news spread quickly throughout the Lower Congo that a prophet and miracle-worker had arisen in the region. By May 1921 crowds could be seen streaming toward the village of Nkamba where Kimbangu was staying. Hospital beds emptied, and workers in the cities and on the plantations left their jobs to make the trek to witness and partake of the new prophet's miracles.****

Kimbangu and his followers obviously took over much Christian myth and symbolism. There is little doubt that he saw himself as a Christ figure. Shortly after his initial miracles he appointed twelve apostles who were to preach, cure, and aid in spreading the word. According to Father Van Wing, he laid down three laws for his adherents: the destruction of all fetishes; the destruction of the drums used in what was considered a lascivious dance and the abolition of the dance itself; and the condemnation of polygamy.[3] These practices, which the missionaries had for years attacked without success, were suddenly in large part abandoned.

---

*Georges Balandier noted similar feelings among Africans in Moyen Congo: "The peasants think that the Fathers have not taught them all that they know about God. They believe that it is through their religion that the Europeans are able to become wealthy and [therefore] none of them wants to reveal this secret. Therefore, they [i.e., the Africans] have decided to seek it themselves, to rely on their own prophets" (Afrique ambigue, p. 227).

**Bengt Sundkler, discussing the causes of Zulu separatism in South Africa, noted that "the African has put up a strong resistance to the missions' attempted conquest. The independent Zulu churches may well be regarded as a symptom of inner revolt against the White man's missionary crusade, and in these churches we shall see many proofs of the vitality of the religious and cultural heritage of the Zulus, which in them is given a more honored place than in the Mission Church" (Bantu Prophets in South Africa, p. 19).

***Kimbangu's father was a fetish priest (nganga) (Joseph Van Wing, "Le Kimbanguisme vu par un témoin," p. 566).

****The words ngunza (prophet) and mvuluzi (saviour, messiah, apostle) were used by the Africans to describe Kimbangu (Ibid., p. 571).

The movement's rapid growth and its inhibiting effects on commerce in the Lower Congo caused the administration, which had initially adopted a tolerant attitude, to come to view it as subversive. The missions, the colons, and the colonial press (especially L'Avenir Colonial Belge) reacted with fear and even panic, and contributed to the government's decision to arrest Kimbangu and the other leaders of the movement.[4]* Kimbangu was finally arrested on September 15, 1921, tried at Thysville, and convicted of fomenting rebellion. He was sent to prison in Elisabethville, more than a thousand miles from his home in the Lower Congo, and there, in 1951, he died.**

Kimbangu became the fountainhead of Bakongo messianism. His removal from the scene failed to bring about the hoped-for demise of his movement. Its impact stirred too many chords within the African for that to happen. For its appeal was not that of an abstract doctrine or belief but that of a means to achieve freedom.*** Kimbanguism and other movements like it effected some significant social and political changes. They diminished deep fear of black magic and witchcraft which tended to undermine mutual trust and cooperation. And they helped undercut the power of the chiefs whom many saw as arms of the colonial authority and keepers of anachronistic tradition.[5]

Stimulated by Kimbanguism and partly in response to its proscription, similar movements developed in the Lower Congo region. Among them were Mpadism (an outgrowth of the Salvation Army),**** Tonsi, and Dieudonné.

Mpadism, also known as L'Eglise des Noirs and Kakisme, was the brainchild of Simon Mpadi, a former officer in the Salvation Army. Beginning in 1939, his movement attracted many adherents in the Lower Congo. It was not long before the Belgians discerned elements of revolt in it. Mpadi, it was alleged, had instructed his followers that the laws of his church were supreme, while those of Bula Matari (the state) were to be ignored.[6] In Mpadi and his movement the continuing protest, the articulate and inarticulate, of the

---

*"At one point the streets of Kinshasa [Léopoldville] were posted with machine guns in hourly expectation of a Kimbanguist attack" (Raymond L. Buell, The Native Problem in Africa, p. 604).

**The judgment handed down by the military tribunal charged that Kimbangu preached against the whites, and that while hiding behind the veil of religion he conducted a campaign aimed at undermining the security of the state by fomenting rebellion (see Jules Chomé, La passion de Simon Kimbangu, pp. 68-70). A sentence of death had been handed down by the tribunal, but this was commuted to life imprisonment by King Albert after a plea of clemency by a group of Protestant missionaries.

***Describing the attitudes of the Bakongo toward the prophet movement, Georges Balandier noted that "what the villagers wish for was not only to master sacred techniques...but to restore their former freedom of action. They wish to reconstruct their civilization, which gives them power and unity" (Afrique ambigue, p. 235).

****The letters AS (Armée de Salut) emblazoned on the uniforms of the organization were translated by the Kimbanguists as Armée de Simon. André Ryckmans noted that Captain Henri Becquet, the first director of the Salvation Army in the Congo, was received as a reincarnation of Simon Kimbangu (André Ryckmans, "Les Mouvements prophétiques Kongo en 1958," p. 4 [unpublished paper, in author's possession]).

Bakongo people against the colonizer found expression.* This threat to their authority caused the Belgians to order his arrest.

The war years (1939-1945) witnessed a resurgence of messianic popular movements in the Congo. As the colonial authorities made greater demands on them, the Congolese were subjected to increased social and economic pressures. Recruitment of porters and workers for the military and for plantations and mines caused widespread social dislocation. Many made their way to the burgeoning cities, there to find both opportunity and hardship. The upheavals in their society during this period made the Congolese more susceptible to prophetism.[7] The Belgians attributed the wartime disturbances at Matadi (1945), Masisi (1944), Luluabourg (1944), and elsewhere at least in part to religio-political movements, which they therefore took steps to suppress.[8] But, as before, repression did not succeed in destroying the various prophet movements, whose durability attests to the meaning they held for their followers. On the contrary, new movements emerged.

One of these, Tonsi or Matonsi, allegedly had strong racist overtones. It looked forward to a millennium when sickness and death would no longer occur, when ancestors would be resurrected, and when the whites would be destroyed or disappear and Africans would be transformed into whites. Following the Christian model, it offered for adoration a holy trinity: Père Esprit, Père Kimbangu, and Père Allemand, the last being a reflection of the contemporary invasion and occupation of Belgium by the Germans, who were seen by some Africans as potential liberators from Belgian domination.

Dieudonné, a somewhat later movement, was begun in 1954 by a Catholic catechist of that name. Preaching against fetishes, he urged the use of Catholic holy water in their stead.[9] The Catholic missionary hierarchy encouraged an attitude of patience and tolerance toward Dieudonné. At the movement's height in 1955 Father Léopold Denis, a well-known Jesuit missionary, suggested that the Church should give holy water when requested but should explain to the recipients that it was of value only to those who accepted its religious meaning. In this way the Catholics hoped to channel the movement into paths that might lead to a return of Dieudonné's Catholic adherents to the fold or to the eventual conversion of the others to Catholicism.[10] The sect was largely peaceful in nature, but it took on more violent overtones in the territories of Kasangulu and Madimba, the area where Kimbanguism and Mpadism were widespread. Bloody riots occurred, and in March 1956 the Dieudonné movement was prohibited by government decree.

The postwar years saw the organization of a movement to unify the various prophetic sects then active in the Lower Congo. This was an attempt to establish a Kimbanguist orthodoxy. Known as the L'Eglise de Jésus-Christ sur la terre par le prophète Simon Kimbangu (EJCSK) and sometimes referred to as Kintwadi, it grew in strength and popularity during the early 1950s. It was formally established in 1956, when the administration lifted its ban on a number of messianic sects in the Lower Congo.[11] In the same year the EJCSK demanded personalité civile (comparable to the granting of a charter by the

---

*Pierre De Vos, writing in 1950, indicated that Mpadi played a leading role in the 1945 disturbances at Matadi (Nation Belge, February 9, 1950). However, the present author could find no confirmation of this.

administration) which would have given it the right to qualify for school subsidies and thus have put it on a par with the Protestant and Catholic missions. It also addressed a memorandum to the United Nations asking that Belgian and Portuguese control over the Lower Congo be ended and the path thus left open for the reestablishment of the Kingdom of the Kongo.[12]* This clear expression of Bakongo nationalism was a reflection in part of the somewhat more urbanized and sophisticated leadership that headed the movement and in part of the changed political atmosphere in the Congo.** Aims that in other prophet movements had been covert now received overt expression. Total EJCSK membership as of December 1958 was estimated at approximately 60,000.[13]***

Kitawala

The Lower Congo, though apparently a fertile area for syncretistic movements, was not the only part of the Congo so affected. In the eastern regions a movement known as Kitawala (Tower or Advent) or Watchtower spread rapidly. Kitawala had roots in the American Watchtower Bible and Tract Society (Jehovah's Witnesses),**** but its origin in the Congo has been attributed to Tomo Nyirenda, an African from Nyasaland. Nyirenda appeared in the Mkushi District of Northern Rhodesia in 1925. There he proclaimed himself a prophet and adopted the name Mwana Lesa (God Child). Successful, he extended his activites in the same year to Southern Katanga, near Kipushi in the Sakania territory. Accused of committing multiple murders there by drowning people whom he contended were witches, he fled back to Northern Rhodesia. Wanted on similar charged there, he was arrested, tried, and hung by the colonial authorities in 1926.

The economic depression in the early 1930s led to many African workers being fired, with predictable consequences of unrest and resentment. This agitation was accompanied by a spurt in religio-political movements in the Katanga, which the alarmed Belgian authorities attributed to Watchtower and to the migrant laborers who appeared to be its chief proponents. In 1934 they proscribed the movement and expelled non-Congolese African workers.[14]*****

---

*One can note here a similarity of views between the EJCSK and ABAKO.

**It would seem that the membership was not exclusively Bakongo. The secretary general of the EJCSK told Raymaekers at one point that there were Bangala and Baluba members as well (Paul Raymaekers, "L'Eglise de Jésus-Christ sur la terre par le prophète Simon Kimbangu," p. 704).

***The EJCSK has recently been admitted to membership in the World Council of Churches.

****In 1926 the Watchtower Bible and Tract Society disavowed any relationship with Kitawala or similar movements (Watchtower Bible and Tract Society, "Memorandum on the Congo Case" [typewritten], n.d., p. 8 [Archives of the Watchtower Bible and Tract Society, Brooklyn, N.Y.]).

*****The Belgians were not the only ones to rather hastily attribute the labor disturbances in the mining areas to Watchtower. The commission of inquiry established by the British to investigate the Copperbelt disturbances of 1935 came to similar conclusions. Taylor and Lehmann are of the opinion that

As in the case of Kimbanguism, the proscription neither destroyed Watchtower nor halted its growth. Instead, the government's repressive policy and its practice of exiling Watchtower members served to spread the movement further. It had started in Elisabethville, Jadotville, Kamina, and other mining towns of Katanga; it now rapidly expanded to the other provinces.*

During World War II a series of major incidents in the eastern Congo were either wholly or partially blamed on Kitawala. In 1941 there were incidents at Boende (Equateur) and Manono (Katanga); in the latter case 925 workers were arrested.[15] The Masisi (Kivu) Revolt of 1944 and the Luluabourg Mutiny in the same year were among the most serious disturbances attributed to Kitawala: "To speak of the Masisi revolt, of those tragic hours that gripped the whites in fear, is to speak of Kitawala.[16]**

Watchtower adherents recognized neither traditional nor European authorities and thus threatened the colonial structure. The Belgians, fearing that Kitawala and Kimbanguism would combine into an anticolonial front, attempted to keep Kimbanguist and Kitawala exiles apart. In 1956 a respected Catholic missionary saw in Kitawala the making of a Congolese Mau Mau, a planned conspiracy to overthrow the Belgians by stirring up a mutiny in the Force Publique.[17] Such was the anxiety evoked by the movement that on January 12, 1949, all organizations called Watchtower were banned by the governor-general.[18]***

---

the commission "laid too much responsibility at the door of the Watchtower movement and accepted many serious allegations on very slender evidence" (John V. Taylor and Dorothea Lehmann, Christians of the Copperbelt, p. 27).

*In 1937 the authorities acknowledged that Kitawala had appeared at Kwamouth only 200 km. from Léopoldville. By 1940 a large part of Equateur was affected (especially the Tshuapa District), camps for exiled Kitawala leaders having been established there. The Kivu also proved fertile for Kitawala. Kitawala exiles, transferred from Equateur in order to prevent them from creating an alliance with Kimbanguist exiles also in that province, were sent to Lubutu in the Kivu. Thus another seed was planted which soon sprouted in the form of increased Kitawala activity (Robert Kaufmann, Millénarisme et acculturation, p. 80).

**The revolt was led by a Kumu named Busizi from Bafaswende (Oriental Province) and his assistant, Alleluia. Claiming to be a messiah, he called for a "war against Muslims and Europeans" (Ibid., pp. 99-100). The Kumu, in particular, were attracted to his preaching and played a notable part in the Masisi Revolt. Kumu involvement has been explained by some writers as an anomic reaction of a society undergoing disintegration and unable to cope adequately with change (see D. Biebuyck, "La société Kumu face au Kitawala," passim; and Kaufmann, Millénarisme, passim). L'Avenir Colonial Belge, August 3, 1948, noted that "Kitawala has given the black the opportunity to transform his customary mentality on his own, a fact which is worth thinking about."

***In 1954, 150 Africans were arrested at Stanleyville for being members of Kitawala (Nation Belge, April 29, 1954). And in 1956 it was reported that 200 arrests were made by the Force Publique in the area of Ponthierville (just south of Stanleyville); however, only 25 were detained on charges of being members of Kitawala (Courrier d'Afrique, February 10, 1956).

As in the case of Kimbanguism, the Protestants were condemned for aiding and abetting a subversive movement. The Catholic missions and their supporters in particular emphasized the American origins of Watchtower.* The <u>Bulletin des Missions</u> of the Benedictine Fathers noted that Watchtower "is strongly supported by American Protestant sects, who have not the slightest hesitation about exciting the worst appetites of the natives, promising them...land, money, and even the wives of their white oppressors."[19] The Congo Protestant Council countered the charges against the Protestant missions by disclaiming any connection with the movement. At its annual meeting in 1946 it went "on record as opposing the spread in the Belgian Congo of the movement variously known as Jehovah's Witnesses, Kitawala, Watchtower, and International Bible Students Association. It recommends to all Protestant Missions active, positive teaching to counteract the anarchistic and irresponsible character of the movement."[20] The Protestant sect which suffered the most, however, was the American-based Watchtower Bible and Tract Society (Jehovah's Witnesses— JW). It repeatedly eschewed any connection with Kitawala (though not denying that their literature may have influenced that movement) or any other movements in the Congo which might call themselves Watchtower. The JW noted that, in spite of attempts in 1932 and 1948, none of their European representatives had been allowed to enter the Congo.[21] It was not until the late 1950s that the Belgians finally recognized that a difference existed between Kitawala and the JW, and even then their skepticism was not entirely overcome.**

In view of the <u>Weltanschauung</u> of the African in his traditional setting, it is not surprising that his response to the forces of social disintegration and repression should have assumed a religious form. In African society, as in many other societies, religious change was a highly sensitive gauge of stability and instability. At a time when the values, traditions, and life style of the African were in question, traditional religion could no longer provide relief from tensions; only messianism offered a way out of despair. It has been noted that "in all ages, the messiah has been a divine apostle of hope. He has infused old dreams with new vitality, pronouncing a regenerated world to those who accepted him. Emphasizing tribal values and virtues, he has, of necessity, been faithful to his culture; he has responded to its demands even while imparting to it fresh meaning."[22]

All these messianic movements seem to have been attempts to overcome feelings of helplessness and impotence in the face of European encroachment which had weakened the African customary institutions and their purposes, to regain personal and social security through the rebuilding and modification of old institutions, and to provide the resentment and hostility felt against European power with an outlet that would not entail self-annihilation. This could be accomplished by building and believing in a Utopia where the Europeans would disappear or be killed and their wealth and power transferred to the believers. It was a world of fantasy, an illusion of a people under

---

*A right-wing Catholic newspaper stressed that "Kitawala...is of American origin" (<u>Le Phare Dimanche</u>, January 22, 1950).

**An official of the JW at their Brooklyn headquarters provided the following membership figures for his organization in the Congo: in 1947, 1; in 1948, 14; in 1956, 156; in 1961, 1,385 (of whom 900 to 1,000 were in Léopoldville).

pressure, whose traditional culture had failed to give them the understanding and capacity to deal with the forces of the rapid change brought about by the colonial situation.* In the messianic and syncretistic movements they found at once vehicles for sociopolitical change and a means of achieving increased self-esteem.**

One writer holds that the Congolese messianic and syncretistic movements were linked to a search for religious and political autonomy and gave birth to a kind of "holy nationalism."[23] This view seems to have merit. With the easing of Belgian repression toward the end of the 1950s some observers detected a more openly political tone in pronouncements by the leaders of these movements. André Ryckmans, writing of the situation in the Lower Congo, noted that "in certain meetings [of messianic sects], prayer seems to occupy less time than discussion, and doctrine at times vanishes before political preoccupations."[24] By 1958, a time when fledgling Congolese political parties had little or no popular following, the messianic and syncretistic movements "could count on mass support."[25] In some areas these movements had assumed quasi-governmental authority, superseding both the customary authorities and the Colonial Administration: "They had their own chiefs, their judges presiding over their tribunals, their police, [etc.]"[26] They had become a revolutionary force and were in some cases destined to become affiliated with such new political parties as the Association Bakongo (ABAKO), which were just beginning to emerge.***

---

*Thomas Hodgkin has said of these movements: "Their main achievement... has undoubtedly been to diffuse certain new and fruitful ideas, in however confused a form, among the African mass, the peasants in the countryside and the semi-proletarianized peasants in the towns,...; the idea of the historical importance of Africans; of an alternative to total submission to European power; of social ties that are based upon common beliefs and purposes rather than upon kinship; of a community in which women enjoy equal rights and duties with men" (Nationalism in Colonial Africa, pp. 113-114). Balandier also has seen messianic movements as "a reaction against the process of disintegration of the group....These movements seek more or less consciously to recreate broken ties, to reform a community; they knit together; they unify" (Georges Balandier, "Messianisme des Bas-Kongo," p. 218).

**Here there is a marked resemblance between these movements and such movements as the Black Muslims and Marcus Garvey's Universal Negro Improvement Association in the United States.

***There are some indications that in many instances the membership of messianic and syncretistic movements diminished as political parties became legitimized and more active. If this is indeed so, it would seem that, as political secular movements grow and offer an alternative means of reintegration, messianic and prophet movements tend to become depoliticized and more religious in character. In the Lower Congo just prior to independence there was a great resurgence of messianism; this diminished with the granting of independence. If, however, the promises of the political parties or independence go unfulfilled and thus fail to serve as a basis for reintegration, then, if this assumption is correct, one is likely to witness a growth in messianism and syncretism even under noncolonial governments. Some of the symptoms of messianism, if not the resurgence of the movements themselves, could be seen during the 1964-1965 rebellion in the Congo.

CHAPTER 14

THE MOVEMENT TOWARD INDEPENDENCE

The End of the Triumvirate

For over half a century the Congo had been controlled by a triumvirate of church, government, and commercial trusts. From this collaboration each partner derived tangible benefits. Such strains and conflicts as arose between them tended to be compromised or suppressed for the sake of maintaining the system. But the policies pursued during the four years of the Buisseret regime shattered the stability and security resulting from this interdependence. Buisseret's attack on missionary dominance over education, his attempt to reduce state subsidies to the missions, and his promotion of secular education for Congolese did much to precipitate a break with the past.

The Catholics were initially shocked and disturbed by the radical change in mission-state relations. They had played an integral and vital part in the development of the Congo. A policy that cast aside those who had contributed so much seemed to them both foolish and irreverent. Yet the unwanted breakup of the triumvirate came at an opportune time for the Catholic missionaries. They, like many other Belgians, had for some time believed the Congo to be an island of peace in a stormy sea. They had been confirmed in this belief by the policy of collaboration, which fostered the impression that the barbarians could be kept from the gates. The battle with Buisseret shook many Catholics from their lethargic conservatism. It shattered the illusion that a Christian society could be built in the Congo with the cooperation of government and business. And the missionaries began to feel the security of old relationships crumble around them.

The growing disaffection of the Congolese elite from the Church (see above, pp. 108-110) had deeply disturbed the missions. The évolués felt that many missionaries were too authoritarian, that they were too closely allied with the state and the large commercial enterprises, and that they were unwilling to relinquish control to the African clergy and laity. In general, they regarded the missionaries as guardians of the status quo.

Aware of the failure of traditional missionary policy, a progressive faction of missionaries saw in Buisseret's anticlerical activities the opportunity to free the Church from the bonds which had for so many years tied it to the colonial regime. Among this group was Father Mosmans, who was disturbed that missionaries "at times hesitated to defend natives against injustices when they are committed, for fear of losing some expected financial benefits." He implored his colleagues to "have the courage to liberate themselves from this stifling servitude and thereby regain their total independence."[1] And the militant lay Catholic leader Jacques Meert, addressing

144

the clergy in the Congo, asserted that "the Church must not appear to be an enemy of progress."[2]

To this clamor for change was added the voice and support of the Papacy. Pope Pius XII, in his encyclical letter _Fidei Donum_, issued in 1957, called attention to the rapid changes taking place in Africa which were leading toward "a new social order." He intimated that the Church in that continent must meet this challenge direct and warned that "any delay or hesitation is full of danger."[3]

By 1956 the colonial dike was leaking badly, and the Catholic missions, faced with the alternative of either swimming willy-nilly with the growing tide of African nationalism or being swept under by it, threw in their lot with the Congolese. In spite of the fact that missionary opinion was far from unanimous on the point, many in the upper reaches of the Catholic hierarchy considered that the time had come to openly declare the Church's support for Congolese nationalist aspirations. This step was taken on June 29, 1956, when the Catholic bishops of the Congo made public a solemn declaration which in clear and explicit terms pronounced their divorce from the government: "Matters purely spiritual are exclusively within the realm of the Church. Purely temporal matters are within the direct competence of the State."[4] This Augustinian solution was further affirmed by the bishops in their plenary conference in session at Léopoldville at the time of the declaration: "In Belgian Africa as elsewhere [the Church] claims a perfect independence in regard to all forms of politics."[5] But what was to be left unto Caesar did not, in the estimation of the bishops, include "notably those problems concerning education and youth organizations," since they directly affected the Church.[6]

The political role the bishops assigned themselves was not entirely passive. They saw the Church as providing the inspirational and moral basis for social and political change. Their declaration concerned itself chiefly with such questions as property rights, family affairs, work and pay, the right to free association, and race relations. But it was their closing paragraphs, devoted to political emancipation, that aroused the greatest interest—and a storm of controversy:

> All of the inhabitants of a country have the duty to actively collaborate in the general welfare. They have, therefore, the right to take part in the conduct of political affairs.
>
> The protecting nation has the obligation to respect this right and to favor the exercise thereof through progressive political education.
>
> The indigenous population has the obligation to become aware of the complexity of their responsibilities and to prepare to assume them.
>
> It is not the province of the Church to indicate how the emancipation of a people should come about. She considers it legitimate from the moment that respect for mutual rights and a sense of charity can be attained.[7]

While cautiously advocating a gradualistic approach to Congolese political development, the bishops had gone far to emphasize that the interests of the Congolese must receive primary attention, that the Congolese had the right to political participation, and that eventually the Congo should achieve political emancipation. For the Catholic missions this was a radical departure from the past. Once they had abandoned the old pattern of relationships, they could not easily revert to it without destroying their image among the Congolese. Often in spite of themselves, they were committed to the course of action outlined in the declaration.*

Le Manifeste de Conscience Africaine

The bishops' declaration had concluded with a statement regarding the role of the laity: "Catholics have the duty to participate in political and social life. They will dedicate themselves to seeing that the institutions that are created respect the rights of Christian conscience."[8] On July 1, 1956, two days following the appearance of this document and as if on cue, a group of Congolese Catholic laymen made public a statement which embodied many of the principles outlined by the bishops. The Manifeste de Conscience Africaine was the first major political statement ever made by Congolese.

The manifesto emphasized the separate national character of the Congolese and urged that this be recognized by the Belgians: "We wish to be civilized Congolese, not Europeans with black skins."[9] It clearly stated the desirability and necessity of political independence, but envisioned a delay of thirty years before its final achievement.[10]**

The appearance of the manifesto was greeted with impassioned support and no less impassioned opposition. It was variously seen as reasonable, moderate, radical, and a clerical plot. The last accusation stemmed from the origins of Conscience Africaine and the associations of its editors. Conscience Africaine was a weekly newspaper identified with CERS (see above, p. 133) and with Father Ceuppens who had been instrumental in obtaining government authorization for its publication.[11]*** At the time of the manifesto the editorial staff included Albert N'Kuli, Dominique Zangabie, Antoine Ngwenza, Victor N'Djoli, Joseph Ngalula, and Joseph Ileo, editor-in-chief.

---

*Marcel Lihau indicated in 1958 that, despite the bishops' declaration, "some priests, even in the face of nationalism...continue today to support outdated doctrines" ("Les aspirations nationales au Congo belge," p. 159).

**The idea of a thirty-year transition period leading to independence was borrowed by the editors of Conscience Africaine from Van Bilsen (see above, p. 20 fn.).

***Conscience Africaine was printed at the Scheutist printing plant and was to some degree under missionary purview. In fact the only outlets available to the Congolese for journalistic expression for some time were either the private (white) missionary- or government-controlled press. It was not until 1957 that the first independent African newspapers appeared: Quinze and Congo, both of which were suppressed that same year. This contrasts with areas of British and French Africa where a vigorous African press had existed for many years (see Thomas Hodgkin, African Political Parties, pp. 31-34). The Catholics had long been aware of the uses of a controlled press as an aid to evangelization and as a vehicle for defending and making their views widely known. The Catholic press, published in French and vernacular languages, enjoyed a large circulation among Congolese. Publication figures for 1958 reveal that the two largest European secular dailies, Le Courrier d'Afrique and L'Avenir Colonial Belge, had 13,000 and 3,000 readers respectively, while Temps Nouveau d'Afrique, published by the White Fathers, had

The initiative for the manifesto seems to have come mainly from the editorial board. The board, however, enlisted the aid of others in formulating its ideas. Meert informed Jean Buchmann and Joseph Nicaise, two professors from Lovanium University at that time giving courses at CERS, that the _Conscience Africaine_ group had decided to publish a political manifesto and would appreciate their advice and counsel.[12] The first meeting of the group included members of the editorial staff, Meert, Nicaise, Buchmann, and Malula. Malula had offered his residence as the meeting place but asserted that he had only acted as an intermediary and did not attend any further meetings of the group. Discussions centered around Van Bilsen's thirty-year plan. Jean Buchmann, acting as spokesman for the group, established contact with Jean Cordy, an important member of the administration in Léopoldville and an advisor to ABAKO. Buchmann informed him of the group's intention of publishing a political manifesto. Cordy responded favorably and did much to convince Governor-General Pétillon and Vice Governor-General Cornelis to allow publication of the manifesto. The governor-general was presented with a copy twenty-four hours before the manifesto appeared on the streets of Léopoldville.

Greeted with enthusiasm by most Congolese, the manifesto was condemned as a missionary plot by the anticlericals who pointed to its Catholic origins and cited the roles of Malula and the European militant Catholic advisors as smacking of the dictate of the Church. It seemed to them more than coincidental that the manifesto should have given evidence of strong influence by the bishops' declaration and should have surfaced only two days after it. Critics saw both documents as expedient tactical moves, designed to maintain the influence of the Church and to undercut an imminent Socialist party statement dealing with political reform in the Congo. This statement was in fact made public the day following the appearance of the _Manifeste de Conscience Africaine_.*

4,500 readers, and _Horizons_ (until 1957 _La Croix du Congo_), published by the Scheutist Fathers, had 6,000 (J. Grosjean, "La presse au Congo," p. 82). The vernacular missionary press attained what was, for the Congo, a rather large circulation. In 1958 _Hodi_ (White Fathers) had 17,000 readers, _Ndongozi_ 20,000, and _Kindugu_ (Xavierians) 35,000 (_Ibid._).

The four major European newspapers were evenly split between pro- and anti-clerical alignments, _Courrier d'Afrique_ and _L'Essor du Congo_ being generally proclerical, while _L'Avenir_ and _L'Echo du Katanga_ were firmly anticlerical.

The government sponsored and published _La Voix du Congolais_ which, while under its control, was staffed and run by Congolese. It was not until August 1959 that freedom of the press was formally accorded, although, as Crawford Young notes, censorship and suppression of the press had effectively ended after the Léopoldville riots of January 1959 (_Politics in the Congo_, p. 279).

*The anticlerical newspaper _L'Echo du Katanga_ asserted at the time that "the manifesto...was distributed in the streets of Léopoldville the first of July, BEFORE the resolution of the Socialist congress had been voted on and could be made known," and that "it was distributed in the provinces by Catholics who had private connections with Lovanium" (_Courrier d'Afrique_, September 1-2, 1956, quoting from _L'Echo du Katanga_). The Socialist program, while more specific in its proposals for political reform than the bishops' declaration,

As to the timing of the two documents, the anticlericals' charge seems to have some validity. Catholic officials were certainly aware of the date of the Socialist congress and of the likelihood that a policy statement on colonial matters would be forthcoming. There are also indications that Meert urged the editors of Conscience Africaine to issue the document before the Socialist conclave.[13] A review of all the evidence available suggests, however, that the Manifeste de Conscience Africaine was not the product of a clerical conspiracy,* but rather arose out of the disaffection of the Congolese editors of Conscience Africaine and their enchantment with Van Bilsen's thirty-year plan. While the authors no doubt enjoyed the support of the Catholic hierarchy and the advice of European lay militants, the document was essentially their own production. Malula seems to have purposely refused to play a role in its formulation in order to avoid giving any appearance that the Church was behind it. In face of the growing antagonism that the Congolese laymen felt toward the missions because of their interference in secular affairs, it would be to the Church's advantage to avoid direct association with the manifesto. But, even if the missionaries had in fact been pulling the strings behind the scenes, the impact of the manifesto would perhaps have remained the same; the content in itself struck a sympathetic chord among Congolese.

For some the manifesto was too mild in its language and too gradualistic in its demands. Kasavubu, president of ABAKO, was of this opinion and attacked the document in a speech delivered on August 23, 1956. He scoffed at the idea of a thirty-year transition period and demanded "immediate independence" for the Congo.[14] Less than two months after its appearance the manifesto, which had been viewed by many as a radical statement of Congolese demands, was already dépassé. But it had played an important role as a springboard for African political expression. It is doubtful whether Kasavubu would have gone as far as he did in his August speech if the Manifeste de Conscience Africaine had not paved the way.

For many whites in the Congo, clericals and anticlericals alike, the pro-Congolese policy of the missions, as expressed in the bishops' declaration and reflected in the manifesto, went beyond principle and became incitement. Some members of the administration denounced the declaration as a "stab in the back,"[15] and viewed the missions as troublemakers who for their own selfish reasons were harboring and promoting radical Congolese nationalists. Even the generally pro-Catholic newspaper L'Essor du Congo, which reflected colon opinions, denounced the missionaries for their political

---

was no more forward-looking than the latter (see "Le programme d'action du PSB," in Le Congo, documents 1956, pp. 24 ff.). It was certainly less radical than the Manifeste de Conscience Africaine.

The PSC had also produced a statement on colonial policy which appeared on February 26, 1956 (see "Le manifeste du PSC sur le Congo," ibid., pp. 18 ff.). In many ways it was a much tamer document than any of the three mentioned above. It emphasized the establishment of a Belgo-Congolese community but did not suggest political autonomy for the Congo.

*René Lemarchand also seems to hold this view (see Political Awakening in the Congo, p. 157).

meddling: "The work of the missionary...pleases us when it concerns the emancipation of men, the construction of schools and hospitals, social reform, and even a degree of temporal domination, etc., but not when it concerns political activity as such."[16] And the Socialist journal Le Peuple accused the Catholic promoters of the manifesto of aiming at "the formation of a Catholic elite and party that will grab the levers of control at the opportune moment."[17]

In the face of such white reaction, the bishops' declaration and their support of the manifesto were at once a radical departure and a frightening new commitment for the Catholic Church in the Congo. At this stage the Catholics had to decide how to short-circuit the efforts of the Liberals and Socialists* whose organizations (amicales and cercles) were attracting members of the Congolese elite, and whether or not to establish Catholic political organizations that would at the propitious time transform themselves into political parties in order to rival those of the anticlerical opposition.

To counteract Liberal and Socialist activities in the colony, the Catholics raised a public protest in both Belgium and the Congo against the intrusion of metropolitan political rivalries, on the ground that it threatened the authority of and respect for the administration and whites among Congolese.[18] At a time when power over colonial matters had passed from Catholic hands into those of the Socialist-Liberal coalition, such pleas had little chance of success. The Catholics therefore sought to convince the Congolese that the appearance of Belgian political parties in the Congo was not only detrimental to their interests but even insulting. The Manifeste de Conscience Africaine reflected this view:

> National union is necessary because the entire population of the Congo must above all become conscious of its national character and its unity.
>
> How could this be possible if the people are appealed to by several parties, which are in conflict with one another?...This leads us to take a position regarding the introduction of Belgian political parties into the Congo. Our position is clear: these parties are bad and useless.[19]

The editors of the manifesto, however, did not limit their condemnation to Belgian political parties. They saw all political parties, whether Belgian or Congolese, as exacerbating the conflicts within society, not as instruments for forging national unity. The manifesto gave succinct expression to

_____

*Ruth Slade has noted that "there was a great deal of Liberal propaganda in the Congo; the Liberals had found the ground prepared among the white settlers, and soon had groups of supporters among the évolués as well. On the whole, the Socialists had still greater success among the Congolese. Both groups preached an anti-paternalism which delighted the Africans" (The Belgian Congo, p. 41). This was motivated in large part by their wish to weaken the position of the Catholic missions, which were under increasing attack by Congolese évolués for their paternalistic attitudes. The PSC on the other hand was wary of getting directly involved in the Congo and tended to follow the lead of the Catholic missions by denouncing the introduction of Belgian political parties into the colony (see "Le manifeste du PSC sur le Congo," in Le Congo, documents 1956, pp. 18-23).

this abhorrence of political parties: "We wish neither party competition nor a single party."[20]

This rejection of party both as an instrument of politics and as an expression of nationalism by a group of the most highly politicized Congolese to be found at that time can only be understood in terms of the group's Catholic and ethnic affiliations. It appears that by 1956 the missionaries and European lay militants in the Congo had reached a decision not to counter the Liberals and Socialists by building a confessional political party. In reply to the question whether Christians should enter party politics, Meert said: "We truly think that this would be an error." But he added: "We are equally convinced that one must not remain inactive."[21]*

Political Associations

The Catholic missions, although eschewing political parties as a means of protecting their interests against the anticlerical onslaught, did not flinch from using other political instruments when necessary. They promoted the establishment of the Fédération des Moniteurs Catholiques as well as the Comité Mixte de la Ligue de Parents Chrétiens, both of which were designed to act as organized pressure groups aimed at forcing the administration to change its policies in regard to educational subsidies and secularized education. These groups, though composed of and staffed by Congolese, were little more than Catholic-front organizations and were often under the direct influence and control of Catholic missionaries.

Support was also sought by the Catholics in another quarter. In 1957 the director of the Bureau de l'Enseignement Catholique invited some members of the Government Council to meet privately with him before the next council session: "I will place myself at your disposal, to inform you of certain educational questions in order to bolster the resolutions that you may have decided to present at the Office of the Council."[22] Canon Moermans' invitation led to the formation of the Intergroupe des Intérêts Chrétiens (IIC) which represented Catholic interests within the Government Council. Among its members were Gaston Diomi** and Emmanuel Kini, both of whom were leading figures in ABAKO. The members of the IIC from time to time consulted with Canon Moermans and Father Ceuppens, director of Agence DIA, on matters that were or were to be brought before the Government Council. The IIC and the various Catholic-front organizations, however, became increasingly irrelevant during 1957, as the political initiative shifted from the administration and the missions to the Congolese.

---

*The necessity of political awareness and participation for the protection of Catholic interests was pressed home by the missionaries as well. One priest warned his readers that "the same thing must not happen in Belgian Africa that occurred in Uganda, where, on the day that political emancipation began, all powers were concentrated in the hands of non-Catholics, because the Catholics had not understood their duty...to prepare themselves for political responsibilities" ("Déclaration de l'épiscopat du Congo Belge et du Ruanda-Urundi," p. 458).

**Leader of the Congolese faction of the IIC. The European leader was Philippe Boulengier.

Shortly after its appearance the Manifeste de Conscience Africaine was vehemently attacked by Kasavubu for its denial of the role and efficacy of political parties, which some had interpreted as a mission-inspired assault not only on the Belgian political parties but on ABAKO as well. Kasavubu acidly commented:

> Notice how confused are our friends of Conscience Africaine. They wish to govern, but disdain the means by which one directs a country. These soldiers like victory but find weapons distasteful. But can one achieve military victory by divesting oneself of arms? Have not the authors of the manifesto taken it into account that by trampling on politics they have made themselves the enemies of their own plans?...Can one participate in the government of a country while dispensing with politics?... Party conflict, although dangerous, is quite necessary in a democracy.[23]

The challenge by ABAKO, which some missionaries and Congolese saw as increasingly anticlerical and dangerously ethnic, helped arouse Catholic interest in building an organization to counter its growing influence among Congolese. Another factor contributing to a reassessment of the attitude toward political parties expressed in the Manifeste de Conscience Africaine was the forthcoming statut des villes which was expected to provide for African participation in elections during 1957.*

In drawing up their manifesto the editors of Conscience Africaine looked forward to the establishment of a program to which all Congolese might adhere.[24] They may in fact be said to have called for the building of a national movement. Shortly afterward, however, in the September-October issue of Conscience Africaine they veered toward the formation of a congress-type political organization,** and announced that a meeting, open to all, would be held in Léopoldville to establish a Mouvement National Congolais (MNC). But when the meeting took place, its promoters put limits to this open invitation. Ileo refused entrance to Cyril Adoula who represented the Socialists.

---

*The statut des villes which provided for "consultation" (the word election was not used because the final approval of those elected remained with the governor-general) was finally issued during March 1957. Africans were to serve on the conseil de ville as representatives of the African population, and African burgomasters were to head the communes to be established in the cité indigène. Less important politically was a decree issued May 10, 1957, which concerned rural areas (Young, Politics in the Congo, passim).

**In Hodgkin's words "the term 'national movement' is used for the most part in a very general sense—to refer to the effort of a colonized people... to liberate itself from colonial rule in all its aspects. A 'national movement' in this sense can exist without any determinate type of organization." By congress Hodgkin meant a political organization "whose principal characteristics are (a) a broad national objective, the elimination of the existing colonial system; (b) looseness of structure...; (c) emphasis on the idea of representing all the people, the national will made articulate; (d) an aggressive strategy, associated with the lack of constitutional mechanisms for the realization of the nationalist objectives" (African Political Parties, pp. 50-51).

This action destroyed the credibility of the pro-Catholic group's assertion that it wished to construct an organization that would encompass Congolese of all political shades. Ileo's action may well have reflected the controversy existing among the Belgian advisors of the Conscience Africaine group.

Following the July manifesto Ngalula and Ileo continued to consult with Meert, Nicaise, Buchmann, and Jean Bruck, head of the Confédération des Syndicats Chrétiens Congo. Opinion among the European counselors* was running in favor of a religiously oriented political party. Meert and Bruck in particular pressed for the establishment of a Christian Democratic party or a Catholic Social party.** Opposition to such a move came mainly from Buchmann who, believing that a confessional party would polarize Congolese opinion around the religious issue and thus harm both the Catholics and the nationalist cause, supported the idea of a secular party with broad membership.

The split among these advisors may have given rise to the seeming ambivalence of the Conscience Africaine group in regard to the nature of their proposed MNC. By excluding the Socialists they had afforded their detractors some evidence to support the charge that their effort was merely a clerical plot to insure Catholic domination over the nationalist movement. The result was that the MNC failed to attract popular support and languished. Its later revival was in an entirely different form (see below, p. 157 fn.).

In Léopoldville the communal elections of December 8, 1957, gave a resounding victory to ABAKO: winning 46 percent of the total vote, it captured 133 out of 170 council seats.[25] Organizationally it had proven itself to be the most effective Congolese political party in the Congo, perhaps the only one worthy of being so labeled. But its weakness, as well as its strength, was to be found in its ethnic homogeneity. It was a Bakongo party and, as such, incurred the enmity of the other ethnic groups in Léopoldville.

The origins of ABAKO are closely linked to the Jesuits and their mission at Kisantu. Father Van Wing played a prominent role in its inception.[26] He had made a profound study of Bakongo history, traditions, and beliefs, and was a forceful advocate of the teaching and development of Kikongo, the language of the Bakongo people. While on a tour of the Congo during 1946 he met with groups of Bakongo évolués in Léopoldville and counseled them to form groups to protect their language.[27] It was at his urging that Edmond Nzeza-Landu had produced the first manifesto of ABAKO,*** which emphasized the unity

---

*Max Bastin, editor of the pro-Catholic Courrier d'Afrique, also acted as a close advisor to this group. (Interview with Jean Buchmann.)

**In Katanga Antoine Rubbens, a European lawyer, helped found Union Congolaise, a party which sought to combine Congolese nationalism with Christian social doctrine (Rubbens, "Political Awakening in the Belgian Congo," pp. 63 ff.). Crawford Young indicates that "it rallied a number of Catholics who were offended at the anti-clericalism of the other candidates" (Politics in the Congo, p. 29). Unsuccessful in the communal elections in Elisabethville, it shortly thereafter faded from the scene.

***The manifesto, although written in 1950, was not made public until 1953, when it was published by Van Wing in the journal Kongo-Overzee (Nos. 2-3, pp. 178-181). For the text of the document see Benoit Verhaegen, ed., ABAKO, 1950-1960, pp. 10-13.

of all Mukongo (people of the Bakongo tribe) based on their common language, historical experience, and origins under the Kingdom of the Kongo (Kongo dia Ntotila).

Nzeza-Landu had been a seminary student at Kisantu, where Van Wing had acted as his spiritual advisor. The schools and seminaries at Kisantu were over the years the major training ground for Bakongo intellectuals from the Kwango area and the entire Lower Congo.* The Kisantu alumni were members of the Association des Anciens Elèves des Pères Jésuites (ASAP) which had "an important role in the training of several of the leaders of ABAKO, by offering them a real chance to develop themselves and to reinforce their ties of solidarity with each other."[28] In addition the two organizations had officials in common: in 1953 Simon Nzeza was the dean of ASAP, while also serving as treasurer of ABAKO, and Joseph Yumba, president of ASAP, was at the same time a member of the Central Secretariat of ABAKO.[29]

ABAKO's ties to Kisantu were also indicated by a manifesto it issued in 1950 inviting missionaries who worked among the Mukongo and spoke their language to become members of ABAKO.[30] In early days some missionaries appear to have done this; among them were two Bakongo clergymen, Abbé Jean Loya and Father Henri Matota, who played important roles as advisors to ABAKO leaders.[31] Jesuit involvement with ABAKO was not, however, entirely marked by fraternal accord. Van Wing, who had helped to bring the organization into being, expressed a feeling of unease about the growing "superiority complex" of the Bakongo: "This [Bakongo] nationalism, which engenders contempt and suspicion, is a factor of division among the urban masses and, as such, contrary to the constitutions of associations of every nature."[32] Missionary support for ABAKO continued, but skepticism about it grew rapidly after 1954, the year Kasavubu was elected its president.

Kasavubu, who was not a Kisantu alumnus, was suspicious of ABAKO's ties to the Jesuits and had refused to join in 1953 when he was proposed for membership. His biographer records that "he wished neither to deliberately join the Jesuit 'clan' nor any association sponsored, openly or secretly, by the clergy, 'because if you have the imprudence to do so, the day will come when you wish to leave and it will be said of you: There goes a bad Christian.'"[33] Although not a member, Kasavubu was drafted by ABAKO to serve as its president in 1954.** From that moment onward, and especially during 1955-1956,

---

*The Jesuits also had a major mission station at Kikwit in the Kwilu region. Kisantu drew its students from this area as well as from the Kwango where it was located. Benoit Verhaegen notes that at Kisantu "a certain ideological affinity was forced between the leaders of different ethnic groups and regions, but who had come under the same missionary influence" ("ABAKO," [unpublished manuscript, n.d., n.p., private papers of M. Verhaegen]). This factor may help in part to explain the collaboration which later took place between ABAKO and the Parti Solidaire Africain.

**Gilis notes that Kasavubu's election as president of ABAKO has been most often explained as an attempt to balance and settle clan rivalries within the association between the Bantandu, pro-Jesuit faction of Nzeza-Landu, and the Bandibu, among whom were many Protestants—Pierre Canon and Simon Tezzo belonged to this faction. Kasavubu was brought in because he was a Muyombe. Gilis considers that, while this explanation is partially

estrangement between ABAKO and the Jesuits grew as the organization became increasingly political and secular. Nzeza Landu, the preceding president,* had had close ties to the Jesuits and felt a debt of gratitude to them, particularly to Van Wing. Kasavubu had no such commitments and was prepared to tear ABAKO away from its clerical restraints. The separation of ABAKO from the Jesuits was, however, neither abrupt nor complete. As late as 1957 Father Matota, Abbé Loya, and Auxiliary Bishop Kimbondo** were said to be still in contact with the leaders of the association.[34] But Kasavubu's distaste for Jesuit-inspired clericalism was matched by the Jesuits' fear and dislike of what they saw as the growing political radicalism of ABAKO under its new leader.

It was this fear that motivated one African priest, a member of ABAKO, to communicate his anxieties about the "revolutionary" nature of the organization to the director of Agence DIA.[35] The Scheutist-dominated Catholic press agency, already antagonistic to ABAKO, was quick to utilize this information to attack the Bakongo group. On February 20, 1957, it released a dispatch entitled "A fanatical revolutionary party."*** A major theme of the press release was that Kasavubu's attack on the Conscience Africaine manifesto was an indication of the aggressive tribal nationalism of ABAKO.**** It

_____

correct, one must take into account the character and talent of the man as well. Kasavubu himself believed that his writings in Kongo dia Ngunga (the ABAKO newspaper) had helped make him popular (Charles-André Gilis, Kasa-Vubu, p. 70).

*He became the full-time editor of Kongo dia Ngunga after his resignation as president of ABAKO.

**When Kimbondo was installed, ABAKO sent him the following congratulatory telegram: "ABAKO Léopoldville and Kongo dia Ngunga warmly greet the nomination of Pierre Kimbondo, Bakongo bishop, worthy successor of Don Henrique de Banga Kongo, ordained in 1513" (Courrier d'Afrique, September 24, 1956). The ethnic chauvinism of ABAKO clearly extended to the Bakongo clergy as well.

***Father Ceuppens reported that he had gone to Cornelis to discuss the article on ABAKO before its release, and that the vice governor-general had tried to persuade him to suppress it. Ceuppens refused. When Governor-General Pétillon returned to the Congo, Ceuppens informed him too of his intentions; he met an attitude of incredulity (interview with Ceuppens). It appears that Ceuppens actually believed that ABAKO was ready to begin an armed insurrection at the opportune moment, although he did not say this in the press release.

****ABAKO was also accused by DIA of supporting and receiving support from the Kimbanguists. An alliance of ABAKO with the Bakongo messianic movement was both suspected and feared by the missionaries, including the Jesuits, who perceived it as a serious threat to their converts in the Lower Congo. In reply to these charges Kasavubu condemned Kimbanguism as "the stain that has blackened the history of the Bas-Congo" (Verhaegen, ed., ABAKO 1950-1960, p. 47).

Benoit Verhaegen believes that the anti-Kimbanguist position initially taken by Kasavubu was opportunistic but necessary in view of the power of

was noted that "all the members of the Committee of Conscience Africaine were Bangala* or Baluba," and that ABAKO's attack was ethnically motivated and designed to establish eventual Bakongo political hegemony in Léopoldville.[36] On April 7, 1957, ABAKO, replying to Agence DIA, defended the Bakongo claim to Léopoldville by citing historical sources.[37] It also derided the Scheutists for their lack of knowledge of Kikongo and for attempting to prevent the political progress of the Congolese by provoking a conflict between Bakongo and Bangala:

> Our compatriots from the Haut Congo have never protested against their brothers of the Bas Congo. But on the contrary, it is you, dear DIA, who, desiring to put into practice the magnificent precept of Christ, "Love One Another," have grouped certain elements, good children of the Church, around your table, in order to urge them to cry out against us in spite of themselves. Formerly you profited from the ignorance of these same elements and you succeeded in making them sign manifestos against Lay Schools.[38]

ABAKO's accusation that the gens du Haut were puppets directed by the Scheutist missionaries was vehemently denied and resented by the leaders of the organizations represented in the Fédérations du Haut Congo.** The presidents of the Fédération des Bangala (Bolikongo) and the Fédération du Kasai (P. Kabayidi) asserted that their differences and conflicts with the Bakongo

---

the colonial structure and of ABAKO's wish to remain legitimate and open. It was an attempt to set at rest the fears of the administration and the missions ("ABAKO" [unpublished]). This seems to be borne out by the fact that during the months just prior to independence ABAKO made a conscious attempt to court the Kimbanguists, although by that time the sect was a legal organization and the former restraints were in part gone.

In April 1960 the leaders of ABAKO (Kasavubu, Daniel Kanza, Diomi, and Nzeza-Landu) took part in the ceremonies surrounding the return to Léopoldville of the remains of Simon Kimbangu. The alleged messiah was eulogized by Kasavubu and others as a Bakongo nationalist (Courrier d'Afrique, April 4, 1960). In addition, Kimbanguists held posts within ABAKO and after independence held government office under the ABAKO label. Among these was Charles Kisolokele, Simon Kimbangu's son, who was vice president of the Province of Kongo Central in 1961 (Pierre Artigue, Qui sont les leaders congolais?, pp. 156-157).

*Crawford Young discussing the term Bangala comes to the conclusion that no such tribe ever existed, and that the existence of the term can be attributed to a number of ethnographic errors which perpetuated a myth. The term was, however, popularly used in Léopoldville where "all gens du Haut [immigrants arriving from up the river] were referred to as Bangala. The Bakongo in particular referred to all non-Bakongo as Bangala, and the term came to be accepted by all but the Kasaiens, Mongo and Kwango-Kwiluites" (Young, Politics in the Congo, p. 244).

**The Fédération des Bangala, the Fédération du Kasai, and the Fédérations de L'Equateur.

antedated the DIA dispatch, and that the grievances of the gens du Haut against ABAKO and its policies were indeed real and not some clerical fantasy.[39] The tension between the Bakongo and the gens du Haut began in the late 1930s as the influx of non-Bakongo peoples into Léopoldville reached significant proportions. Lingala became the major language of the non-Bakongo group and, being also the "official" administrative language, spread rapidly, even among the Bakongo in the cité. Its usage was aided and promoted by the administration and by the Scheutist missions in the capital.

The Scheutists, whose major missions were to be found in the Lac Léopold II district (Apostolic Vicariate of Inongo), Equateur (Apostolic Vicariate of Lisala), and the Kasai (Apostolic Vicariates of Luluabourg and Kabinda), naturally aligned themselves with those from these areas who settled in Léopoldville.* Reportedly, they even refused to conduct prayers or hear confessions in Kikingo[40] or to use it in their schools, giving preference to Lingala.** These Scheutist actions embittered the Bakongo population, especially its évolués. They also antagonized the Jesuits who had become the patrons and defenders of Kikongo.

Faced by what appeared to them to be a combined Scheutist-administration attack on the Bakongo and their language, Father Van Wing and other Jesuits urged Bakongo intellectuals to establish an organization to defend their linguistic and cultural interests. It was under this impulsion that first Renaissance Bakongo and later ABAKO were founded.***

Parochial Nationalism

The missions did not originate the feuding between Bakongo and Bangala elements in Léopoldville, but they certainly contributed to and exacerbated it by fostering feelings of linguistic and ethnic exclusivity that were to have far-reaching effects on Congolese political development.

The promotion of parochial nationalism was not confined, however, to the Jesuits. Missionaries throughout the Congo had become over the years exponents

---

*The Scheutist Fathers also had control of the Apostolic Vicariate of Boma, which included the Mayombe, where the population was Bakongo. However, the vicariate was somewhat of a stepchild in the eyes of the directors of the Scheutist missions, due in part to the fact that it was the only Scheutist vicariate operated by the French-speaking minority within the Scheutist order, which is strongly flamingist.

**The African Linguistic Commission, meeting at Tervuren (Belgium) in 1952, decided that Kikongo should become the language of instruction in the primary schools of Léopoldville. Its decision was opposed by Father de Boeck (a Scheutist member of the commission) and Msgr. Six (Scheutist apostolic vicar of Léopoldville).

***Renaissance Bakongo (Renaibako) was founded in 1944 by J. Mavuela. Its membership was mainly drawn from former students of the Jesuits (Kisantu) who lived in Léopoldville at the time (Verhaegen, ABAKO 1950-1960, p. 10). It was succeeded in 1950 by ABAKO, whose full title was the Association of Bakongo for the Unification, Conservation, Perfection, and Expansion of the Kikongo Language.

and advocates for this or that culture and language. What Van Wing had done
for the Bakongo, Fathers Boelaert, Hulstaert, and de Rop did for the Mongo,
De Boeck for the Ngombe, De Sousberghe for the Bapende, and Vandermeirin and
Verhulpen for the Baluba.[41] In general, the most vocal missionary proponents
of linguistic and cultural revival among various Congolese tribes were Flemish. Coming from a motherland where they had felt themselves an oppressed
people that saw salvation in its own cultural traditions and language, they
tended to react sympathetically to ethnic nationalism in the Congo.

The Bakongo-Bangala dispute had parallels elsewhere in the Congo. In
the Luluabourg area there was growing antagonism between Baluba and Lulua.
The Lulua resented the fact that, although the area was traditionally Lulua,
the Baluba had managed to attain predominance.* Balubas were to be found oc-
cupying many of the government, mission, and commercial posts open to Congolese. Their adaptability and aggressiveness made them favorites with both
missionaries and administrators. They had early become targets for evangelization by both Catholics and Protestants, and many became catechists. They
also had been quicker than the Lulua to respond to the educational opportunities offered by the missions and were therefore better qualified for skilled
jobs. Responding to the challenge, in 1952 the Lulua formed an organization,
Lulua Frères, designed to protect and promote their interests.   Meanwhile
the Catholic missions' identification with the Baluba caused the Lulua to
look upon the missionaries with suspicion and hostility.** Problems also
arose elsewhere in the Kasai among the Bakuba,[43] whose experience with the
Baluba was similar to that of the Lulua. In the Katanga the pattern was repeated. The lure of jobs in the mining towns, especially Elisabethville,
drew Baluba to the area. There they established close contact with the missions. During the months prior to independence these tribal rivalries came
to be translated into open political competition along ethnic party lines***—
Balubakat, Lulua Frères (later changed to Parti de la Défense du Peuple Lulua),
ABAKO, and Union Mongo being among the most prominent of these parties.

It seems clear that the ethnocultural polices and attitudes of the missionaries contributed to the political fragmentation along tribal or ethnic
lines which took place in the Congo just prior to and after independence.

---

*In 1954 the Baluba constituted about 57 percent of the cité indigène
of Luluabourg (H. Nicolai and J. Jacques, La transformation des paysages congolais par le chemin de fer, Brussels, 1954, p. 82, quoted in Lemarchand,
Political Awakening, p. 97).

**Joseph Nkongolo, the first Congolese bishop in the Kasai (ordained
1959) was a Mulaba. As such, he was unpopular with the Lulua and Bakuba in
that province, who saw his appointment as further evidence of Baluba encroachment.

***Supraethnic parties were also formed, but for the most part they were
merely intertribal coalitions. The only really successful national party was
the MNC. This was a revival of the MNC formed by the group of Conscience Africaine, but in an entirely new form. It was founded in 1958, partly in response to the ABAKO sweep in the December 1957 elections in Léopoldville. It
initially drew its leadership from Catholic (Ileo and Ngalulu), Socialist
(Cyril Adoula), and Liberal (Patrice Lumumba) factions. Lemarchand records
that in 1958 Lumumba was also a member of CERS (Political Awakening, p. 20).

Also partly responsible were the colonial authorities who refused to allow the existence of Congolese political organizations or Congolese participation in government until the eleventh hour, when, for lack of time to organize, they turned to the ready-made constituencies to be found in the tribe.

The Léopoldville Riots

Toward the end of 1958 several events combined to heighten the tension, anticipation, and impatience within the African cité of Léopoldville. In Brazzaville, just across the Congo River, Charles de Gaulle had offered France's African colonies a choice between complete independence or membership within the French Community. For those on the Léopoldville bank of the river this gesture poignantly illustrated the gap between their own political situation and that of their brothers in Brazzaville, a fact of which they had been increasingly aware since France's passage of the Loi Cadre in 1956.*

During the spring and summer of 1958 évolués from all parts of the Congo attended the Brussels Exposition, where they had a unique opportunity to discover a sense of kinship founded on shared grievances, frustrations, and hopes. They also came into contact with Belgians of the anticolonial Left and became more aware of the weaknesses and fissures within the métropole, an awareness that was to help them in the coming months. In that same spring of 1958 the PSC took control of the reins of the Belgian Government, and in an unprecedented move Governor-General Pétillon was appointed minister of colonies (he soon changed his title to that of minister of Congo and Ruanda-Urundi). His most notable action was to appoint a groupe de travail, composed of leaders from each major Belgian political party, to conduct an inquiry into the situation in the Congo and submit recommendations for political reform. When the groupe de travail returned to Belgium in November 1958, after a stay in the Congo, it found that Pétillon had been replaced as minister by Maurice Van Hemelrijck (PSC). It proceeded with the preparation of its report, and Van Hemelrijck promised a government declaration on January 13, 1959.

During the last months of 1958, while the Belgian Government was planning the liberalization of its colonial policies, the political attitudes of many Congolese were hardening and becoming more radical. In August 1958, following President de Gaulle's speech in Brazzaville, the leaders of the MNC sent Pétillon a letter calling for reforms leading to the eventual political emancipation of the Congo.[44] On December 28, 1958, Lumumba, just returned from the All-African Peoples' Conference in Accra, made a speech to a meeting of MNC supporters in which he made it repeatedly clear that the Congolese were demanding independence in the immediate future,[45] a theme that Kasavubu had been voicing for some time.

On January 4, 1959, a mass meeting, scheduled by ABAKO in the African cité of Léopoldville, was postponed after the crowd had already gathered.[46]

---

*This law gave Africans in France's colonies greater control over their internal affairs. For an excellent discussion of the Loi Cadre reforms see Ruth Schachter Morgenthau, Political Parties in French-Speaking West Africa, pp. 65-74.

In the ensuing confusion the pent-up frustrations of the participants turned to fury, and what had been a crowd became a mob. The riots which spread throughout the cité were suppressed by the Force Publique, but not before a number of Congolese had been killed. The rioters' burning and looting was particularly directed at Portuguese-owned stores and the buildings of the Catholic missions in the cité.

The missionaries were disturbed and perplexed by this display of hostility. They had entered the cité to help the Africans—and had been rewarded by their wrath. The reasons for this seem twofold. Firstly, the missionaries were Belgian whites; as such, they and their institutions were identified, not without some cause, with colonial rule and attitudes. In lashing out at the missions the Congolese were attacking all the injustices they had suffered at the hands of the Belgians. Father Mosmans was of the opinion that "many missionary establishments were sacked for the sole reason that they were the symbols of the European presence. In many cases, the missionaries are considered to belong to the White clan."[47] A second reason was advanced by the parliamentary commission which later investigated the disturbance: a widespread feeling among évolués that the Catholic missions, while opposing lay education for Congolese, had at the same time limited the development of the education they themselves offered by turning away many Africans who wished to enter their schools. The PSC-dominated commission absolved the missions of these charges and placed the blame on the Buisseret ministry: "missionary education...was braked by a policy of restrictions, applied in a draconian manner by the public authorities in 1958."[48]

This view had the support of the Association des Parents d'Elèves des Écoles Catholiques de Léopoldville which claimed that mission buildings had been singled out by the rioters who had been dropped by the lay schools, where they had been taught to hate the Catholic missions, and had formed gangs of roving youths.[49] Adequate evidence to corroborate or invalidate this allegation is lacking, but there can be no doubt that the destruction of mission structures was both conscious and deliberate. The depth of suspicion and mistrust felt toward the missionaries in the cité is confirmed by an African priest who, in his testimony before the committee of inquiry, noted that the Africans believed "that the missions were against a raise in salaries, and that confession permitted the missionaries to spy for the Government."[50] Kimbanguism also was singled out as a cause of the riots.[51] Kimbanguists were accused of being among those who destroyed mission property, and their link with ABAKO was emphasized.[52]

Whatever the rioters' motives, their attacks on the missions were a clear indication that missionary relations with the Congolese were at a low ebb. The riots themselves widened the chasm between the missionaries and their flock and were a severe blow to missionary self-confidence. A Protestant pastor, attending services in Luluabourg a week after the disturbances in the capital, noted a tenseness, which other missionaries also must have felt in those tumultuous days.

> Before the service I could sense the unbearable tension in the air as some of my closest African friends seemed unusually cool toward me. They had not heard news of relatives in Léo but they heard that the soldiers and policemen, under the leadership of white officers, had fired upon the mobs, killing numbers of Africans. As a white man I was a symbol of repression even to these friends of long standing.[53]

Political Disengagement of the Missions

Sensing the confusion and despair of their colleagues and aware of the promise of independence made in the government's declaration of January 13, 1959,[54] the progressives within the Catholic missions once again exhorted the Church to reevaluate its policies in the Congo.* Father Mosmans warned that "the Church cannot remain indifferent to this powerful current of emancipation."[55] At the same time he emphasized that priests and missionaries should stay out of politics.[56] The same view was expressed and made more explicit by another Catholic missionary in a speech to the Afrika Kring in Louvain. The speaker exhorted his fellow missionaries to refrain from promoting tribalism, from supporting a particular candidate or party, and from acting as judges in palavers.[57]**

On August 15, 1959, some three months prior to the government announcement that a conference would meet in Brussels to work out the details of Congolese independence,*** the bishops of the Congo issued an apostolic letter dealing with the Church's position in regard to independence. In it they eschewed any political role for the clergy: "Politics is essentially a lay affair, and the Church as such intends to interfere neither in the establishment nor functioning of [political] institutions."[58]**** The bishops

----

*Shortly after the riots Bernard Leclaire, Jacques Neyns, and Jean Buchmann, all from the faculty of Lovanium University, arranged a conference with Msgr. Scalais and others to discuss the riots. It was decided to send a telegram to the minister of colonies urging that he offer independence to the Congolese. (Interview with Jean Buchmann.)

**In this respect the Protestants reiterated their traditional attitude toward separation of Church and state. Writing in the Congo Mission News, Dr. E. R. Wide emphasized that "events of [the] last month have proved once again how very dangerous it is for missions to be linked with politics, and we must see to it that the CPC maintains its tradition in this respect" (The Presidential Address," p. 3).

***The Round Table Conference took place in Brussels from January 20 to February 20, 1960. It was decided that the Congo would be granted its independence on June 30, 1960.

****In the Kwango-Kwilu region, during 1959 the Parti Solidaire Africain (PSA) emerged as the most important political entity in the area. It had close connections with the Jesuit alumni association (ASAP) at Kikwit. Cléophas Kamitatu, the president of ASAP-Kikwit, became the president of the PSA's Kikwit branch. The organizers of the PSA in the region made a number of visits to Catholic and Protestant missions during the summer of 1959 for recruitment purposes. From their reports it would appear that in most cases they were well received by the missionaries and African abbés. However, the attitude of the Catholic missions in the area seems to have changed after the apostolic letter of August 15, 1959, was issued. When the PSA asked to hold a meeting at one of the Catholic missions in the Kwilu in August 1959, the Father Superior of the mission "suggested" that since the meeting was of a "public and political character" it be held in the commercial center and not on mission property. The Father Superior stressed that "the mission did

made clear, however, that they would encourage Congolese Catholics to exercise their political responsibilities.* The Church pledged its loyalty to the leaders of the new nation, but it warned of three perils: a one-party system; a religious party—the bishops wished to discourage a confessional party but made it clear that they would support a particular party if it was the only party that "offered guarantees indispensable from a Christian point of view"; and the suppression of minority groups and the political opposition.[59] The greatest fear of the Church, as expressed in this apostolic letter, was that the new state would be laicizing and antireligious.**

The Léopoldville riots of January 4, 1959, did much to convince the Catholic missions that their active participation in politics was undesirable. Many were disturbed by the burning and sacking of mission structures in or near the African cité, and not a few feared the consequences of a more liberal policy. Others saw in the attacks on missionary property evidence that the missions should have been even more deeply involved. In general, however, the riots made the missions more wary of involving themselves in the nationalist movement and in politics in general.

As independence drew near, the Church took steps to insure its survival and the maintenance of its interests and position in the new political and social setting. It believed that, in the existing state of Congolese politics it could best achieve these aims by adjusting to the new order, maintaining a neutral position in the realm of politics, and becoming involved only if threatened by its enemies. This was a radical departure from the

----

not wish to lend its support to any particular party" and wanted to dissociate itself from all political parties. In October 1959 Antoine Gizenga, general president of the PSA, saw fit to warn the Catholic missionaries in the Kwango that an unwelcome fate might be their lot if they did not support the PSA: "The first victims of the January 4, 1959 disturbances in Léopoldville and of other disturbances as well, were, unhappily, priests and nuns. Shouldn't that give you something to think about?" (Herbert Weiss and Benoit Verhaegen, eds., Parti Solidaire Africain (PSA), pp. 49, 1945, and passim). It would appear that the call of the Catholic bishops for missionary abstention from political and party involvement was at least partially heeded, even by the African clergy.

*In addition, the apostolic letter expressed five major concerns of the Church on the eve of independence: (1) the need of respect for the traditions and customs of the people; (2) the protection of minority groups in the face of political, social, and economic change; (3) that the rights of "certain races and categories of citizens" should be considered; (4) that foreigners should be welcome as long as they were loyal to the new nation; and (5) that the Congo should participate in the community of nations (Ibid., p. 338).

**Msgr. Malula, addressing the Congolese elite two months before independence, warned against the adoption by the elite of an antireligious philosophy: "For true Congolese nationalists, for all those who sincerely love this country, laicism is an attack on the religious life of the Bantu people whose private, family, and public life is entirely impregnated with a religious sense" (Vers l'Avenir, April 3, 1960).

historical posture of the Catholic missions in the Congo. During the colonial period they played a direct and often primary role in politics. But their influence had been largely derived from their special relationship with certain political forces in the métropole—forces which were no longer important. Henceforth any political influence the Catholics might wield in the new state would have to be won entirely within a Congolese context. An era had come to an end.

The period from 1954 to 1960 was marked by the Catholics' disengagement from their traditional policy in regard to the colonial regime and by their search for a new relationship that would recognize and emphasize Congolese desires and demands. The more progressive faction of the Church was thus able to make its influence felt, and the ideas of Father Mosmans and others became more widely accepted. The shift in policy is evident from the bishops' declaration of 1956 which clearly put the Church in favor of greater Congolese political autonomy, and from lay Catholic sponsorship of the Manifeste de Conscience Africaine and of the original MNC.

Yet in spite of this growing political involvement of Catholic missionaries and lay militants no religiously based political parties formed in the Congo. This is especially surprising in view of the fact that well over a third of the population was reputedly Christian.* In other African colonies Christians, both Catholic and Protestant, had formed nationalist parties around the core of shared religious identification.** In the Congo this did not occur. Proposals were twice made to institute such political parties, but they came to nothing.*** One reason for this failure may be found in the very fact that the missions evangelized so widely and so well. Proselytization was not limited to one or two tribes, or to a limited area of the colony. Thus no one group came to be identified as Christian, nor did a religiously trained or oriented elite become coterminous with one tribe or region, as happened in the French Cameroons and Dahomey.[60] Had this been the case, it might have worked to aid in the building of a confessional political party. A heterogeneously composed and nationally oriented Catholic elite might have built a party with a supratribal emphasis. This did not come to pass, however, because the missionaries fostered cultural and linguistic exclusivity,

---

*In 1958 there were 4,546,160 Catholics and 825,625 Protestants, out of a total population of 13,658,185 (Inforcongo, Belgian Congo, vol. 2, pp. 12 and 165).

**The Democratic party (Catholic) in Uganda, the Christian Democratic party (Catholic, later merged with the Congress Labour party to form the Christian Liberation party) in what was Nyasaland, and the Parti des Démocrates Camerounais (Catholic) are examples of such parties (see D. A. Low, Political Parties in Uganda 1949-1962, p. 22; Herbert J. Spiro, "The Rhodesias and Nyasaland"; and Victor Le Vine, "Cameroun").

***In addition to the suggestion made by some of the lay militant advisors of the Conscience Africaine group (see above, p. 151) there was a post-independence attempt to form such a party; this idea for a Union des Croyants Congolais also failed.

not universality.*

In general the missionaries came to identify strongly with their flocks. Their hopes and aspirations for promoting a particular African language and culture often exceeded even those of the indigenous peoples themselves. In this sense, Flemish parochial nationalism was often, as in the case of ABAKO, projected by Catholic missionaries on to the African setting. The Catholic theory of the universality of the Church failed to overcome the rivalry of the various missionary orders working in the Congo. The clearest example of such rivalry was the conflict between the Scheutists and the Jesuits, who respectively supported for control of the African cité of Léopoldville the Bangala and Bakongo factions of the African population. This feud was often as bitter and vituperative as any between Catholics and Protestants. The African clergy of the Catholic Church also failed to overcome their own ethnic or tribal parochialism. The missions tended to send them to work among their own people; when they did venture elsewhere, both they and the local parishioners often tended to be guarded in their relations. The indigenous Church itself was never nationalized and therefore found it difficult to promote national cohesion.**

The Protestant role in the movement toward independence was negligible when compared with that of the Catholics. The assertion that "there were strong suggestions of covert official support of Catholic African groups in the Belgian Congo as a counterweight to the more nationalist-minded Protestant African groups,"[61] simply does not hold up under close scrutiny. It is true that the administration aided Catholic African groups, but this was done not so much to counter the Protestants as to check unrest among the évolués in general, both Catholic and Protestant. In addition, a glance at the first years of the nationalist movement in the Congo suggests that nearly all the political agitation and action was organized with the aid and abetment of

---

*"Insofar as they did communicate to the Africans a sense of pride in their culture, and a conviction that their culture was as worthy of recognition as that of the Belgians, Christian missionaries in effect gave the Congolese elites a justification for their fight against Belgian colonialism. But in so doing they also gave an ethnic direction and focus to nationalist assertions" (R. Lemarchand, "Congo (Léopoldville)," in James S. Coleman and Carl G. Rosberg, Jr., Political Parties and National Integration in Tropical Africa, p. 563).

**A Mukongo Catholic priest who was the head of a secondary school in the Lower Congo related to the author that, when he was sent among another tribe in the Kwilu, his parishioners had looked upon him as a foreign intruder; and it was apparent from his comments that he reciprocated their hostility. Their mutually shared Catholicism did little to forge a bond between them.

At the time of this interview (1964) the provincial government of Kongo Central had passed a law that allowed only those children whose parents or parent resided in the province to attend schools located in it. The mission schools were faced with a problem, since some of them had a substantial number of students who would have to be expelled. The school director mentioned above, however, was not at all chagrined by this; he felt it to be quite just that only Bakongo children be allowed to attend schools in the Lower Congo.

either the Catholic missionaries or lay militants, as in the case of the
Conscience Africaine, ABAKO, and the first MNC, or was led by Congolese
Catholics, as was ABAKO under Kasavubu, or the Parti Solidaire Africain
under Gizenga and Kamitatu. Nothing comparable to this degree of political
involvement is to be found among the Protestants, except perhaps for Jason
Sendwe, the former leader of the Balubakat party in Katanga.

The Catholics tended on the whole to be more politically and national-
istically oriented, if for no other reason than that Catholic évolués were
far more numerous than their Protestant counterparts. That, however, is
only a partial explanation. Another important factor was the apolitical or
even antipolitical attitude of many Protestant missionaries which they communicated to their African adherents. As a result many African Protestants
were embittered and hostile toward the missionaries when, as independence
arrived, they perceived that local and national political offices tended to
be dominated by African Catholics.

The Christian missions in the Congo had nurtured the elite that was responsible for the nationalist movement, but they could not provide a focus
for national integration. On the contrary, in many ways they fostered the
disintegrative forces which have been at play in the Congo at various periods
since independence, and which remain a potential danger.

SUMMARY AND CONCLUSION

For years after attaining independence on June 30, 1960, the Congo experienced unremitting political and human agony. Racked from the outset by
revolt and rebellion, its people endured social and economic dislocation,
and untold numbers of them died from violence, disease, or malnutrition. In
many areas its administrative apparatus broke down. Its political institutions as conceived in 1960 were in disarray, and the numerous attempts to
redesign and revitalize them remained, until recently, unrewarding.* Above
all, the Congolese have failed to forge a nation from the varied and dispar-
ate tribes and peoples within their boundaries. Whether the Congo survives
as a political entity will depend to a large degree on whether or not it
succeeds in forging such a nation in the future.
    In the drama that led to Congo's present situation the missions played
an important part that started during the colonial period. By helping to
establish and legitimize the Free State they became intimately tied to the
colonial administration. In the case of the Belgian Catholic missions this
bond was apparent; in the case of the Protestant missions its existence,
though real, was less obvious. Both tended to see the state as an ally in
the struggle to establish a new Christian society and welcomed the protection of the civil authorities while emphasizing, in their teachings to the
Congolese, subservience and loyalty to Bula Matari (the state). In a spiritual sense Belgium's path in the Congo was seen as that of manifest destiny.
Writing in 1947, Father J. Roussel exhorted his countrymen "to sweep away
savagery by progressively making the light of civilization shine..., by
leading a new crusade: God wishes it!"1
    The conditions prevailing in Belgian social and political life gave the
Catholic missions significant power and influence in matters concerning the
Congo. In conjunction with the Catholic party (the Parti Social Chrétien),
they and their friends exerted great leverage in political matters. They
led the way in forcing the resignation of Governor-General Lippens whom they
deemed hostile to their interests; they gained a monopoly over educational
subsidies, freezing out the Protestants for nearly twenty-five years; they
forced such changes in administrative policies as the revocation of Lippens'
circulars; and sometimes they succeeded in influencing colonial administrators to do their bidding. The Catholic missions were, in fact, a power to
be reckoned with in the Congo, and on occasion were practically a law unto

────────────

    *As of 1971, the regime of President Joseph Mobutu seems to have halted
and even begun to reverse the process of social, economic, and political disintegration. Whether he can succeed where others have failed remains to be
seen.

themselves. To the Africans, the Catholic missionaries often appeared in the dual role of men of religion and of symbols and representatives of the colonial power—with the emphasis often on the second. This is not to say that these Catholic missionaries were omnipotent in political affairs; on the contrary, they frequently failed to achieve their objectives. But their influence was nonetheless a constant and important factor that no student of Belgian colonial politics can afford to overlook.

As long as collaboration with the state appeared to aid them in the achievement of their aims, the missions were willing to support it. In so doing, they often turned a blind eye on certain contradictions between words and deeds inherent in the authorities' actions toward the Congolese—just as, less consciously, they tended to ignore similar contradictions of their own.

An anticlerical campaign led by Minister of Colonies Auguste Buisseret forced the Catholic missionaries to reassess their position and policies and brought them face to face with the fact that to continue their own contradictions between wish and reality was to endanger their objectives. While far from impotent in fighting Buisseret on his own ground—witness their success in forcing him to restore cuts he had made in their educational subsidies or in inducing his turnabout on the question of Lovanium University's right to grant valid degrees—they found it prudent, in fact necessary, to turn to the Congolese for support. Up to that time many of them had posed before their flocks as powerful and all-knowing fathers; now, through their own admitted weakness, paternalism had to yield to cooperation. That cooperation involved equality was not so easily perceived by the missionaries who wished to hold onto their role in what they saw as a master-pupil relationship. But cooperation meant the abandonment of all claim to such a relationship, and the Congolese, who were being wooed by Liberals and Socialists as well, recognized this fact.

On the other hand, if the missionaries were slow to extend responsibility to their followers or to Congolese members of the clergy, it was nonetheless they who had helped to nurture the elite that revolted against paternalism, whether of the state or of the Church. It was the missions' work in education, both religious and secular, that had produced the Westernized and articulate Congolese évolués. The missionaries not only ran a vast system of lower schools but were in the forefront of the moves to establish secondary and university education for the Congolese. In these activities they often clashed with a reluctant and recalcitrant Colonial Administration. Full credit should be given to them and to their supporters for overcoming this resistance. Even before this the missions had for many years provided the Congolese with their only avenue to higher education. Mission seminaries produced not only an African clergy but also some of the future political leaders of the Congo, among them Joseph Kasavubu.

The missionaries were also the first to set up, at Kisantu, an institution to train Congolese in the techniques of public administration; here again they acted against the wishes, sometimes in the teeth of the bitter hostility, of the Colonial Administration. The École des Sciences Administratives à Kisantu was concrete evidence of the fact that some missionaries at least were alert to the need for direct Congolese participation in the political process, even in a colonial setting. Again, the politicization of the Congolese elite was advanced through the various voluntary organizations promoted by the missions. The alumni associations, parent groups, trade-unions, and evening programs affiliated with the missions gave many Congolese a greater sense of political and social awareness, as well as providing them with the skills needed for effective political organization. It was their utilization by the missions in their battle against the anticlericals that made the members of these organizations aware of their own potential for political action.

The astute advice of certain progressive churchmen and the increasing willingness of the leaders of the Catholic hierarchy to accept it led the missions to adopt a policy designed to assure the survival of the Church in the Congo by a clear separation of it from the colonial government and from the large corporations. By identifying with Congolese aspirations, they sought to channel feelings of rebellion and hostility away from themselves and against the system. The bishops' declaration of June 29, 1956, and their support for the Manifeste de Conscience Africaine are proof of this policy. That it was not wholly successful is evidenced by the selection of mission property as a target by the participants in the Léopoldville riots of January 4, 1959. The missions' consequent recoil was the signal not so much of a return to past policies as of a withdrawal from politics. They had begun to despair of influencing the course of Congolese political development. In any case their ability to exercise such influence had already been surpassed by the emerging secular political organizations. Some of these had had their origins in such mission-sponsored or mission-supported groups as ABAKO and the various organizations of the gens du Haut in Léopoldville; and many of their leaders had received their political baptism in the voluntary organizations fostered by the missions. Kasavubu, Ngalula, Kamitatu, and Ileo are examples.

Yet the missions, while injecting strength into the emerging Congolese polity also contributed to its basic weakness. Their attitudes and actions often promoted ethnic and parochial nationalism. Their linguistic policies and their close identification with the people whom they were evangelizing were apt to emphasize tribal over supratribal loyalties. Their view of the Congo and its problems often tended to be parochial, even microscopic. Had they been able to subordinate themselves and their experience to the doctrines they taught, they might have been a more vital force for national integration. As it was, they saw themselves in the role of Plato's philosopher-kings who dispensed justice and forged the good polity. They attempted to provide a theological basis for government and society. Assured of their own cultural superiority and of the value of the message they bore, they often had little compunction about attacking basic elements of African societies. In consequence they succeeded in fragmenting the traditional basis of those societies while providing no adequate substitute for the personal and social integration that had been sacrificed. The promises of equality and the other goals they held out to the Africans rarely seemed possible of fulfillment in the colonial setting. The missionaries were at once reformers in regard to African tradition and traditionalists in regard to the colonial situation. Conservative innovators, they acted as instruments of social change and modernization yet wished to preserve their positions within the status quo.

The failure of the missionaries to provide for the promised personal and communal integration led the Congolese to seek other solutions. In the messianic movements both spiritual and secular goals were assured through charismatic religious leadership. In a sense these protonationalist movements provided a halfway house on the road to politicization, modernization, and nationalism, midway between a traditional theocracy and a political religion.

Yet the failure thus far of national integration in the Congo should not be laid entirely at the door of the missions. The persistence of tradition over more universal appeals, and the policies and practices of the Belgian colonial government and the large commercial firms were additional and major contributory factors. All three elements combined to limit the growth of Congolese political development until the last few years of Belgian rule. During those latter years the missionaries experienced a shock of recognition—the Congolese, perhaps for the first time, became in their eyes not merely mass but men.

APPENDIX A

EXCERPTS FROM TREATIES AND LEGISLATION
AFFECTING THE BELGIAN CONGO

The General Act of Berlin, February 26, 1885: Article VI.

para. 2. They [the Signatory Powers] shall, without distinction of creed or nation, protect and favour all religious, scientific, or charitable institutions, and undertakings created and organized for the above ends, or which aim at instructing the natives and bringing home to them the blessings of civilization.

para. 3. Christian missionaries, scientists, and explorers with their followers, property and collections, shall likewise be the objects of especial protection.

para. 4. Freedom of conscience and religious toleration are expressly guaranteed to the natives, no less than to subjects and to foreigners.

para. 5. The free and public exercise of all forms of Divine worship, and the right to build edifices for religious purposes, and to organize religious missions belonging to all creeds, shall not be limited or fettered in any way whatsoever.[1]

The Act of Brussels, July 2, 1890:* Article II.

para. 3. [The Signatory Powers pledge themselves] to protect, without distinction of creed, the missions which are already or may be hereafter established.[2]

The Treaty of Saint Germain-en-Laye, September 10, 1919:* Article XI.

para. 2. They [the Signatory Powers] will protect and favour, without distinction of nationality or of religion, the religious, scientific or charitable institutions and undertakings created and organised by the nationals of the other Signatory Powers and of States, Members of the League of Nations, which may adhere to the present Convention, which aim at teaching the natives

---

*The Act of Brussels, 1890, and the Treaty of Saint Germain-en-Laye were revisions of the Act of Berlin, 1885.

169

to follow the path of progress and civilisation. Scientific missions, their property and their collections, shall likewise be the objects of special solicitude.

para. 3. Freedom of conscience and the free exercise of all forms of religion are expressly guaranteed to all nationals of the Signatory Powers and to those under the jurisdiction of States, Members of the League of Nations, which may become parties to the present Convention. Similarly, missionaries shall have the right to enter into, and to travel and reside in, African territory with a view to prosecuting their calling.

para. 4. The application of the provisions of the two preceding paragraphs shall be subject only to such restrictions as may be necessary for the maintenance of public security and order, or as may result from the enforcement of the constitutional law of any of the Powers exercising authority in African territories.[3]

La Charte Coloniale, 1908: Article 5.

Le Gouvernement-Général veille à la conservation des populations indigènes et à l'amélioration de leurs conditions morales et matérielles d'existence. Il favorise l'expansion de la liberté individuelle, l'abandon progressif de la polygamie et le développement de la propriété. Il protège et favorise, sans distinction de nationalités ni de cultes, toutes les institutions et entreprises religieuses, scientifiques ou charitables, crées et organisées à ces fins ou tendants à instruire les indigènes et à leur faire comprendre et apprécier les avantages de civilisation.

Les missions chrétiens, les savants, les explorateurs,[4] les escortes, avoirs et collections sont l'objet d'une protection spéciale.

APPENDIX B

EXCERPTS FROM THE CONCORDAT OF 1953

The most controversial clauses of the convention are given below:

<u>Art. 11</u>.   Constatant l'importance primordiale de la stabilité de la famille pour le développement harmonieux de la societé au Congo, le Gouvernement belge continue à assurer, sur le plan législatif et réglementaire, son appui au mariage catholique.

<u>Art. 15</u>.   Tenant compte de l'importance des charges assumées par les missions dans le domaine de l'enseignement, le Gouvernement met les institutions scolaires placées sous le régime de l'"agrégation" à même d'assurer le maintien de l'enseignement à un niveau élevé dans des établissements convenables et bien équipés.

Le Gouvernement assure à ces institutions une aide financière qui leur permettra de procurer à leur personnel enseignant et administratif des conditions de vie décentes analogues à celles dont bénéficie le personnel de l'enseignement d'Etat.

Les institutions de régime "officiel" sont mises sur le même pied que les établissements analogues directement gérés par le Gouvernement.

Toutefois, les rapports juridiques qui unissent le personnel enseignant et administratif de ses institutions aux circonscriptions ecclésiastiques ou aux associations religieuses sont les mêmes que ceux qui unissent aux mêmes circonscriptions ou associations le personnel des établissements placés sous le régime de l'"agrégation".

<u>Art. 16</u>.   Les interventions financières du Gouvernement consenties aux institutions scolaires, médicales et sociales qui fonctionnent soit sous le régime de l'"agregation", soit sous le régime "officiel", tiendront compte des conditions de vie du personnel religieux appelé à desservir ces institutions.

<u>Art. 19</u>.   Le Gouvernement cédera ou concédera gratuitement aux institutions religieuses définies dans la présente convention ou aux établissements des missions catholiques les terres nécessaires à leur functionnement et au développement de leurs oeuvres.

<u>Art. 20</u>.   En reconnaissance du caractère d'intérêt général qui représente le concours de l'Eglise catholique à son oeuvre civilisatrice, le Gouvernement belge consent les avantages suivants:

aux prêtres séculiers de nationalité belge, affectés au culte dans les circonscriptions ecclésiastiques reconnues, une allocation pécuniare annuelle les aidant à remplir leur tâche et à vivre décemment;

aux associations missionnaires, une allocation annuelle proportionnelle au nombre de leurs membres de nationalité belge, exception faite de ceux pour lesquels une rémunération permanente est déjà allouée par le Gouvernement pour des activités exercées à son profit.

En outre, le Gouvernement apportera sa contribution à la construction des églises desservants une population importante.

Toutes ces allocations et contributions seront fixées selon un barème et dans des conditions à déterminer d'un commun accord.

Art. 21. L'aumônerie militaire catholique du Congo belge pourverra aux besoins du culte et à l'assistance religieuse des membres catholiques des unités et des services de la Force publique, ainsi qu'à leurs familles, conformément aux dispositions canoniques en la matière.

La nomination ecclésiastique de l'aumônier en chef est faite par le Saint-Siège.

Avant d'y procéder, celui-ci s'informera confidentiellement auprès du Gouvernement afin de s'assurer qu'il n'existe au sujet du candidat aucune difficulté de caractère politique générale.

L'aumônier en chef recoit sa juridiction directement du Saint-Siège. Après s'être mis d'accord, d'une part, avec l'ordinaire du candidat, et, d'autre part, avec les autorités militaires compétentes, il nomme les aumôniers militaires au titre ecclésiastique.

La nomination de l'aumônier en chef et des aumôniers militaires par le Gouvernement en tant que fonctionnaires sera faite simultanément avec la nomination ecclésiastique.

Art. 23. Les circonscriptions ecclésiastiques et les associations religieuses étant d'utilité publique sont exemptées de l'impôt personnel et foncier.

Art. 26. Au cas où des difficultés viendraient à surgir entre les autorités civiles et le personnel ecclésiastique et religieux, elles seront réglées à l'amiable entre les autorités locales respectives et, si l'entente ne pouvait s'obtenir, les mêmes autorités locales en référeront aux autorités supérieures.[1]

APPENDIX C

CARTE D'IMMATRICULATION AND CARTE DE MERITE CIVIQUE

The Belgians held out the promise of equality to the Africans but made it clear that their economic, social, and moral standards would have to match, if not exceed, those of the Belgians before social and political equality could be assumed. The government hoped to produce a stable middle-class base for further development by instilling Belgian bourgeois values into a sufficient number of Congolese. This objective was stated in Aristotelian terms by one writer who urged that Belgian policy seek to instill into the Congolese the "Belgian characteristics of our middle way, which is nothing but the search for the golden mean."[1] Middle-class values and Christian morality were to be the foundation of the new Congolese elite.

Inevitably the next issue to be faced was that of how and when the Congolese were to become civilisés on a par with the whites. The Léopoldian regime had given a special immatriculé* status to some Africans living outside the customary milieux (for example, urban workers, soldiers, and those living on mission stations). The main effect was to bring the immatriculés under the jurisdiction of the Belgian civil code without to any great degree enhancing their position vis-à-vis the whites. In the two decades following Belgian annexation of the Congo little had been done to promote this policy. But with the growth of industry and commerce and the consequent movement, during the late 1920s, of many Congolese to plantations or mining or urban areas interest in immatriculation revived.[2]

Missionary opinion at the time was split. Many felt that Christianity and, by definition, civilization could only succeed if the influence of the traditional authorities were weakened. The granting of immatriculé status seemed a step in this direction, for it seemed calculated to insure Congolese development by insulating its holders from their customary milieux. Many missionaries also considered immatriculation desirable as constituting objective proof of the success of their work. It gave validity to their dream of constructing a truly Christian society in the heart of Africa. To deny it was to deny their vision, their very raison d'être. But there were other missionaries who, while not denying that one day the Congolese would become true civilisés, believed that extension of immatriculé status at that time was premature. This attitude was especially prevalent among the more conservative missionaries. Their chief theoretician and spokesman was Msgr. de Hemptinne who reflected the view of the powerful colon interests in Katanga.

---

*The term used to designate an African who by virtue of his education, job, or location was recognized by the colonial government as having a different and higher status under the law than those Africans who were governed by the customary codes and the laws concerning indigènes.

173

It was not until 1948 that the administration attempted to change the status of the évolués. The method then adopted was the carte de mérite civique.* This carte, however, proved to be little more than honorific and extended no significant rights and privileges to the holder. Africans became reluctant to apply for it, and a British writer has noted that "only some 452 Africans had received the privileges of the Carte by the end of 1952."[3]

A new decree on immatriculation was issued in May 1952, but the évolués were disenchanted with it. Its provisions would restrict it to a very few, and the concessions to the immatriculés were of limited and dubious value. Moreover the very process of applying for immatriculation under the 1952 decree was regarded as embarrassing and insulting by many Congolese who therefore did not apply for it.** Applicants were asked such questions as: "What do you understand by immatriculation? What is your object in applying for it? What are its legal advantages? What do you do in your spare time? What sort of friends do you consort with? What books do you read and by what authors? If you had a disagreement with your husband, would you leave your husband in order to go to your relatives? How do you share your meals with your husband? Does he beat you? What does your husband do with the money he earns? Does he entrust you with the management of the home?"[4]

For the Congolese the carte d'immatriculation and the carte de mérite civique had become symbols of futility and frustration, of equality offered but deferred, of disdain cloaked by such high-sounding but empty phrases as Belgo-Congolese community.*** The Belgians extended the promise of political and social participation, ostensibly they educated the évolués for it; but they never fulfilled the promise. Their treatment of the Congolese elite was ambivalent; it at once lauded and condemned, legitimized and bastardized.

---

*The carte de mérite civique was to be available on application to those who had a record free of "uncivilized" practices, such as polygamy and sorcery, and crimes, such as theft or fraud, that indicated a lack of integrity. Literacy was required, except for individuals with twenty-five years of "good and faithful service" in the administration or twenty years' service as a chief (Crawford Young, Politics in the Congo, p. 78).

**"African priests, the first category deemed fit to acquire the civilization cards, refused en masse to apply. They felt that their educational attainments spoke for themselves, without any other external badge than their soutanes, and also that acceptance of this status would create an artificial barrier between themselves and their communicants" (G. Malengreau, "Chronique de politique indigène," Zaire, p. 964, quoted in Young, Politics in the Congo, p. 84). Those few paramount chiefs who had been highly educated likewise found an immatriculation card beneath their dignity. At the end of 1958, only 217 family heads had received the cards (Belgium, Chambre des Représentants, Rapport annuel sur l'administration du Congo belge, 1958, p. 104, quoted in Ibid.).

***From 1952 to 1958 the communauté belgo-congolaise became the much-vaunted central theme of Belgian colonial policy. Never clearly defined, it was seemingly used to describe a system where there would be mutual respect between Belgians and Congolese and where the latter could expect increasing, though limited, political participation in the Provincial and Government Councils, etc. (see Belgian Congo, Conseil du Gouvernement, Compte-rendu analytique, 1955, speech by Governor-General Pétillon, n.d., passim).

NOTES

Abbreviations for collections of unpublished materials cited in these notes:

BEC Archives of the Bureau de l'Enseignement Catholique, Kinshasa, Congo.

CPC-BB Archives of the Brussels Bureau of the Congo Protestant Council, Brussels, Belgium.

CPC-KIN Archives of the Congo Protestant Council, Kinshasa, Congo.

DIA Archives of the Agence DIA (Documentation et Information Africaine), Kinshasa, Congo.

NCC-AC Archives of the Africa Committee of the Division of Overseas Ministries (formerly Division of Foreign Missions) of the National Council of Churches, New York, U.S.A.

Chapter 1

1. Ruth Slade, English-Speaking Missions in the Congo Independent State (1878-1908), pp. 15-16. Also of interest are her other works on the Léopoldian period: King Léopold's Congo and L'Attitude des missions protestantes vis-à-vis les puissances européennes au Congo avant 1885.

2. Slade, L'Attitude des missions protestantes, p. 689.

3. The Missionary Herald, 1881, p. 18.

4. United Missionary Conference on the Congo, Léopoldville, 1909, p. 26.

5. Pall Mall Gazette, May 20, 1884, quoted in Slade, English-Speaking Missions, p. 7 fn.

6. D. Fr. de Meeus and D. R. Steenberghen, Les missions religieuses au Congo Belge, p. 28.

7. J. Du Plessis, The Evangelization of Pagan Africa, p. 241.

8. Slade, English-Speaking Missions, p. 244.

9. United Missionary Conference, Léopoldville, 1902, pp. 44-45.

10. Ibid., p. 46.

11. Slade, English-Speaking Missions, p. 308.

12. Ibid., p. 297.

13. United Missionary Conference, Léopoldville, 1906, p. 187.

14. Emile Vandervelde, Les derniers jours de l'Etat du Congo, p. 179.

15. P. Vermeersch, La question congolaise, passim.

16. de Meeus and Steenberghen, Les missions religieuses, p. 38.

17. Slade, English-Speaking Missions, p. 350.

18. United Missionary Conference, Luebo, Kasai, 1918, p. 116.

19. Ibid., p. 123.

Chapter 2

1. Emile Tibbaut, "L'Assistance sociale au Congo," pp. 683-684.

2. Deuxième conférence plénière des ordinaires des missions du Congo Belge et du Ruanda-Urundi, p. 71.

3. For a discussion of this problem see Edward Caldwell Moore, "Some Aspects of the Relations of Missions to Civilization," pp. 362-363. Also, for an excellent study of the evangelical tradition in American society see Richard Hofstadter, Anti-Intellectualism in American Life.

4. A. Victor Murray, "Christianity and Rural Civilization," pp. 388, 391.

5. P. Schebesta, "Blancs et noirs au Congo belge," p. 334.

6. Félix Scalais, "L'Eglise devant les banlieues congolaises," p. 48.

7. J. Van Wing, "Une évolution de la coutume Bakongo (Congo Belge)," p. 240.

8. Sylvain Van Hee, "Rapport sur la mission des R. P. jésuites au Congo," p. 315.

9. R. P. Vandenbulke, "Comment traiter les chefs noirs," p. 171.

10. L. LeGrand, "Les missionnaires catholiques du Kwango et les institutions indigènes," p. 506.

11. Ibid., p. 508.

12. V. Roelens, "Le respect de la coutume indigène," p. 500.

13. LeGrand, "Les missionnaires catholiques," pp. 527, 533.

Chapter 3

1. Anton F. Marzorati, "L'Evolution des relations entre les communautés européennes et la société indigène du Congo Belge," p. 939.

2. Fontainas, "Le droit de colonisation," p. 716.

3. Marzorati, "L'Evolution des relations," p. 939.

4. B. S. Chlepner, <u>Cent</u> <u>ans</u> <u>d'histoire</u> <u>sociale</u> <u>en</u> <u>Belgique</u>, pp. 19, 359. Also see Roger E. de Smet and Réné Evalenko, <u>Les</u> <u>elections</u> <u>belges</u>, <u>explication</u> <u>de</u> <u>la</u> <u>répartition</u> <u>géographique</u> <u>des</u> <u>suffrages</u>, pp. 17, 43; and Val R. Lorwin, "Belgium: Religion, Class and Language in National Politics."

5. François Perin, <u>La</u> <u>démocratie</u> <u>enrayée</u>, pp. 127-128.

6. "Le budget des colonies aux chambres," p. 418.

7. "Le Congo en 1934 d'après le rapport annuel aux chambres," <u>Congo</u>, January 1936, pp. 53-54.

8. <u>Ibid</u>., January 1935, pp. 62-63.

9. <u>Ibid</u>., January-February 1937, p. 139.

10. <u>Ibid</u>., p. 169.

Chapter 4

1. "Decret de 2 mai, 1910," <u>Bulletin</u> <u>officiel</u>, 1910, pp. 456 ff.

2. L. Guebels, "Relation complète des travaux de la Commission Permanente pour la Protection des Indigènes," p. 371.

3. <u>Ibid</u>., p. 239.

4. Jean de Hemptinne, "Le gouvernement du Congo belge—projet de réorganisation," p. 341.

5. Louis Franck, "La politique indigène, le service territorial, et les chefferies," p. 189.

6. See Lord Lugard, <u>The</u> <u>Dual</u> <u>Mandate</u> <u>in</u> <u>British</u> <u>Tropical</u> <u>Africa</u>.

7. Emory Ross, "Memorandum of Interview with the Governor-General of the Belgian Congo," July 6, 1922 (Archives of the Congo Protestant Council, Kinshasa [hereafter cited as CPC-KIN]).

8. For the complete text of these circulars, see Belgian Congo, Gouvernement Général, <u>Recueil</u> <u>mensuel</u> <u>des</u> <u>circulaires</u>, <u>instructions</u> <u>et</u> <u>ordres</u> <u>de</u> <u>service</u>, Boma, 1922.

9. <u>Ibid</u>., p. 6, M. Lippens, <u>Circulaire</u> <u>de</u> <u>25</u> <u>janvier</u>, <u>1922</u>.

10. <u>Ibid</u>., p. 151, M. Lippens, <u>Circulaire</u> <u>de</u> <u>30</u> <u>septembre</u>, <u>1922</u>.

11. "The Governor-General of the Congo Belge and Missions," p. 10.

12. L. LeGrand, "De la légalité des villages chrétiens," p. 2.

13. Stanislas De Vos, "La politique indigène et les missions catholiques," pp. 635-637.

14. L. LeGrand, "Les missionnaires catholiques du Kwango," p. 527.

15. V. Roelens, "Le respect de la coutume indigène," p. 498.

16. Henri Anet, "Debate on the Congo Administration in the Belgian Senate," p. 13.

17. <u>Ibid</u>.

18. D. Edouard Neut, "Au Congo Belge: évangelisation et colonisation," p. 408.

19. Martin Rutten, "Circulaire du Gouverneur Général sur les relations avec les missions," p. 711.

20. <u>Ibid</u>., pp. 711-712.

21. <u>Ibid</u>., pp. 712-714.

Chapter 5

1. <u>Congo Mission News</u> (hereafter cited as CMN), November 1912, p. 8.

2. <u>Ibid</u>., August 1913, p. 4.

3. <u>Ibid</u>., November 1915, p. 13.

4. "Minutes, Meeting 7," Léopoldville, Jan. 22-24, 1930, p. 13 (CPC-KIN).

5. Emory Ross, memo. to minister of colonies, Léopoldville, Feb. 14, 1933, p. 21 (CPC-KIN).

6. Raymond Leslie Buell, <u>The Native Problem in Africa</u>, vol. 2, p. 437.

7. G. Dufonteny, "La méthode d'évangelisation chez les non-civilisés," p. 31.

8. "Protestantism in the Congo."

9. H. W. Coxill, "Une protestation des protestants," Léopoldville, Apr. 16, 1936, p. 2 (CPC-KIN).

10. "Roman Catholicism in the Congo," pp. 33-34.

11. Buell, <u>Native Problem</u>, p. 599.

12. Memo. to prime minister, Léopoldville, Aug. 11, 1942, p. 4 (CPC-KIN).

13. Ross, memo. to minister of colonies, Léopoldville, Feb. 14, 1933, pp. 17-18 (CPC-KIN).

14. Conseil Colonial, <u>Compte-rendu analytique des séances</u>, 1948, pp. 998-1000.

15. <u>Ibid</u>., 1947, p. 66.

16. <u>Ibid</u>., 1948, pp. 1684, 1690.

17. Preliminary draft of memo. to colonial minister, Léopoldville, Sept. 22, 1932 (CPC-KIN).

18. <u>Het Handelsbad</u>, Oct. 14, 1950.

19. <u>CMN</u>, October 1934, p. 17.

20. J. M. Springer, "The CMCMEC Surveys Its Field," p. 18.

21. <u>Ibid</u>.

22. "Minutes, Meeting 8," Léopoldville, Feb. 13-19, 1931, p. 6 (CPC-KIN).

23. "Minutes, Meeting 7," Léopoldville, Jan. 22-24, 1930, p. 4 (CPC-KIN).

24. Ross, "The Roman Catholic Situation in Congo Belge," Léopoldville, Apr. 21, 1931, p. 11 (CPC-KIN).

25. World Missionary Conference, Edinburgh, 1910, Carrying the Gospel, vol. 1, p. 313.

26. Hyac Vanderyst, "Les instituts missionnaires universitaires," p. 416.

27. F. Malengreau, L'Enseignement médical aux indigènes du Congo Belge, p. 5.

28. F. Malengreau, Une fondation médicale au Congo Belge, pp. 7-8.

29. Ibid., p. 153.

30. Ibid., pp. 17-18.

31. Ibid., pp. 34-35.

32. Ibid., p. 17.

33. Ibid., pp. 71-73.

34. Nkome, "La Cadulac," pp. 225-226.

35. Henri Beckers, "Le fonds du bien-être indigène," p. 791.

36. Annales parlementaires du Belgique: Chambre des Représentants, 1950-1951, p. 3.

37. Clement C. Chesterman, "Possibilities of Government Cooperation in our Medical Work," p. 9.

38. Ibid., p. 10.

39. "Conseil Protestant du Congo," CMN No. 78, 1932, p. 12.

40. Memo. to minister of colonies, Léopoldville, Feb. 14, 1935, p. 30 (CPC-KIN).

41. Ibid., p. 4.

42. Ibid., p. 7.

Chapter 6

1. World Missionary Conference, Edinburgh, 1910, Report of Commission III, Education in Relation to the Christianisation of National Life, p. 372.

2. Ibid., pp. 374-375.

3. "Christian Missions and Colonial Policy," pp. 361-362.

4. CMN No. 14, 1916, letter to editor, p. 14.

5. Robert Keable, "The Worth of an African," p. 326.

6. Pierre Charles, "Exposé général: le pourquoi de l'enseignement dans les missions," p. 13.

7. Ibid., p. 318.

8. "L'Instruction publique au Congo Belge," pp. 501, 529.

9. Paul Coppens, "Les missions du Congo vues par un laïque," pp. 417-418.

10. Edouard D. Neut, "Au Congo Belge: évangelisation et colonisation," p. 409.

11. Ibid.

12. CMN, January 1923, pp. 3-4.

13. "L'Instruction publique," pp. 529, 530.

14. L. Guebels, "Relation complète des travaux de la Commission Permanente pour le Protection des Indigènes," p. 312.

15. H. W. Coxill, memo. to prime minister, Léopoldville, Aug. 11, 1942 (CPC-KIN).

16. Belgium, Ministère des Colonies, Organisation de l'enseignement libre au Congo Belge et au Ruanda-Urundi avec le concours des sociétés des missions nationales, Brussels, 1929.

17. Ibid., p. 45.

18. Ibid., pp. 46-47.

19. Première conférence plénière des ordinaires des missions du Congo Belge et du Ruanda-Urundi, p. 58.

20. Ibid., p. 76.

21. Ibid., p. 61.

22. A. Debra, "Préambule," p. 1.

23. Théodore Nève, "En visite à la préfecture apostolique du Katanga," p. 45.

24. Jean de Hemptinne, quoted in Anton F. Marzorati, "Certains aspects du problème social au Congo Belge," p. 709.

25. Ibid.

26. Michel Merlier, Le Congo, de la colonisation belge à l'indépendance, p. 220.

Chapter 7

1. "Equality," p. 2, quoting from an article by de Hemptinne in L'Essor du Congo.

2. "Minutes, Meeting 21," Léopoldville, Mar. 12-18, 1943, p. 17 (CPC-KIN).

3. Emory Ross, "The Roman Catholic Situation in Congo Belge," Léopoldville, Apr. 21, 1931, p. 14 (CPC-KIN).

4. "Notes on Roman Catholic Activities," p. 28.

5. Oldham to Ross, Apr. 4, 1933 (CPC-KIN).

6. Ross, memo. to minister of colonies, Léopoldville, Feb. 14, 1933, pp. 9, 13 (CPC-KIN).

7. "Consultation de Monsieur Marzorati," Nov. 1939, pp. 203 (CPC-KIN).

8. "Extrait d'une note du Comte M. Lippens," 1939 (CPC-KIN).

9. Note in reply to memo. of Feb. 14, 1933, Brussels, Sept. 14, 1933, p. 3 (Archives of the Brussels Bureau of the CPC [hereafter cited as CPC-BB]).

10. Coxill, "Interview with Governor-General Ryckmans," Léopoldville, May 31, 1944 (CPC-KIN).

11. Ross to Godding, N.Y., Dec. 11, 1945 (Archives of the Africa Committee, National Council of Churches [hereafter cited as NCC-AC]).

12. Godding to Ross, Brussels, Feb. 23, 1946 (CPC-BB).

Chapter 8

1. Guy Mosmans, "Les impératifs de l'action missionnaire en Afrique Belge," p. 6.

2. Hyac Vanderyst, "Les futurs universités catholiques au Congo," p. 258.

3. Guy Malengreau, untitled paper, unpublished, typewritten, n.d., p. 5 (private papers of M. Malengreau).

4. Mosmans, "Les impératifs," p. 7.

5. Joseph Van Wing, "Évolués et clergé indigène," p. 167.

6. Pierre Ryckmans, "Les évolués," p. 28.

7. Troisième conférence plénière des ordinaires des missions du Congo Belge et du Ruanda-Urundi, pp. 153, 156.

8. Ibid., pp. 156-157.

9. Ibid., p. 39.

10. Paul Brasseur, "La formation d'une élite universitaire indigène," p. 116.

11. Malengreau, unpublished paper, p. 6.

12. Interview with Father Van Wing.

13. Malengreau, unpublished paper, p. 9.

14. Ibid., p. 60.

15. Ibid., p. 28.

16. Ibid., p. 121 bis.

17. L'Avenir Colonial Belge, May 4, 1949.

18. La Métropole, September 14, 1949.

19. La Libre Belgique, Apr. 13, 1950.

20. G. Mosmans, "Action de l'église au plan social en Afrique," p. 285.

21. Interview with Father Van Wing.

22. L'Avenir Colonial Belge, September 19, 1952.

23. Malengreau, unpublished paper, p. 50.

24. Ibid., p. 60.

25. Ibid., p. 68.

26. Ibid., p. 33.

27. Ibid., p. 44.

28. Ibid., p. 138.

29. Ibid., pp. 120-121.

30. Ibid., p. 122.

31. Ibid., p. 124.

32. Ibid., p. 125.

33. Ibid., p. 127.

34. Coxill to Rev. Hans P. Emming, Alliance des Missions Protestantes, Usumbura, Ruanda-Urundi, Brussels, Oct. 30, 1953 (CPC-KIN).

35. Interview with R. J. Decker, former rector of the University of Stanleyville.

Chapter 9

1. XXX, "La politique scolaire au Congo du point de vue missionnaire," p. 299.

2. Annales parlementaires de Belgique: Chambre des Représentants, 1950, p. 3.

3. La Flandre Liberale, July 1, 1950.

4. "Rapport sur la question scolaire au Congo Belge et Ruanda-Urundi depuis l'avènement de M. Buisseret (avril, 1954, jusqu'au 25 janvier, 1955)," Brussels, 1955, unpublished, typewritten, p. 31 (in the possession of the author; hereafter cited as "Rapport sur la question scolaire").

5. L'Echo du Katanga, August 10, 1954.

6. L'Avenir Colonial Belge, July 24, 1952.

7. "Rapport sur la question scolaire," p. 30.

8. L'Avenir Colonial Belge, September 27, 1951.

9. Annales parlementaires: Chambre, 1954, p. 433.

10. Ibid., p. 490.

11. Ibid., p. 436.

12. Ibid., p. 490.

13. Ibid., pp. 435-436.

14. Ibid., pp. 467, 469.

15. Ibid., pp. 434, 473.

16. Ibid., p. 439.

17. Ibid.

18. Ibid., p. 487.

19. Ibid., p. 437.

20. Ibid., p. 472.

21. "Rapport à l'intention du Conseil de la Fédération et du Conseil Protestant du Congo," n.d., p. 2 (NCC-AC).

22. George W. Carpenter to H. W. Coxill, N.Y., April 5, 1954 (CPC-KIN).

23. Coxill to Carpenter and Ohrneman, Brussels, Feb. 18, 1954 (CPC-KIN).

24. Coxill to minister of colonies, Bruges, Feb. 19, 1954 (CPC-KIN).

25. Ibid.

26. Coxill to Carpenter, Brussels, Feb. 18, 1954 (CPC-KIN).

27. Annales parlementaires: Chambre, 1954, p. 471.

28. Ibid., p. 493.

29. Interviews with various Belgian missionaries.

Chapter 10

1. A. A. J. Van Bilsen, "Quatre années de politique congolaise," p. 462.

2. "Education," p. 2.

3. "State Schools for Africans," p. 3.

4. Ministère des Colonies, Mission pédagogique Coulon-Deheyn-Renson, p. 12.

5. Ibid., p. 13.

6. Ibid., pp. 15, 17.

7. Ibid., pp. 166-167.

8. Ibid., p. 127.

9. Guy Malengreau, "La réforme de l'enseignement, mission pédagogique Coulon-Deheyn-Renson," p. 406.

10. Ministère des Colonies, Plan décennal pour le développement économique et social du Congo Belge, p. 63.

11. Ministère des Colonies, Mission pédagogique, p. 116.

12. Ibid., pp. 282-283.

13. Ibid., p. 39.

14. Ibid., p. 38.

15. Ibid., p. 209.

16. Ibid., p. 207.

17. Malengreau, "Le réforme de l'enseignement," p. 408.

18. *Ibid.*, p. 410.

19. *Ibid.*, pp. 406-407.

20. *Ibid.*, p. 406.

21. E. Vandenbussche, ed., *Objectivité "sur mésure,"* p. 10.

22. *Ibid.*, pp. 23-24.

23. "Rapport sur la question scolaire," p. 50.

24. *Ibid.*, p. 70, quoting from 24th session of the Conseil du Gouvernement, 1954.

25. G. Moulaert, "Instruction et éducation," p. 528.

26. "Conférence plénière des ordinaires du Congo Belge et du Ruanda-Urundi, Léopoldville, 21-30 juin," 1956, p. 1 (Archives of the Bureau de l'Enseignement Catholique, Kinshasa [hereafter cited as BEC]).

27. *Annales parlementaires de Belgique: Chambre des Représentants*, 1954, p. 6.

28. *Ibid.*

29. *Ibid.*, 1956, pp. 507-508.

30. *Ibid.*, 1954, p. 10.

31. *Ibid.*, pp. 149-150.

32. *Ibid.*, p. 147.

33. Ministère de Colonies, *Mission pédagogique*, pp. 116-117.

34. *Ibid.*, p. 212.

35. Van Bilsen, "Quatre années," p. 465.

36. *Annales parlementaires: Chambre*, 1954, p. 119.

37. "Rapport sur la question scolaire," pp. 33-34.

38. *Ibid.*, p. 84.

39. *Annales parlementaires: Chambre*, 1954, p. 115.

40. *Ibid.*, p. 112, speech by De Vleeschauwer.

41. *Ibid.*, 1955, p. 1068.

42. *Ibid.*, 1954, p. 118.

43. K. Plessers, "L'Evolution religieuse au Congo Belge, l'église face à ce tournant, journées d'études missionnaires centrale Jociste, 9-12 avril, 1956," unpublished, mimeo., Brussels, 1956, p. 13 (in possession of the author).

44. Ministère de Colonies, *Mission pedagogique*, p. 215.

45. "Minutes, Meeting 29," Feb. 19-26, 1950, Léopoldville, p. 9 (CPC-KIN).

46. Omar L. Hartzler, "Notes of a Report on Education in the Belgian Congo," Sept. 17, 1958, p. 4 (NCC-AC).

47. "Rapport sur la question scolaire," p. 112.

48. "Minutes," N.Y., June 10, 1955, p. 14 (NCC-AC).

49. Coxill to Ohrneman, Brussels, Jan. 22, 1955 (CPC-KIN).

50. Doc. No. A785-E, n.d., p. 5 (NCC-AC).

51. Extract of minutes of CPC meeting held in Léopoldville, Feb. 27-Mar. 6, 1955 (CPC-KIN).

52. Carpenter to Coxill, N.Y., July 26, 1954 (CPC-KIN).

53. Buisseret to Coxill, Brussels, Aug. 17, 1955 (CPC-BB).

54. P. Rigard, Mission Protestante Belge, Ruanda, to Ohrneman, Remera Ruboma, Kigali, n.d. (CPC-KIN).

55. Coxill to Ohrneman, Brussels, Feb. 22, 1955 (CPC-KIN).

56. R. K. Orchard to Coxill, London, Aug. 1955 (CPC-BB).

57. "Rapport sur la question scolaire," p. 9.

58. Ibid.

59. Ibid., pp. 9-10.

60. Ibid., p. 10.

61. Ibid.

62. Ibid., p. 11.

63. Coxill to Carpenter, Brussels, May 5, 1955 (CPC-KIN).

64. "Rapport sur la question scolaire," p. 182.

65. Ibid.

66. Annales parlementaires: Chambre, 1957, p. 493.

67. Interview with Father Van Wing.

68. "Rapport sur la question scolaire," p. 139.

69. Ibid., p. 141.

70. Ibid., p. 199.

71. Guy Mosmans, "Impressions de voyage," p. 117.

72. "Comment on conçoit l'égalité en matière d'enseignement à la 8e Direction Générale," Léopoldville, 1956 (BEC).

73. Mosmans, "Impressions," p. 116.

74. See De Vleeschauwer's comments, Annales parlementaires: Chambre, 1954, p. 147.

75. Ministère des Colonies, Mission pédagogique, p. 12.

76. Ibid., p. 117.

77. Ibid., p. 57.

78. "Rapport sur la question scolaire," p. 73.

79. Annales parlementaires: Chambre, 1954, p. 147.

80. Ministère des Colonies, *Mission pédagogique*, p. 88.

81. Buisseret to Ohrneman, Brussels, Apr. 11, 1956 (CPC-BB).

82. "Rapport de la commission pour la révision des dispositions générales, avril 11-25, 1956," Léopoldville, n.d. (BEC).

83. "Rapport sur la question scolaire," p. 199.

84. *Annales parlementaires*: *Chambre*, 1955, p. 1054.

85. *Ibid.*, 1954, p. 113.

86. *Ibid.*

87. *Ibid.*, p. 114.

88. *Ibid.*, 1956, p. 489.

89. "Rapport sur la question scolaire," p. 143, quoting letter from Msgr. Mels to governor-general, Luluabourg.

90. *Ibid.*, pp. 177-180, quoting letter from Cornelis to Ohrneman, Léopoldville, Dec. 8, 1954.

91. *Ibid.*, p. 180.

92. *Ibid.*, p. 193.

93. Conseil Permanent des Ordinaires du Congo Belge et du Ruanda-Urundi to Pétillon, Léopoldville, Jan. 11, 1955 (CPC-KIN).

94. Hendrik Cornelis to Moermans, Léopoldville, Dec. 8, 1952 (BEC).

95. "Rapport sur la question scolaire," p. 184.

96. *Ibid.*, p. 190.

97. Conseil Permanent des Ordinaires to Pétillon, Léopoldville, Jan. 10, 1955 (CPC-KIN).

98. Pétillon to Conseil Permanent, Léopoldville, Jan. 11, 1955 (CPC-KIN).

99. "Rapport sur la question scolaire," p. 232.

100. *Ibid.*

101. *La Libre Belgique*, Jan. 17, 1955, quoted in "Rapport sur la question scolaire," p. 238.

102. Verwimp to Catholic Ordinaires, Kisantu, Jan. 27, 1955 (BEC).

103. "Rapport sur la question scolaire," p. 265.

104. Verwimp to Buisseret, Léopoldville, Jan. 25, 1955 (BEC).

105. "Rapport sur la question scolaire," p. 270.

106. Buisseret to Verwimp, Léopoldville, Jan. 26, 1955 (CPC-BB).

107. Verwimp to Pétillon, Léopoldville, Feb. 18, 1956 (BEC).

108. "Note redigée par le Directeur du Bureau de l'Enseignement Catholique au sujet de l'appel à la concurrence en matière de construction scolaire au Congo Belge et soumise à la bienveillante attention de M. le Ministre des Colonies," Annex I, Léopoldville, Mar. 6, 1956 (BEC).

109. Moermans, "Note expliquant les accords intervenus entre le Comité Permanent des Ordinaires et le Ministre des Colonies, suite aux entretiens du 9 mars et à la convention du 13 mars, 1956," Léopoldville, n.d. (BEC).

110. Verwimp and Scalais to Buisseret, Léopoldville, Apr. 4, 1956 (BEC).

111. Moermans, "Execution de l'accord signé à Bruxelles le 9 mars 1956 entre M. le Ministre Buisseret et M. le Chanoine Moermans, Directeur de Bureau de l'Enseignement Catholique, compte-rendu des entretiens des 26 et 27 mai entre M. le Chanoine Moermans et le Chef de Cabinet du Gouverneur-Général," Léopoldville, n.d. (BEC).

112. Moermans, "Remarques destinées à M. le Ministre des Colonies au sujet de mes notes," Léopoldville, n.d. (BEC).

113. "Audience with the Governor-General on Wednesday, 6th June, 1956," n.d. (CPC-BB).

114. Van Bilsen, "Quatre années," p. 466.

Chapter 11

1. "Rapport de la commission pour l'étude du problème de la main d'oeuvre au Congo Belge," Congo, June 1925, p. 6.

2. "La formation d'une élite noire au Congo belge," p. 9.

3. Dominer pour servir, p. 5.

4. Quatrième conférence plénière des révérendissimes ordinaires du Congo Belge et du Ruanda-Urundi, p. 66.

5. J. M. Carret, "La colonisation mise au point," p. 70.

6. Marcel Lihau, "Les aspirations nationales au Congo Belge," p. 157.

7. Courrier d'Afrique, March 20, 1958.

8. Lihau, "Les aspirations nationales," p. 161.

9. Antoine Sohier, "Le sacré des évêques noirs," p. 235.

10. Ibid., p. 234.

11. K. Plessers, "L'Evolution religieuse au Congo Belge, l'église face à ce tournant, journées d'études missionnaires centrale Jociste, 9-12 avril, 1956," unpublished, mimeo., Brussels, 1956, p. 11 (in author's possession).

12. Pascal Ceuterick, "Evolution psychologique du noir," p. 60.

13. Placide Tempels, Bantu Philosophy, p. 110.

14. Guy Mosmans, "Les impératifs de l'action missionnaire en Afrique belge," p. 10.

15. Plessers, "L'Evolution religieuse," p. 8.

16. Mosmans, "Les impératifs," p. 11.

17. Plessers, "L'Evolution religieuse," p. 8.

18. M. X, "Les déterminismes de la situation coloniale," p. 25.

19. Lihau, "Les aspirations nationales," p. 162.

20. See Anne Fremantle, ed., The Papal Encyclicals in Their Historical Context, p. 306.

21. Troisième conférence plénière des ordinaires des missions du Congo Belge et du Ruanda-Urundi, p. 22.

22. Quatrième conférence plénière, p. 76.

23. Plessers, "L'Evolution religieuse," p. 15.

24. James Covin, "The Christian Missions and the African Churches in Africa South of the Sahara," May 23, 1952 (NCC-AC).

25. "Minutes," N.Y., Sept. 28, 1948 (NCC-AC).

26. Trevor Shaw, "A Pertinent Question," p. 11.

27. E. M. Braekman, Histoire du protestantisme au Congo, pp. 342-343.

28. "Congo Protestant Council Meeting, February 1954," N.Y., Apr. 29, 1954 (NCC-AC).

29. Inforcongo, Belgian Congo, vol. 2, p. 164.

30. Crawford Young, Politics in the Congo, p. 199.

31. James S. Coleman, Nigeria, p. 104.

32. Joseph Van Wing, "Père Van Wing traite ensuite des événements de Léopold-ville et de la nouvelle politique congolaise," p. 14.

33. A. Huys, "Statuts du clergé indigène," p. 41.

34. Ibid., p. 42.

35. Ibid., p. 58.

36. Jacques Meert, L'Eglise au Congo face à son avenir, p. 52.

37. Mosmans, "Les impératifs," p. 19.

38. Plessers, "L'Evolution religieuse," p. 20.

39. Inforcongo, Belgian Congo, vol. 2, p. 164.

40. Quatrième conférence plénière, p. 79.

41. Antoine Sohier, "Le problème des indigènes évolués et la commission du statut des congolais civilisés, p. 879.

Chapter 12

1. See Thomas Hodgkin, Nationalism in Colonial Africa; Kenneth Little, West African Urbanization; and Immanuel Wallerstein, Africa.

2. Hodgkin, Nationalism, pp. 84-85.

3. Jacques Meert, "Le jocisme face à l'avenir noir," pp. 351-352.

4. "Rapport sur la question scolaire," p. 203.

5. Ibid.

6. Guy Mosmans, "Les impératifs de l'action missionnaire en Afrique belge," p. 12.

7. Benoit Verhaegen, "ABAKO," unpublished manuscript, n.d., n.p. (private papers of M. Verhaegen).

8. S. Comhaire-Sylvan, "Food and Leisure Among the African Youth of Léopold-ville," p. 120.

9. J. Roussel, "Les conditions psychologiques et morales de l'Action Sociale au Congo Belge," p. 121.

10. Deuxième conférence plénière des ordinaires des missions du Congo Belge et du Ruanda-Urundi, p. 130.

11. Cinquième conférence plénière des ordinaires des missions du Congo Belge et du Ruanda-Urundi, p. 34.

12. Michel Merlier, Le Congo, p. 220.

13. Verwimp, "Note concernant la création du Conseil Fraternal et du service national de la jeunesse au Congo," 1956 (BEC).

14. Ioan Davies, African Trade Unions, p. 32.

15. CMN, May 1913, p. 4.

16. Ibid., January 1926, p. 3.

17. Henri Anet, Vers l'avenir, p. 51.

18. "Rapport annuel sur l'administration de la colonie du Congo Belge pour 1928," p. 56.

19. See Raymond L. Buell, The Native Problem in Africa, vol. 2, p. 506; and E. Jaspers, "Le discours de M. le Premier Ministre Jaspers à la Chambre," pp. 459 ff.

20. Joseph Van Wing, "Le Congo déraillé," p. 619.

21. A. Brys, "Situation sociale et action sociale au Congo Belge," ca. 1951, p. 11 (Archives of the Agence Documentation et Information Africaine, Kinshasa [hereafter cited as DIA]).

22. Davies, African Trade Unions, p. 32.

23. J. Nicaise, "Chronique sociale congolaise," p. 157.

24. Pierre Charles, Etudes missiologiques, p. 289.

25. Deuxième conférence plénière, pp. 151-152.

26. Merlier, Le Congo, pp. 179-180.

27. Van Wing, "Le Congo déraillé," p. 621.

28. Brys, "Situation sociale," pp. 14-15.

29. See Charles, Etudes missiologiques, p. 290; and Placide Tempels, "Justice sociale," p. 72.

30. Grand Séminaire, Kabwe, "Rapport, 1945," n.d. (DIA).

31. "Déclaration solennelle de l'épiscopat congolais," p. 8.

32. <u>Troisième conférence plénière des ordinaires des missions du Congo Belge et du Ruanda-Urundi</u>, pp. 257-258.

33. <u>Ibid.</u>, p. 44.

34. Charles Cleire, "Considérations sur la justice sociale," <u>Zaire</u>, July 1949, pp. 803-804.

35. Henri Pauwels, <u>Le syndicalisme et la colonie</u>, p. 88.

36. R. Poupart, <u>Première esquisse d l'évolution du syndicalisme au Congo</u>, p. 24; and Pauwels, <u>Le syndicalisme</u>, p. 88.

37. Louis Ballegeer, "Syndicalisme indigène au Congo Belge," pp. 100-101.

38. Poupart, <u>Première esquisse</u>, p. 39.

39. Jean Bruck, "Problèmes congolais et action syndicale chrétienne," p. 683.

40. Poupart, <u>Première esquisse</u>, p. 42.

41. See <u>Le Congo</u>, <u>documents</u>, <u>1956</u>, <u>passim</u>.

42. "Déclaration solennelle," p. 9.

43. "Rapport sur la question scolaire," pp. 213-214.

44. <u>Courrier d'Afrique</u>, January 16 and 17, 1956.

45. "Rapport sur la question scolaire," p. 226.

46. Vicariat de Luluabourg, "Compte-rendu des journées d'étude des moniteurs catholiques," Mikalayi, Dec. 21-25, 1954, pp. 2-3 (BEC).

47. "Conférence plénière des ordinaires du Congo Belge et du Ruanda-Urundi, Léopoldville, June 21-30: Rapport chronologique de la mission de l'enseignement," n.d. (BEC).

48. "Conférence des missionnaires inspecteurs, Province Orientale, Stanleyville, Nov. 14-17, 1957" (BEC).

49. Inforcongo, <u>Belgian Congo</u>, vol. 1, pp. 474-475.

50. Poupart, <u>Première esquisse</u>, p. 48.

51. Bruck, "Problèmes congolais," p. 684.

52. "Allocution radiophonique de 1er mai," April 30, 1959 (DIA).

53. Merlier, <u>Le Congo</u>, p. 183.

54. Jacques Meert, <u>L'Eglise au Congo face à son avenir</u>, p. 1.

55. <u>Ibid.</u>, p. 50.

56. <u>Ibid.</u>, pp. 82-83.

57. Crawford Young, <u>Politics in the Congo</u>, p. 292.

58. Charles-André Gilis, <u>Kasa-Vubu</u>, p. 62.

59. <u>Ibid.</u>, p. 63.

60. <u>Ibid.</u>

61. Verhaegen, "ABAKO" (unpublished manuscript).

62. René Lemarchand, <u>Political Awakening in the Congo</u>, p. 181.

63. Young, <u>Politics</u>, p. 295 (quoting Pierre Clement, "Patrice Lumumba, Stanleyville 1952-1953," <u>Présence Africaine</u>, No. 40, 1962, p. 73).

64. CSP, "Réunion du comité de direction, May 8 and 29, 1952," Léopoldville (DIA).

65. CSP, "Projet statuts," 1952 (DIA).

66. CERS, "Objet, activités, organization," Sept. 20, 1955 (DIA).

67. <u>Ibid</u>.

68. <u>Le Peuple</u>, November 3, 1957.

Chapter 13

1. George W. Carpenter, "Whose Congo?," p. 282.

2. Charles-André Gilis, <u>Kimbangu, fondateur d'église</u> (Brussels: Editions Europe-Afrique, 1960), pp. 21-22.

3. Joseph Van Wing, "Le Kimbanguisme vu par un témoin," pp. 568-570.

4. Jules Chomé, <u>La passion de Simon Kimbangu</u>, <u>passim</u>.

5. Effraim Andersson, <u>Messianic Popular Movements in the Lower Congo</u>, p. 234.

6. Van Wing, "Le Kimbanguisme," p. 596.

7. <u>Ibid</u>., pp. 608-609.

8. <u>Ibid</u>., p. 609.

9. Jean Kestergat, ed., <u>André Ryckmans</u>, p. 167.

10. Léopold Denis, "Cas de conscience sur l'eau bénite," p. 571.

11. Paul Raymaekers, "L'Eglise de Jésus-Christ sur la terre par le prophète Simon Kimbangu," p. 679.

12. Van Wing, "Le Kimbanguisme," p. 615.

13. Raymaekers, "L'Eglise de Jésus-Christ," p. 728.

14. Robert Kaufmann, <u>Millénarisme et acculturation</u>, p. 74.

15. <u>L'Avenir Colonial Belge</u>, July 31-August 1, 1948.

16. <u>Ibid</u>.

17. K. Plessers, "L'Evolution religieuse au Congo Belge, l'église face à ce tournant, journées d'études missionnaires Centrale Jociste, Brussels, 9-12 avril, 1956," unpublished, Brussels, 1956 (in author's possession).

18. Kaufmann, <u>Millénarisme</u>, p. 81.

19. "Le mouvement pan-nègre," p. 289.

20. "Minutes, Meeting 24," Léopoldville, Feb. 24-Mar. 3, 1946, p. 28 (CPC-KIN).

21. Watchtower Bible and Tract Society, "Memorandum on the Congo case," n.d., p. 9 (Archives of the society, Brooklyn, N.Y.).

22. Wilson D. Wallis, _Messiahs_, p. 4.

23. Georges Balandier, "Contribution a l'étude des nationalismes en Afrique noire," p. 388.

24. "Les mouvements prophétiques Kongo en 1958," p. 126, mimeo. (in author's possession).

25. _Ibid._, p. 20.

26. _Ibid._, p. 27.

Chapter 14

1. Guy Mosmans, "Les impératifs de l'action missionnaire en Afrique Belge," p. 14.

2. Jacques Meert, _L'Eglise au Congo face à son avenir_, p. 45.

3. Anne Fremantle, ed., _The Papal Encyclicals in Their Historical Context_, p. 308.

4. "Déclaration solennelle de l'épiscopat congolais," quoted in _Le Congo, documents, 1956_, p. 9.

5. _Cinquième conférence plénière des ordinaires des missions du Congo Belge et du Ruanda-Urundi_, p. 219.

6. "Déclaration solennelle," p. 7.

7. _Ibid._, p. 9.

8. _Ibid._

9. "Le manifeste de Conscience Africaine," p. 10.

10. _Ibid._

11. Cours de Philosophie et de Sociologie, "Procès verbal de la réunion du comité en date du 8/5/52" (DIA).

12. This account is derived mainly from an interview with Prof. Jean Buchmann.

13. _Ibid._

14. Charles-André Gilis, _Kasa-Vubu_, p. 78.

15. A. A. J. Van Bilsen, "Quatre années de politique congolaise," p. 465.

16. _L'Essor du Congo_, quoted in _Courrier d'Afrique_, September 13, 1956.

17. _Le Peuple_, November 3, 1957.

18. See _Courrier d'Afrique_, February 28, 1956, quoting a speech given by Father Van Wing.

19. "Le manifeste," p. 15.

20. _Ibid._

21. Meert, _L'Eglise au Congo_, p. 38.

22. Moermans to members of the Government Council, Léopoldville, June 24, 1957 (BEC).

23. Congo, 1959, p. 17.

24. Ibid., p. 15.

25. Crawford Young, Politics in the Congo, p. 118.

26. See Joseph Van Wing, Etudes Bakongo, 2d. ed., pub. 1959. The first edition appeared in two volumes, one published in 1921 and the other in 1938.

27. Interview with Father Van Wing.

28. Benoit Verhaegen, "ABAKO," unpublished manuscript, n.d., n.p. (private papers of M. Verhaegen).

29. Ibid.

30. Benoit Verhaegen, ed., ABAKO 1950-1960, p. 12.

31. Verhaegen, "ABAKO," unpublished manuscript.

32. Joseph Van Wing, "Le Congo déraillé," p. 623.

33. Gilis, Kasa-Vubu, p. 68.

34. Verhaegen, "ABAKO," unpublished manuscript.

35. Interview with Father Joseph Ceuppens.

36. Gilis, Kasa-Vubu, p. 84 n.

37. Verhaegen, ABAKO, pp. 104-105.

38. Ibid., pp. 106-107.

39. Ibid., p. 113.

40. Interview with Father Van Wing.

41. See E. Boelart, Nsong'a Lianga; G. Hulstaert, Les Mongo; E. P. A. de Rop, Bibliographie over de Mongo; and E. Verhulpen, Baluba et Balubaisés du Katanga.

42. René Lemarchand, Political Awakening in the Congo, pp. 206-207.

43. Young, Politics, pp. 260 ff.

44. See Congo 1959, pp. 26-28.

45. Ibid., pp. 28-33.

46. See Gilis, Kasa-Vubu, pp. 121-122.

47. Guy Mosmans, "Le problème de l'incompréhension," p. 39.

48. A. Dequae et al., "Rapport de la commission parlementaire chargé de faire une enquête sur les évènements qui sont produits a Léo en janvier 1959," p. 89.

49. "Echos et nouvelles," May 1959, pp. 286-288.

50. Dequae et al., "Rapport de la commission," p. 89.

51. Ibid., p. 90.

52. See "Echos et nouvelles," March 1959, pp. 191-192.

53. H. W. Crane, "Revolution and the New Tribe in Africa," p. 7.

54. See _Congo 1959_, pp. 43-49.

55. Guy Mosmans, "Pour un authentique laïcat africain," p. 567.

56. _Ibid._, p. 562.

57. Endriatis, "L'Eglise au Congo après le 4 janvier 1959," p. 27.

58. Apostolic letter of August 15, 1959, quoted in "Trois lettres pastorales concernant le Congo Belge et le Ruanda-Urundi," p. 337.

59. _Ibid._, p. 339.

60. See Victor Le Vine, "Cameroun," _passim_; and Virginia Thompson and Richard Adloff, _French West Africa_, p. 580.

61. James S. Coleman, "Sub-Saharan Africa," p. 279.

Summary and Conclusion

1. J. Roussel, _Déontologie coloniale_, pp. 25-26.

Appendix A

1. Raymond Leslie Buell, _The Native Problem in Africa_, vol. 2, p. 895.

2. _Ibid._, p. 910.

3. _Ibid._, p. 940.

4. O. Louwers and G. Touchard, _Recueil usuel de la législation_, vol. 6, 1907-1908, Brussels, 1911, p. 567.

Appendix B

1. "Texte du Concordat conclu entre le Saint-Siège et la Belgique," _Le Messager Evangelique_, No. 136, Brussels, May 5, 1954, pp. 75-78.

Appendix C

1. Louis Ballegeer, "Pour une politique congolaise," p. 8.

2. For an excellent discussion of the problem of _immatriculation_ see Crawford Young, _Politics in the Congo_, pp. 75-89.

3. Lord Hailey, _An African Survey_, p. 226.

4. Patrice Lumumba, _Congo, My Country_, p. 53.

BIBLIOGRAPHY

Unpublished Materials

Except as otherwise noted, the unpublished materials cited are located in the following collections:

New York, U.S.A.

Archives of the Africa Committee, Division of Overseas Ministries (formerly Division of Foreign Missions), National Council of Churches. (Referred to in the notes as NCC-AC)

Brussels, Belgium

Archives of the Brussels Bureau of the Congo Protestant Council. (Referred to in the notes as CPC-BB)

Kinshasa, Congo

Archives of the Agence DIA (Documentation et Information Africaine). (Referred to in the notes as DIA)

Archives of the Bureau de l'Enseignement Catholique. (Referred to in the notes as BEC)

Archives of the Congo Protestant Council. (Referred to in the notes as CPC-KIN)

Government Publications

BELGIUM:

Annales parlementaires de Belgique: Chambre des Représentants, 1908-1960. Brussels.

Annales parlementaires de Belgique: Sénat, 1908-1960. Brussels.

Chambre des Représentants. Rapport annuel sur l'administration du Congo Belge, 1920-1959. Brussels.

Conseil Colonial. Compte-rendu analytique des séances, 1946-1960. Brussels.

Ministère des Colonies. Mission pédagogique Coulon-Deheyn-Renson: la réforme de l'enseignement. Brussels, 1954.

_____. Organisation de l'enseignement libre au Congo Belge et au Ruanda-Urundi avec le concours des sociétés des missions nationales. Brussels, 1929.

_____. *Plan décennal pour le développement économique et social du Congo Belge*, vol. 1. Brussels, 1949.

BELGIAN CONGO:

Conseil du Gouvernement. *Compte-rendu analytique*, 1935-1960. Léopoldville.

Gouvernement Général. *Bulletin officiel*, 1908-1960. Léopoldville.

_____. *Recueil mensuel des circulaires, instruction et ordres de service.* Boma, 1922.

Reference Works and Bibliographies

Bingle, Ernst J., and Grubb, Kenneth, eds. *World Christian Handbook.* London: World Dominion Press, 1957.

Corman, Alfred, ed. *Annuaire des missions catholiques au Congo Belge.* Brussels: Librairie Albert Dewit, 1924.

_____. *Annuaire des missions catholiques au Congo Belge.* Brussels: L'Edition Universelle, 1935.

de Rop, E. P. A., comp. *Bibliographie over de Mongo.* Brussels: ARSOM, Sci. Mor. et Pol., N.S., vol. 8, fasc. 2, 1956.

Inforcongo. *Belgian Congo*, 2 vols. Brussels, 1959 and 1960.

International African Institute. *Selected Annotated Bibliography of Tropical Africa.* New York: Twentieth Century Fund, 1956.

Lehmann, Robert L., and Price, Frank W., comps. *Africa South of the Sahara: A Selected and Annotated Bibliography of Books in the Missionary Research Library on Africa and African Countries South of the Sahara.* New York: Missionary Research Library, 1961.

Piron, Pierre, and Devos, Jacques. *Codes et lois de Congo Belge, matières civiles, commerciales, pénales.* Brussels: F. Larcier, 1960.

Rommerskirchen, Johannes, and Dindinger, Johannes, comps. *Bibliografia Missionaria.* Rome: S. Congregazione de propaganda fide e publicata à cura dell' Unione Missionaria del Clero in Italia (annually since 1933).

Van Wing, J., and Goemé, V., eds. *Annuaire des Missions Catholiques au Congo Belge et au Ruanda-Urundi.* Brussels: L'Edition Universelle, 1949.

Books and Pamphlets

Ade, J. F. *Christian Missions in Nigeria 1841-1891: The Making of a New Elite.* London: Longmans, Green, 1965.

Almond, Gabriel, and Coleman, James S., eds. *The Politics of Developing Areas.* Princeton: Princeton University Press, 1960.

Andersson, Effraim. *Messianic Popular Movements in the Lower Congo.* Uppsala: Uppsala University Press, 1958.

Anet, Henri. Vers l'avenir: Rapport de la conférence jubilaire des missions protestantes du Congo et de la conférence missionnaire de l'Afrique occidentale. Léopoldville: Congo Protestant Council, 1929.

Apter, David E. Ghana in Transition. New York: Atheneum, 1963.

Artigue, Pierre. Qui sont les leaders congolais? Brussels: Editions Europe-Afrique, 1961.

Ayandele, E. A. The Missionary Impact on Modern Nigeria. New York: Humanities Press, 1967.

Balandier, Georges. Afrique ambigue. Paris: Plon, 1957.

_____. Sociologie actuelle de l'Afrique noire. Paris: Presses Universitaires de France, 1955.

Baron, Salo Wittmayer. Modern Nationalism and Religion. New York: Meridian Books, 1960.

Bentley, W. Holden. Pioneering in the Congo. 2 vols. New York: Revell, 1900.

Boelart, E. Nsong'a Lianga: l'épopée nationale des Nkurdo-Mongo. Antwerp: De Sikkel, 1949.

Braekman, E. M. Histoire du protestantisme au Congo. Brussels: Librairie des Eclaireurs Unionistes, 1961.

Brausch, Georges. Belgian Administration in the Congo. London: Oxford University Press, 1961.

Buell, Raymond Leslie. The Native Problem in Africa. 2 vols. New York: Macmillan, 1928.

Burke, Thomas J. M., ed. Catholic Missions: Four Great Encyclicals. New York: Fordham University Press, 1957.

Carter, Gwendolyn, ed. Five African States. Ithaca: Cornell University Press, 1963.

Charles, Pierre. Etudes missiologiques. Brussels: Muséum Lessianum, 1956.

Chlepner, B. S. Cent ans d'histoire sociale en Belgique. Brussels, 1956.

Chomé, Jules. La passion de Simon Kimbangu. Brussels: Les Amis de Présence Africaine, 1959.

Cinquième conférence plénière des ordinaires des missions du Congo Belge et du Ruanda-Urundi, Léopoldville, June 21-July 1, 1956. Léopoldville, 1956.

Coleman, James S. Nigeria: Background to Nationalism. Berkeley and Los Angeles: University of California Press, 1958.

Coleman, James S., and Rosberg, Carl G., Jr. Political Parties and National Integration in Tropical Africa. Berkeley and Los Angeles: University of California Press, 1965.

Le Congo, documents 1956. Brussels: De Linie, 1956.

Dahl, Robert A., ed. <u>Political Oppositions in Western Democracies</u>. New Haven and London: Yale University Press, 1966.

Davies, Ioan. <u>African Trade Unions</u>. Baltimore, Md.: Penguin Books, 1966.

de Hemptinne, Jean. <u>La politique des missions protestantes au Congo</u>. Elisabethville: Editions de l'Essor du Congo, 1929.

de Meeus, D. Fr., and Steenberghen, D. R. <u>Les missions religieuses au Congo Belge</u>. Antwerp: Editions Zaire, 1947.

Denis, Léopold. <u>Les jésuites belges au Kwango, 1893-1943</u>. Brussels: Muséum Lessianum, 1943.

de Smet, Roger E., and Evalenko, René. <u>Les élections belges, explication de la répartition géographique de suffrages</u>. Brussels: Université Libre de Bruxelles, Institut de Sociologie Solvay, 1956.

<u>Deuxième conférence plénière des ordinaires des missions du Congo Belge et du Ruanda-Urundi, Léopoldville, June 16-28, 1936</u>. Léopoldville, 1936.

Du Plessis, J. <u>The Evangelization of Pagan Africa</u>. Capetown and Johannesberg: Juta, 1929.

<u>L'Education chrétienne aux missions</u>: Rapports et compte-rendu de la onzième semaine de missiologie de Louvain. Louvain: Muséum Lessianum, 1933.

Fremantle, Anne, ed. <u>The Papal Encyclicals in Their Historical Context</u>. New York: New American Library, 1963.

Gérard-Libois, ed. <u>Congo 1959: Documents Belges et Africains</u>. Brussels: Centre de Recherche et d'Information Socio-Politique, 1962.

Gilis, Charles-André. <u>Kasa-Vubu: au coeur du drame congolais</u>. Brussels: Editions Europe-Afrique, 1964.

Groves, Charles Pelham. <u>The Planting of Christianity in Africa</u>. 4 vols. London: Lutterworth Press, 1948-1958.

Hailey, Lord. <u>An African Survey</u>. Revised 1956. London: Oxford University Press, 1957.

Halewyck, Michel. <u>La charte coloniale</u>. Vol. 1. Brussels, 1910.

Herskovits, Melville J. <u>The Human Factor in Changing Africa</u>. New York: Alfred A. Knopf, 1962.

Heyse, Th. <u>Associations religieuses au Congo Belge et au Ruanda-Urundi</u>. Brussels: Institut Royal Colonial Belge, Section des Sciences Morales et Politiques, Mémoires Collection, vol. 15, fasc. 3, 1948.

Hodgkin, Thomas. <u>African Political Parties</u>. Baltimore, Md.: Penguin Books, 1961.

_____. <u>Nationalism in Colonial Africa</u>. New York: New York University Press, 1957.

Hofstadter, Richard. <u>Anti-Intellectualism in American Life</u>. New York: Vintage, 1966.

Hulstaert, G. <u>Les Mongo: aperçu général</u>. Tervuren, Belgium: Musée Royal de l'Afrique Centrale, 1961.

Jones, Thomas Jesse, ed. Education in Africa. New York: Phelps-Stokes
    Fund, 1922.

Joye, Pierre, and Lewin, Rosine. Les trusts au Congo. Brussels: Société
    Populaire d'Editions, 1961.

Kardiner, Abram, et al. The Psychological Frontiers of Society. New York:
    Columbia University Press, 1945.

Kaufmann, Robert. Millénarisme et acculturation. Brussels: Institut Sol-
    vay, 1964.

Kestergat, Jean, ed. André Ryckmans. Paris: Editions du Centurion, 1961.

Kuper, Leo. An African Bourgeoisie. New Haven: Yale University Press, 1965.

Lanternari, Vittoria. Les mouvements des peuples opprimés. Paris: François
    Maspéro, 1962.

Latourette, Kenneth S. The Great Century in the Americas: Australasia and
    Africa: A.D. 1800-A.D. 1914. Vol. 5 in the series A History of the
    Expansion of Christianity. New York: Harper, 1943.

Laveille, E. L'Evangile au centre de l'Afrique: Le P. Van Henexthoven, S.J.
    Brussels: Muséum Lessianum, 1926.

Lemarchand, René. Political Awakening in the Congo: the Politics of Fragmen-
    tation. Berkeley and Los Angeles: University of California Press,
    1964.

Little, Kenneth. West African Urbanization. London: Cambridge University
    Press, 1965.

Lory, M. J. Face à l'avenir: l'Eglise au Congo belge et au Ruanda-Urundi.
    Tournai: Casterman, 1958.

Low, D. A. Political Parties in Uganda 1949-1962. Commonwealth Papers No. 8.
    London: University of London Institute of Commonwealth Studies, 1962.

Lugard, Lord. The Dual Mandate in British Tropical Africa. London: Black-
    man, 1922.

Lumumba, Patrice. Congo, My Country. New York: Praeger, 1962.

Malengreau, F. L'Enseignement médical aux indigènes du Congo Belge. Louvain:
    Fomulac, 1944.

_____. Une fondation médicale au Congo Belge: La Fomulac (1926-1940).
    Louvain: Fomulac, n.d.

Malengreau, Guy. Les droits fonciers chez les indigènes de Congo Belge.
    IRCB, Mémoires, vol. 15, fasc. 2. Brussels, 1947.

Malinowski, Bronislaw. The Dynamics of Culture Change: An Inquiry into Race
    Relations in Africa. New Haven: Yale University Press, 1961.

Masses urbaines et missions: Rapports et compte-rendu de la XXVI semaine de
    missiologie. Brussels: Desclée, De Brouwer, 1957.

Meert, Jacques. L'Eglise au Congo face à son avenir. Léopoldville: Secré-
    tariat Général de la JOC, 1956.

199

Merlier, Michel. Le Congo: de la colonisation belge à l'indépendance. Paris: François Maspéro, 1962.

Morgenthau, Ruth Schachter. Political Parties in French Speaking West Africa. London: Oxford University Press, 1964.

Mosmans, Guy. L'Eglise à l'heure de l'Afrique. Tournai: Casterman, 1961.

Nkrumah, Kwame. Ghana: An Autobiography. Edinburgh: Thomas Nelson and Sons Ltd., 1961.

Oliver, Roland. The Missionary Factor in East Africa. London: Longmans, Green, 1952.

Pauwels, Henri. Le syndicalisme et la colonie. Brussels: Editions de la C.S.C., n.d.

Perin, François. La démocratie enrayée. Brussels: Institut Belge de Science Politique, 1960.

Poupart, R. Première esquisse de l'évolution du syndicalisme au Congo. Brussels: Institut Solvay, 1960.

Première conférence plénière des ordinaires des missions catholique du Congo Belge et du Ruanda-Urundi, Léopoldville, October, 1932. Léopoldville, 1932.

Quatrième conférence plénière de réverendissimes ordinaires du Congo Belge et du Ruanda-Urundi, Léopoldville, March 5-11, 1951. Léopoldville, 1951.

Report of the Church Conference on African Affairs: Christian Action in Africa. Otterbein College, Westerville, Ohio, June 19-25, 1942. New York, 1942.

Report of the West African Regional Conference: Abundant Life in Changing Africa. Léopoldville, July 13-24, 1946. New York: Africa Committee, 1946.

Le rôle des laïcs dans les missions: Rapport et compte-rendu de la XXII semaine de missiologie de Louvain, 1952. Louvain: Muséum Lessianum, 1953.

Rotberg, Robert I. Christian Missionaries and the Creation of Northern Rhodesia, 1880-1924. Princeton: Princeton University Press, 1965.

_____. The Role of Nationalism in Central Africa: the Making of Malawi and Zambia. Cambridge, Mass.: Harvard University Press, 1965.

Roussel, Jean. Déontologie coloniale. Namur, Belgium: A Wesmael-Charlier, 1956.

Rubbens, Antoine, ed. Dettes de guerre. Elisabethville: Editions de l'Essor du Congo, 1945.

Ryckmans, Pierre. Dominer pour servir. Brussels: Librairie Albert Dewit, 1931.

Shepperson, George, and Price, Thomas. Independent African. Edinburgh: University of Edinburgh Press, 1958.

Slade, Ruth. L'Attitude des missions protestantes vis-à-vis les puissances européennes au Congo avant 1885. Brussels: IRCB, 1954.

_____. The Belgian Congo. London: Oxford University Press, 1961.

_____. English-Speaking Missions in the Congo Independent State (1878-1908). Brussels: ARSC, Mémoires in 8° N.S., vol. 16, fasc. 2, 1959.

_____. King Leopold's Congo. London: Oxford University Press, 1962.

Stonelake, Alfred R. Congo: Past and Present. New York: World Dominion Press, 1937.

Sundkler, Bengt G. M. Bantu Prophets in South Africa. London: Lutterworth Press, 1948.

_____. Bantu Prophets in South Africa. 2d. edition. London: Oxford University Press, 1964.

Taylor, John V., and Lehmann, Dorothea. Christians of the Copperbelt. London: SCM Press, 1961.

Tempels, Placide. Bantu Philosophy. Paris: Présence Africaine, 1959.

Thompson, Virginia, and Adloff, Richard. French West Africa. Stanford: Stanford University Press, 1958.

Troisième conférence plénière des ordinaires des missions du Congo Belge et du Ruanda-Urundi, Léopoldville, June 25-July 8, 1945. Léopoldville, 1945.

United Missionary Conference on the Congo, Léopoldville, 1902. Matadi: Swedish Mission Press, 1902(?).

United Missionary Conference on the Congo, Léopoldville, 1904. Bolobo: Bolobo Mission Press, 1904.

United Missionary Conference on the Congo, Léopoldville, 1906. Bolobo: Bolobo Mission Press, 1907.

United Missionary Conference on the Congo, Léopoldville, 1909. Bolobo: Bolobo Mission Press, 1909.

United Missionary Conference on the Congo, Bolenge, 1911. Bolobo: Bolobo Mission Press, 1911.

United Missionary Conference on the Congo, Luebo, Kasai, 1918. Bolobo: Bolobo Mission Press, 1918.

Van Bilsen, A. A. J. Vers l'indépendance du Congo et du Ruanda-Urundi. Brussels: Casterman, 1958.

Vandenbussche, E., ed. Objectivité "sur mésure": la mission pédagogique Coulon-Deheyn-Renson envoyée au Congo Belge par Monsieur le Ministre Auguste Buisseret. Introduction par le R. P. Van Wing. Louvain: I.S.A.D., 1955.

Vandervelde, Emile. La Belgique et le Congo. Paris: F. Alcan, 1911.

_____. Les derniers jours de l'Etat du Congo. Paris: La Société Nouvelle, 1909.

Vansina, Jan. Les anciens royaumes de la savane. Léopoldville: IRES, 1965.

Van Wing, Joseph. Etudes bakongo. 2d. edition. Louvain: Muséum Lessianum, 1954.

Verhaegen, Benoit, ed. ABAKO, 1950-1960 Documents. Brussels: CRISP, 1962.

Verhulpen, E. Baluba et Balubaisés du Katanga. Antwerp: L'Avenir Belge, 1936.

Vermeersch, P. La question congolaise. Brussels: Imprimerie Scientifique, 1906.

Wallerstein, Immanuel. Africa, The Politics of Independence. New York: Vintage, 1961.

Wallis, Wilson D. Messiahs: Their Role in Civilization. Washington, D.C.: American Council on Public Affairs, 1943.

Weiss, Herbert, and Verhaegen, Benoit, eds. Parti Solidaire Africain (PSA): Documents 1959-1960. Brussels: CRISP, 1963.

Welbourne, F. B. East African Rebels. London: SCM Press, 1961.

World Missionary Conference, Edinburgh, 1910. Carrying the Gospel. Vol. 1. New York: Oliphant, Anderson and Ferrier, 1910.

_____. The Report of Commission III: Education in Relation to the Christianization of National Life. New York: Oliphant, Anderson and Ferrier, 1910.

Young, Crawford. Politics in the Congo: Decolonization and Independence. Princeton: Princeton University Press, 1965.

Articles

Anet, Henri. "Debate on the Congo Administration in the Belgian Senate." Congo Mission News (hereafter cited as CMN) 43: 12-14; April 1923.

"A propos du Kibangisme." Congo 30: 380 ff.; October 1924.

"L'Avenir du Congo." Congo 1: 396 ff.; March 1924.

Balandier, Georges. "Contribution à l'étude des nationalismes en Afrique noire." Zaire 8: 379 ff.; April 1954.

_____. "Messianisme des Bas-Kongo." Encyclopédie Coloniale et Maritime Mensuelle 1: 216-220; August 1951.

_____. "Messianismes et nationalismes en Afrique noire." Cahiers Internationaux de Sociologie 14: 41-65; 1953.

Ballegeer, Louis. "Pour une politique congolaise." CEPSI 4: 3 ff.; 1946-1947.

_____. "Syndicalisme indigène au Congo Belge." CEPSI 6: 99 ff.; 1948.

Beckers, Henri. "Le fonds du bien-être indigène." Zaire 5: 787-812; October 1951.

Biebuyck, D. "La société Kumu face au Kitawala." Zaire 11: 7 ff.; January 1957.

Brashley, Peter J. "Congo's Changing Culture." CMN 149: 12-13; January 1950.

Brasseur, Paul. "La formation d'une élite universitaire indigène." Lovania 13: 113 ff.; 1948.

Brown, H. D. "The Church and Its Missionary Task in the Congo." International Review of Missions (hereafter cited as IRM) 41: 301 ff.; 1952.

Browne, Stanley G. "The Indigenous Medical Evangelist in Congo." IRM 35:
59 ff.; 1946.

Bruck, Jean. "Problèmes congolais et action syndicale chrétienne." Les Dossiers de l'Action Sociale Catholique 8: 677 ff.; October 1959.

"Le budget des colonies aux chambres." Congo 2: 418 ff.; August 1921.

Carpenter, George. "Bantu Education and European Influence in Congo." CMN
96: 13 ff.; October 1936.

_____. "Church and State in Africa." Civilisations 3: 519-543; 1953.

_____. "Whose Congo?" IRM 2: 271 ff.; 1961.

Carret, J. M. "La colonisation mise au point." Signum Fidei 3: 70-72; April
1946.

"Centralisation et décentralisation." Congo 2: 727 ff.; December 1921.

Ceuterick, Pascal. "Evolution psychologique du noir." CEPSI 14: 59 ff.;
1950.

Charles, Pierre. "Exposé général: le pourquoi de l'enseignement dans les
missions." In L'Education chrétienne aux missions, pp. 13-31. Louvain: Muséum Lessianum, 1933.

Charles, V. "Chronique sociale congolaise." Zaire 5: 959 ff.; September
1951.

Chesterman, Clement C. "Possibilities of Government Cooperation in Our Medical Work." CMN 76: 8 ff.; October 1931.

"Christian Missions and Colonial Policy." IRM 2: 361-363; April 1912.

Clarke, John Alexander. "The Education of the African People." CMN 144: 14-
15; October 1948.

Coleman, James S. "Sub-Saharan Africa." In Gabriel Almond and James S.
Coleman, The Politics of Developing Areas, pp. 247 ff. Princeton:
Princeton University Press, 1960.

Comhaire, Jean. "Evolution politique et sociale du Congo Belge en 1950-1952."
Zaire 6: 1041 ff.; 1952.

Comhaire-Sylvan, S. "Food and Leisure Among the African Youth of Léopoldville." In UNESCO, Social Implications of Industrialization and Urbanization in Africa South of the Sahara, pp. 113-121. Paris:
UNESCO, 1956.

Congo Protestant Council. "Findings of the Léopoldville General Conference."
CMN 88: 13-21; October 1934.

Coppens, Paul. "Les missions du Congo vues par un laïque." Congo 2: 413-418;
October 1924.

Cornelis, Floribert. "L'Instruction et l'éducation de la population indigène
masculine d'Elisabethville." CEPSI 4: 142 ff.; 1955.

Crane, W. H. "Revolution and the New Tribe in Africa." CMN 18: 7 ff.;
    January 1960.

Debra, A. "Préambule." CEPSI 6: 1-2; 1948.

"Déclaration de l'épiscopat du Congo Belge et du Ruanda-Urundi." Revue du
    Clergé Africain 11: 449-458; September 1956.

"Déclaration solennelle de l'épiscopat congolais." In Le Congo, documents
    1956. Brussels: De Linie, 1956.

de Hemptinne, Jean. "Le gouvernement du Congo Belge: projet de réorganisa-
    tion." Congo 1: 337-343; 1920.

_____. "La politique indigène." Congo 2: 187 ff.; July 1929.

_____. "La politique indigène du gouvernement belge." Congo 2: 359 ff.;
    October 1928.

De Jonghe, Edmond. "L'Instruction publique au Congo Belge." Congo 1: 501-
    530; April 1922.

Denis, Léopold. "Cas de conscience sur l'eau bénite." Revue du Clergé Afri-
    cain 10: 568-572; November 1955.

Dequae, A., et al. "Rapport de la commission parlementaire chargé de faire
    une enquête sur les évènements qui sont produits à Léo en janvier
    1959." CEPSI 46: 75 ff.; September 1959.

De Vos, Stanislas. "La politique indigène et les missions catholiques."
    Congo 2: 635 ff.; December 1923.

Dufonteny, G. "La méthode d'évangelisation chez les non-civilisés." Bulle-
    tin des Missions 8: 337 ff., September-October 1927; and 10: 21-31,
    March 1930.

"Echos et nouvelles." Revue du Clergé Africain 14; April, May 1959; 15: 293
    ff., May 1960.

"Education." CMN 167: 2; July 1954.

Endriatis. "L'Eglise au Congo après le 4 janvier 1959." Afrika Kring 2: 19
    ff.; 1959.

"Enquiry on the Missionary Educational System in Congo Belge." CMN 43: 20;
    April 1923.

"L'Enseignement en Afrique Belge." (Editorial) Problèmes d'Afrique Centrale
    36: 96; 1957.

"Equality." CMN 125: 2; January 1944.

Fontainas. "Le droit de colonisation." Congo 1: 693 ff.; May 1934.

Frame, W. B. "Prophets on the Lower Congo." CMN 37: 6-9; October 1921.

Franck, Louis. "La politique indigène, le service territorial et les chef-
    feries." Congo 2: 189 ff.; 1921.

"Le Garveyisme en action dans notre colonie." Congo 2: 575 ff.; November
    1921.

Garvie, Alfred E. "The Education of Missionaries." IRM 5: 27 ff.; 1916.

"The Governor-General of the Congo Belge and Missions." CMN 40: 10; July 1922.

Grevisse, F. "Le centre extra-coutumier de Elisabethville." CEPSI 15; 1951.

Grosjean, J. "La presse au Congo." Afrika Kring 2: 81-87; 1957-1958.

Guebels, L. "Relation complète des travaux de la Commission Permanente pour la Protection des Indigènes." CESPI 20: 1-225; 21: 227-390; 22: 391-616; and 23: 619-754, 1953.

Heenan, Gaston. "Considérations au sujet de notre politique indigène." Congo 1: 77-91; January 1929.

Heyse, T. "Cessions et concessions foncières du Congo." Congo 1: 515 ff., June 1931; 1: 485 ff., June 1932; 2-179 ff., July 1933.

_____. "Concessions du Mayumbe." Congo 1: 648 ff.; May 1928.

Houtart, F. "La pastorale des grandes villes." In Rapports et compte-rendu de la XXVI semaine de missiologie: Masses urbaines et missions, pp. 34 ff. Louvain: Muséum Lessianum, 1957.

Huys, A. "Statuts du clergé indigène." In Deuxième conférence plénière des ordinaires des missions du Congo Belge et du Ruanda-Urundi, pp. 39-82. Léopoldville, June 1936.

Huysmans, Camille. "La tribune de l'amicale socialiste au Congo, les rongeurs de la politique." L'Avenir Colonial Belge, June 21, 1952.

Jaspers, E. "Le discours de M. le Premier Ministre Jaspers à la Chambre." Congo 1: 459 ff.; March 1929.

Keable, Robert. "The Worth of an African." IRM 3: 319-332; 1918.

LeGrand, L. "De la légalité des villages chrétiens." Congo 1: 1-8; January 1922.

_____. "Les missionnaires catholiques du Kwango et les institutions indigènes." Congo 2: 506 ff.; July 1921.

Le Vine, Victor. "Cameroun." In James Coleman and Carl G. Rosberg, Jr., Political Parties and National Integration in Tropical Africa, pp. 132-184. Berkeley and Los Angeles: University of California Press, 1965.

Liesenborghs, Oswald. "L'Instruction publique des indigènes du Congo Belge." Congo 1: 233 ff.; March 1940.

Lihau, Marcel. "Les aspirations nationales au Congo Belge." In Aspirations nationales et missions: Rapports et compte-rendu de la XXVIIIe semaine de missiologie, Louvain, 1958, pp. 157-164. Paris: Desclée, De Brouwer, 1958.

Linton, Ralph. "Nativistic Movements." American Anthropologist 45: 230 ff.; April-June 1943.

Lorwin, Val R. "Belgium: Religion, Class and Language in National Politics." In Robert A. Dahl, ed., Political Oppositions in Western Democracies. New Haven and London: Yale University Press, 1966.

Mabie, C. "Dr. C. Mabie Reports on the ABFMS." CMN 51: 15; July 1925.

Mair, L. P. "Independent Religious Movements in Three Continents." Comparative Studies in Society and History 1: 113-136; January 1959.

Malengreau, Guy. "Chronique de politique indigène." Zaire 6: 957-971; November 1952.

_____. "La réforme de l'enseignement, mission pédagogique Coulon-Deheyn-Renson." Zaire 10: 405 ff.; April 1956.

Malinowski, Bronislaw. "Native Education and Culture Contact." IRM 25: 480 ff.; 1936.

"Le manifeste de Conscience Africaine." In J. Gerard-Libois, ed., Congo 1959, pp. 9-16. Brussels: Centre de Recherche et d'Information Socio-Politique, 1962.

"Le manifeste du PSC sur le Congo." In Le Congo, documents 1956. Brussels: De Linie, 1956.

Marzorati, Anton F. "Certains aspects du problème social au Congo Belge." Congo 2: 701-713; December 1936.

_____. "L'Evolution des relations entre les communautés européennes et la société indigène du Congo Belge." Zaire 6: 929-939; November 1952.

Massion. "Relations humaines entre belges et congolais." Afrika Kring 5: 11-18; 1958.

Matthews, Shailer. "Missions and the Social Gospel." IRM 2: 432 ff.; 1914.

Maurice, Albert. "Social Policy and the Belgian Congo." CMN 163: 22-23; July 1953.

Maus, Albert. "A propos de la réforme scolaire de l'UMHK." CEPSI 81: 138 ff.; 1949.

Meert, Jacques. "Le jocisme face à l'avenir noir." Revue du Clergé Africain 9: 341-358; July 1954.

Miessen. "Assistance sociale indigène au Congo." In Le rôle des laïcs dans les missions. Rapport et compte-rendu de la XXIIᵉ semaine de missiologie de Louvain, 1952, pp. 356 ff. Louvain: Muséum Lessianum, 1953.

Mill, A. G. "Report of the Commission for the Protection of the Natives." CMN 69: 19 ff.; January 1930.

"Minutes of the Committee on Work in the Congo (New York)." CMN 40: 8 ff.; July 1922.

Moeller, A. J. "Note concernant l'étude de Msgr. de Hemptinne sur la politique indigène." Congo 2: 209 ff.; July 1922.

_____. "Précisions sur le problème de la politique indigène." Congo 2: 769 ff.; December 1929.

Moore, Edward Caldwell. "Some Aspects of the Relations of Missions to Civilization." IRM 4: 353-370; 1915.

Morrison, John. "Annual Meeting of the Congo Protestant Council." CMN 155: 4-5; April 1952.

Mosmans, G. "Action de l'église au plan social en Afrique." Revue Nouvelle 22: 276 ff.; October 1954.

_____. "L'Eglise à l'heure de l'Afrique." Revue Nouvelle 29: 225 ff.; March 1959.

_____. "Les impératifs de l'action missionnaire en Afrique Belge." Revue Nouvelle 24: 3 ff.; July-August 1956.

_____. "Impressions de voyage." Afrika Kring 2: 115-126; 1957-1958.

_____. "Pour un authentique laïcat africain." Revue Nouvelle 29: 561-573; July 15, 1959.

_____. "Le problème de l'incompréhension." Afrika Kring 7: 29-40; 1959.

Moulaert, G. "Instruction et éducation." Zaire 10: 525 ff.; May 1956.

"Le mouvement pan-nègre." Bulletin des Missions 7: 289 ff.; May-June 1925.

M. X. "Les déterminismes de la situation coloniale." Afrika Kring 7: 13-27; 1959.

Murray, A. Victor. "Christianity and Rural Civilization." IRM 19: 388 ff.; 1930.

Neut, D. Edouard. "Au Congo Belge: évangelisation et colonisation." Bulletin des Missions 6: 408 ff.; January-February 1923.

Nève, Théodore. "En visite à la préfecture apostolique du Katanga." Bulletin des Missions 7: 44 ff.; March-April 1924.

Nicaise, J. "Chronique sociale congolaise." Zaire 9: 153 ff.; February 1955.

Nkome. "La Cadulac." Revue de l'Aucam 15: 225 ff.; April 1940.

"Notes and Comments." CMN 62: 3; April 1928.

"Notes on Roman Catholic Activities." CMN 78: 25 ff.; April 1932.

Oldham, J. H. "The Christian Opportunity in Africa." IRM 14: 173 ff.; 1925.

Perraudin, J. "Le Cardinal Lavigerie et Léo II." Zaire 12: 901-932; 1957.

"Protestant Missions in the Congo: Summary of Statistics for 1919." CMN 32, Supplement; July 1920.

"Protestantism in the Congo." CMN 55: front cover; July 1926. (Quoting from De Standaard, February 2, 1926.)

"Rapport annuel sur l'administration de la colonie du Congo Belge pour 1928." Congo 1: 55 ff.; January 1930.

"Rapport du Conseil Colonial sur le projet de décret relatif aux centres extra-coutumiers." Congo 1: 686 ff.; July 1932.

Raymaekers, Paul. "L'Eglise de Jésus-Christ sur la terre par le prophète Simon Kimbangu: contribution à l'étude des mouvements messianiques dans le Bas-Kongo." Zaire 13: 675 ff.; 1959.

Roelens, V. "Le respect de la coutume indigène." Congo 2: 496 ff.; July 1921.

"Roman Catholicism in the Congo." CMN 80: 32 ff.; 1932.

Roussel, J. "Les conditions psychologiques et morales de l'Action Sociale du Congo Belge." CEPSI 8: 83 ff.; 1949.

Rubbens, Antoine. "L'Evolution administrative et politique de la colonie." Revue Nouvelle 14: 504-520; December 15, 1951.

_____. "Political Awakening in the Belgian Congo." Civilisations 10: 63 ff.; 1960.

Rutten, Martin. "Circulaire du Gouverneur Général sur les relations avec les missions." Congo 2: 711 ff.; December 1923.

Ryckmans, Pierre. "Les évolués." Revue de l'Aucam 1: 26 ff.; 1946-1947.

Scalais, Felix. "L'Eglise devant les banlieues congolaises." In Les missions et le prolétariat, pp. 45 ff. Paris: Desclée, De Brouwer, 1954.

Schebesta, P. "Blancs et noirs au Congo Belge." Congo 1: 321 ff.; March 1934.

Shaw, Trevor. "A Pertinent Question." CMN 180: 11-12; October 1957.

Slauffacher, Raymond. "Regional Conference of the Church of Christ in Congo." CMN 149: 4-5; January 1950.

Sohier, Antoine. "Le problème des indigènes évolués et le commission du statut des congolais civilisés." Zaire 3: 843 ff.; October 1949.

_____. "Le sacré des évêques noirs et la politique coloniale belge." Bulletin des Missions 18: 233 ff.; 1939.

Spiro, Herbert J. "The Rhodesias and Nyasaland." In Gwendolyn Carter, ed., Five African States, pp. 361-470. Ithaca, N.Y.: Cornell University Press, 1963.

Springer, J. M. "The CMCMEC [Congo Mission Conference of the Methodist Episcopal Church] Surveys Its Field." CMN 70: 17 ff.; April 1930.

"State Schools for Africans." CMN 169: 3; January 1955.

Tabb, W. A. "The Indigenous Church." CMN 77: 16 ff.; January 1932.

Tempels, Placide. "Justice sociale." In Antoine Rubbens, ed., Dettes de guerre, pp. 71-75. Elisabethville: Editions l'Essor du Congo, 1945.

Tibbaut, Emile. "L'Assistance sociale au Congo: l'évolution juridique de la société indigène." Congo 2: 669 ff.; December 1926.

"Translation of an Interview with Msgr. de Hemptinne, R.C. Bishop of Elisabethville, Congo Belge." Het Handelsbad, October 14, 1950.

"Trois lettres pastorales concernant le Congo Belge et le Ruanda-Urundi." Revue Nouvelle 30: 331 ff.; 1959.

Van Bilsen, A. A. J. "Pour une nouvelle politique de mouvement en Afrique." Revue Nouvelle, November 1954, pp. 395 ff.

_____. Quatre années de politique congolaise." Revue Nouvelle 27: 449 ff.; 1958.

Vandenbulke, R. P. "Comment traiter les chefs noirs." In Expectatio Gentium: Rapports et compte-rendu de la XIII semaine de missiologie de Louvain 1935, pp. 150-171. Brussels: l'Edition Universelle, 1935.

Vanderyst, Hyac. "Les futurs universités catholiques au Congo." Bulletin des Missions 9: 254 ff.; November-December 1928.

_____. "Les instituts missionnaires universitaires." Congo 1: 415 ff.; March 1930.

Van Hee, Sylvain. "Rapport sur la mission des R. P. Jésuites au Congo." Congo 1: 310 ff.; February 1930.

Van Wing, Joseph. "Le Congo déraillé." IRCB [Institut Royal Colonial Belge] Bulletin des Séances 3: 609-626; 1951.

_____. "Evolués et clergé indigène." Revue Coloniale Belge 59: 167-169; March 15, 1948.

_____. "Une évolution de la coutume Bakongo (Congo Belge)." In Les élites en pays de missions, compte-rendu de la 5me semaine de missiologie de Louvain, 1927, pp. 235-247. Louvain: Muséum Lessianum, 1927.

_____. "La formation d'une élite noire au Congo Belge." CEPSI 5: 3 ff.; 1947-1948.

_____. "Le Kimbanguisme vu par un témoin." Zaire 12: 563 ff.; 1958.

_____. "Père Van Wing traite ensuite des événements de Léopoldville et de la nouvelle politique congolaise." Assistance aux maternités et dispensaires du Congo, pp. 14-21; April 1953.

Verbeken, A. "La crise de l'évolution indigène." CEPSI 5: 23 ff.; 1947-1948.

Wallace, F. C. "Revitalization Movements." American Anthropologist 58: 264 ff.; April 1956.

Weiss, Herbert. "Comparisons in the Evolution of Pre-Independence Elites in French-Speaking Africa and the Congo." In Willard H. Lewis, ed., French-Speaking Africa, pp. 130-142. New York: Walker, 1965.

Wide, E. R. "The Presidential Address." CMN 186: 3 ff.; April 1959.

XXX. "La politique scolaire au Congo du point de vue missionnaire." Revue Nouvelle 21: 296-301; March 15, 1955.

Newspapers and Press Agencies

Agence Belga (press agency)

L'Avenir Colonial Belge (Léopoldville)

Conscience Africaine (Léopoldville)

Courrier d'Afrique (Léopoldville)

La Croix du Congo (Léopoldville)

La Dernière Heure (Brussels)

De Standaard (Brussels)

DIA (Documentation et Information Africaine—press agency)

L'Echo du Katanga (Elisabethville)

L'Essor du Congo (Elisabethville)

La Flandre Libérale (Antwerp)

Het Handelsbad (Antwerp)

Horizons (Léopoldville)

La Libre Belgique (Brussels)

La Métropole (Brussels)

La Nation Belge (Brussels)

Le Peuple (Brussels)

Le Phare Dimanche (Brussels)

Le Soir (Brussels)

Temps Nouveau d'Afrique (Bukavu)

La Voix du Congolais (Léopoldville)

Periodicals

Afrika Kring (Louvain, Belgium)

Bulletin des Missions (Lopem, Belgium)

CEPSI (Bulletin du Centre d'Etude des Problèmes Sociaux Indigènes) (Elisabethville)

Civilisations (Brussels)

Comparative Studies in Society and History (The Hague)

Congo (Brussels)

Congo Mission News (Léopoldville)

Les Dossiers de l'Action Sociale Catholique (Brussels)

International Review of Missions (Edinburgh)

Lovania (Elisabethville)

The Missionary Herald (BMS, London)

Pourquoi-Pas (Brussels)

Pourquoi-Pas Congo (Léopoldville)

Problèmes d'Afrique Centrale (Brussels)

Revue de l'Aucam (Louvain)

Revue du Clergé Africain (Mayidi, Congo)

La Revue Nouvelle (Tournai)

Signum Fidei (Léopoldville)

Zaire (Brussels)

INDEX

ABAKO (Association Bakongo), <u>see</u> Voluntary associations, Political parties
ADAPES (Anciéns Elèves des Pères du Scheut), <u>see</u> Voluntary associations, alumni
Administratifs de l'Enseignement, 92-93
Administrative chain, 25
Adoula, Cyril, 151, 157n
African Inland Mission, 42
African Linguistic Commission, 156n
Agence DIA, 154, 155, 156
Aide Médicale aux Mission Catholiques, 49
Albert (King of Belgium), 138n
American Baptist Foreign Missionary Society (ABFMS), 38
American Presbyterian Congo Mission, 41, 53
Anet, Henri, 8-9
Annexation, Act of, 8, 11, 38, 123
Anticlericalism, 26, 42; and A. Buisseret, 83, 94, 97, 103; among évolués, 107,
    108-9, 110, 159; and Concordat of 1953, 80, 82; in education, 71, 74, 77,
    84-90; effect on lay organizations, 121, 122; effectiveness of, in
    Belgium, 20, 22, 30; and Louis Franck, 35, 36; and Robert Godding, 76; and
    Maurice Lippens, 33, 34, 35; and Guy Smet, 91n, 92
Anticolonialism, 17-18, 20, 22, 103, 110-11
Anti-Léopoldian campaign, 5-8, 10, 20, 38
Antiprotestantism, 4, 7-9, 41, 45, 49; from Catholics, 38, 39; in education,
    55, 56, 63, 64; toward natives, 40, 45, 50
Antislavery movement, 1, 5, 47
Antiwhite sentiment, 159
Apostolic Vicariate of the Congo, 3
Arabs, the, 4, 5, 12
Association Universitaire Catholique d'Aide aux Missions, 48
Augouard, Prosper-Philippe, 2
Bakongo, 152; -Bengala dispute, 155-57, 163; and messianic movements, 137-39;
    nationalism, 140, 153, 155; political party, <u>see</u> Voluntary associations
Balandier, Georges, 135, 137n, 138n, 143
Baluba people and language, 155, 157
Bandibu clan, 153n
Bankaert, J., 32n
Banque Lambert, 20
Bantandu clan, 153n
Bantu tribe, 109n
Bapende language, 157
Baptist Missionary Society (BMS), 1-2, 4-6, 38, 53
Barrett, David, 136
Bastin, Max, 153n

Bata school for nurses, 47

Baynes, A. H., 5

Becquet, Henri, 138n

Belgian International Association, 2, 3

Belgian parliament, 22-23

Benedict XV, 112, 114

Benedictine Missions, 61, 62

Bengala dispute with Bakongo, 155-57, 163

Bentley, W. Holden, 4, 5n, 6

Berlin West African Conference, the, 4; see also General Act of Berlin

Bishops' conferences (Conferences of the Catholic Bishops of the Congo and Ruanda-Urundi): second plenary, 1936, 12, 117, 122, 125; third plenary, 1945, 68, 112, 126-27; fourth plenary, 1951, 106; fifth plenary, 1956, 129, 145-46

Bishops' declaration of 1956, 145, 146, 147, 148, 162, 167

Bishops, Permanent Committee of Catholic: 1955 meeting, 100-102, 128

Bizala, Cléophas, 129

Black Muslims, 143n

Boelaert, E., 157

Bolikongo, Jean, 132, 133, 155

Boma, 2, 32-33, 35, 46

Bomboko, Justin, 70

Boudouinville (Kivu) séminaire, 114

Boulengier, Philippe, 150n

Bozlee, M., 93

Brasseir, André, 94

Brasseur, Paul, 69

Brausch, Georges, 93

Brazzaville independence, 158

British, the, 15, 20, 39; and Léopold II, 2-4, 6-8, 10; and separation of church and state, 52-53

Brochure jaune, 58

Brothers of Our Lady of Lourdes-Obstacker, 48

Bruck, Jean, 152

Brussels Exposition, 158

Brys, Albert, 124, 126

Buchmann, Jean, 147, 152, 160n

Budgets, 25, 99; for schools, 60, 95-96

Buisseret, Auguste, 84-88, 90-95, 97-99, 159, 166; and anticlericalism, 73-74, 76, 103, 110, 166; and Coulon Commission, 84-86; and discontent of évolués, 106, 107; and education, 70, 83, 86-88, 95-98, 101-102; and foreign and "national" missions, 90-91; and land grants, 98-99; and ministère gris, 93-94; and Synod of the Union des Eglises, 91-92

Buisseret-Moermans-Thompson Agreement, 102

Buisseret Regime, 120, 126, 128, 130, 144

Bureau de l'Enseignement Catholique (BEC), 97n

Burgomasters, 151

Bunia (Lac Albert), 48

Business interests, 42-46, 61, 111, 124n, 138

Busizi, 141n

CADULAC (Centre Agronomique de l'Université de Louvain au Congo), 48, 67, 69

Cambier, Em., 32n

Canon, Pierre, 153n
Cão, Diego, 1
Cardijn, 130
Carpenter, George, 91, 92, 109n, 113
Casement, Robert, 6
Catechists, 45, 52, 157; and evangelizations, 14, 15, 114; and native policy,
    34, 37, 126
Catholic Party, see PSC
Cattoor, (Col.), 94
c-d-t, see Labor
census, 47
Cento, Fernand, 78
Centre Agronomique de l'Université de Louvain au Congo, see CADULAC
Centre Universitaire Congolais Lovanium, see CUCL
Ceuppens, Joseph, 133, 146, 150, 154
Ceuterick, Pascal, 109
CGS (Confédération Général des Syndicats), see Voluntary associations, labor
    unions
Chanois du Latran, 62
Charles, Pierre, 47, 53, 125
Chefferies, 31, 33, 61
Church of Christ in the Congo, 113
Colonial Administration, 35, 116; and Catholics, 120-121; in collaboration with,
    12, 30n, 50, 64; and education, 64, 65, 67, 70, 72, 83; in opposition to,
    33, 129; and Protestants, 10, 42, 109n
Colonial Charter, 17n, 22, 79, 85
Colonial Council, 25, 41, 42
Colonial Ministry, 9, 26, 30, 49, 76, 99
Colons, 42, 77, 80, 126, 148; view of Colonial Administration, 32, 33, 83; view
    of education, 67, 68, 72, 84
Comber, Thomas, 1
Comité Permanent des Ordinaires du Congo Belge et du Ruanda-Urundi, 40
Commission on Education, 1924, 58
Commission for the Protection of the Natives, 6, 31-32, 45, 49, 56, 123
Compagnie du Kasai, 9
Concordat of 1906, 7, 11, 41, 52, 65, 77-78, 79
Corcordat of 1953, 77-80, 113
Confédération des Syndicats Chrétiens (CSC), see Voluntary associations, labor
    unions
Congo Free State, 4, 5, 8, 36, 165
Congo Mission News, The, 34
Congo Protestant Council, see CPC
Congo Reform Association, 7
Congolese, 42, 166; chiefs, 15, 17, 31-32, 33, 34, 35, 37, 90, 138; cultural
    institutions, 33, 137, 143, 163; cultural selectivity, 15-16, 17, 32;
    education and training, 46-47, 72, 166; effects of evangelization, 14, 15;
    and missions, 16, 107, 135-136, 167; polygamy, 18, 35, 37, 88; viewed by:
    Europeans, 67, 71, missionaries, 13-15, 35, 39, 53, 166; see also Language
Congregation of the Holy Ghost, 2
Congregation of the Immaculate Heart of Mary, 2
Conscience Africaine, see Newspapers
Conseil Supérieur de l'Enseignement, 74n

213

Convention of 1948, 95n, 97, 99
Convention of 1950, 72n
Convention of 1952, 95n, 97, 100
Conventions De Jonghe, 58, 95
Coppens, Paul, 55
Coquilhatville professional school for nurses, 47
Cordy, Jean, 147
Cornelis, Hendrik, 99-100, 147, 154
Coulon Commission, 84-86, 87, 97
Coxill, H. Wakelin, 41, 65, 75, 81, 90, 92, 93, 102
CPC (Congo Protestant Council), 80, 114, 160n; and antiprotestantism, 38, 45,
    142; and Synod, 91, 92
CSC (Confédération des Syndicats Chrétiens), see Voluntary associations, labor
    unions
CUCL (Centre Universitaire Congolaise Lovanium), 70, 71, 75
de Boeck, 156n, 157
De Cleene, N., 32n
De Clerq, Auguste, 60
Decree of April 4, 1950, 18n
Decree of May 2, 1910, 31, 32, 61
de Gaulle, Charles, 158
de Hemptinne, Jean, 32-33, 42, 45, 62, 126
De Jonghe, Edmond, 55, 56
Dellepiane, Giovanni, 40, 61, 69, 122, 127
Dennis, Leopold, 137
Dequae, André, 72, 74, 79, 87, 92, 93
Déracinés, 17, 104, 105, 159
Dericoyard, Jean Pierre, 132
de Rop, E. P. A., 157
De Schrijver, Auguste, 100
de Smedt, (Senator), 74
De Sousberghe, 157
De Tiecken, Breuls, 94
De Vleeschauwer, Albert, 74, 79, 87, 88, 98, 99
Devos, 49n
De Vos, Pierre, 139
de Worm, H., 80, 91
Dibaya (Haut Kasai) CADULAC Center, 48
Diomi, Gaston, 131, 133, 150, 155n
Direction de Culte et de l'Enseignement, 92, 93
Disciples of Christ Mission in Equator Province, 38
Dispositions Générales of 1948, 95n
Dominican Fathers, 3, 69
Dungu (Uele) secondary school, 69
Dutch, the, 34
École de Pasteurs et d'Instituteurs, 114
École des Sciences Administratives à Kisantu (EAK), 69, 70, 166
Écoles chapelles, see Education
Education, 45, 64, 65, 84-85; Catholic, 45, 52-62, 63, 100-101, 166; church-
    state separation, 52-53, 54-55; for elite, 104, 153; financing, 7, 53-54,
    55, 56, 58, 60, 64, 65-66, 69, 80, 85, 95-96; inspection service, 56, 68;
    Protestant, 45, 63, 90; reforms, 36, 68; schools, 60n, 61, 101, 102n,

Gradualism, 20n, 48, 67, 105-107, 125, 146n, 148
Grenfell, George, 1, 4, 6
Grison, Gabriel, 32n
Groupe de travail, 158, 159
Guerre scolaire, 76, 81, 86, 92, 95
Guffens, J. (Msgr.), 106
Harmel, Pierre, 74
HCB, see Lever Brothers
Henri, E. J. M., 32n
Hodgkin, Thomas, 143, 151
Housiaux, Georges, 79
Hulstaert, G., 157
Huys, Auguste, 117
Idzumbuir, Theodore, 70
Ileo, Joseph, 131, 133, 146, 151, 152, 157n
Independence, 20n, 160, 161n, 163-165; government declaration of January 13,
    1959, 158, 160; movements, 39, 47
Independent State, 52
Indirect rule, 15, 33, 35, 37
International Association, 4
International Bible Students Association, 142
International Missionary Council (IMC), 91
Internats, 99, 101
Islam, 1, 12
Jadot, Jean, 117
Jehovah's Witnesses, 140
Jesuit missions, 14, 47, 52
Jesuits, 2-3, 7, 52n, 156, 163; and ABAKO, 152, 153, 154; and education, 62,
    69, 70, 73
JOC (Jeunesses Ouvriers Chrétiens), see Voluntary associations, labor unions
John XXIII, 112
Jungers, Eugène, 76, 77
Kabamba, Eugène, 132
Kabayidi, P., 155
Kakisme (Mpadism), 138
Kalombo, Anatole, 88
Kamponde (Kasai), 69
Kanitatu, Cleophas, 160n, 164
Kanza, Daniel, 155n
Kanza, Thomas, 72n
Kaoze, Stephano, 114
Kasai Company, 7
Kasai District, 94, 95, 98, 156, 157
Kasangulu Territory, 139
Kasavubu, Joseph, 132, 148, 151, 153, 154, 155n, 164, 166
Katana, Kivu, 47
Katanga, 32-33, 45, 140, 141, 157
Keesen, (Msgr.), 55
Kidnapping, 37, 38
Kilo-Moto gold mines, 123
Kimba, Evariste, 107
Kimbangu, Simon, 39, 137, 138, 155n

Lumumba, Patrice, 132, 157n, 158
Lundula, Victor, 88
Madimba territory, 139
Malengreau, F., 70
Malengreau, Guy, 69, 70, 72, 74, 84, 85-86
Malinowski, Bronislaw, 13n, 16n
Malula, Joseph, 133, 147, 148
Manifeste de Conscience Africaine, 146, 147, 148, 149, 151, 154, 162, 167
Manono (Katanga) disturbance, 141
Marist Brothers, 62
Marzorati, Anton F., 19, 65
Masisi Revolt, 139, 141
Massa, Jacques, 133
Matadi disturbance, 125, 139
Matonsi (Tonsi), see Messianic movements
Matota, Henri, 153, 154
Mavuela, J., 156n
Maximum Illud, 112, 114
Mbanza-Boma, Bas Congo, 69
Meert, Jacques, 118, 130, 131, 133, 144-145, 147, 148, 150, 152
Mels, Bernard, 94, 99, 129
Merlier, Michel, 123
Messianic movements, 12, 134, 143n, 167; Dieudonne, 138, 139; L'Eglise de
    Jésus-Christ sur la terre par le prophète Simon Kimbangu (EJCSK), 139, 140;
    Kimbanguism, 12, 139, 141, 142, 154, 155, 159; Kitawala, 140-143; Mpadism,
    138-139; and Protestantism, 39, 136; Salvation Army, 138; Tonsi, 139;
    Watchtower, 140-141, 142; see also Kimbangu, Simon
Métropole, 35-36, 71, 76-77, 158; involvement with Congo, 19-22, 30, 55, 56;
    relationship of mission to, 34, 46, 61, 162
Migration to urban centers, 68, 104n, 121, 124, 139
Mill Hill Fathers, 7, 34
Minister of Colonies, office of, 25, 35, 41n
Ministère de l'Instruction Publique, 97
Ministry of Colonies, 50; anticlericalism in, 64, 83, 92; and the Catholic
    Party, 22, 77; and education, 65, 70
Missionary Herald, The, 2
Missionary Sons of Scheut, 2
MNC (Mouvement National Congolais), see Voluntary associations, political
    associations
Mobutu, Joseph, 165n
MOC (Mouvement Ouvrier Chrétien), see Voluntary associations, labor unions
Moermans, Joseph, 97n, 101-102, 150
Moody, T., 6
Morel, Edmund D., 7, 8
Morrison, William, 9
Mosmans, Guy, 67, 71, 95, 110-111, 119, 121, 144, 159, 160, 162
Moyersoen, M., 100
Mpadism, 138-139
Mugeri (Kivu) secondary school, 69
Munongo, Godefroid, 70
Mwamba, Remy, 88

Mwana Lesa, 140
"National missions," 8, 41, 49, 50, 58, 61, 65, 90
Nationalism, 120, 143, 162; Bakongo, 140, 153; fear of, 35, 103; vs parochialism, 163, 167, 168; role of Catholic Church in, 119, 131, 145, 146, 161, 163; see also Voluntary associations, political
Native rights, 6
N'Djoli, Victor, 146
Newspapers, 146-147; Congo, 146n; Conscience Africaine, 146, 147, 148, 151, 152, 154-155,164; Courrier d'Afrique, 152n; Kongo dia Ngunga, 154n; Quinze, 146n; Revue du Clergé Africain, 119
Ney, Jean, 75, 93, 106
Neyns, Jacques, 160n
Ngalula, Joseph, 131, 133, 146, 152, 157n
Ngwenza, Antoine, 146
Nicaise, Joseph, 147, 152
Nkamba, 137
Nkongolo, Joseph, 157n
N'Kuli, Albert, 146
Nyirenda, Tomo, 140
Nzeza, Joseph, 70
Nzeza, Simon, 153
Nzeza-Landu, Edmond, 152-153, 154, 155n
Ohrneman, Joseph, 91, 92, 102
Oldham, J. H., 65
Oriental province, 61, 114
Pan-African movements, 12
Parliament, Belgian, 25n, 36
Parti du Liberte et Progres, see Liberal Party
Parti Liberal Belge (PLB), see Liberal Party
Parti Social Chrétien, see PSC
Parti Socialiste Belge (PSB), see Socialist Party
Pauwels, 130
Permanent Commission for the Protection of the Natives, see Commission for the Protection of the Natives
Permanent Committee of Catholic Bishops, see Bishops
Pétillon, Léon, 72, 93, 100, 101, 147, 158
Phelps-Stokes Commission, 53
Philipp, Ross, 32n
Pishal, Ed., 91
Pius XI, 54, 111, 112, 122n, 145
Platonism, 105n
PLB, see Liberal Party
Plessers, K., 108-109, 111
Political parties, African, 162; Belgian, 21-22, 26
Politics, Congolese, 120, 164, 165; education and, 70, 71, 85; see also Voluntary associations
Portuguese, the, 1, 2, 3, 4, 140, 159
Premonstrants, 3
Princeps Pastorum, 112n
Propaganda (Sacred Heart Congregation for the Propagation of the Faith), 3, 40
PSB, see Socialist Party

PSC (Catholic Party), 149n, 165; and annexation, 8, 11-12; and Belgian politics, 21, 22-24, 72, 76, 93, 158; and A. Buisseret, 74, 94; and Colonial Administration, 26-29, 93; and Concordat of 1953, 78, 81, 82, 113; and Congo reform, 128, 148n, 159; and education, 70, 87, 97; and guerre scolaire, 77, 81, 82
Raymaekers, Paul, 140
Redemptorists, 3
Reform, 22, 158; and Catholic Church, 108-110, 160; in education, 53, 67, 72, 84-85; elite demands for, 107-110; Protestant demands for, 9, 38, 108n-109n; of Rubber Regime, 6-8
Renaibako, see Voluntary associations, political associations
Renkin, Jules, 8, 9, 11, 32
Reppresentati in Terra, 54
Rey, J., 81
Rivalry between missions, 163
Rochedieu, Paul, 9
Roelens, V., 16, 17n, 35
Roosevelt, Theodore, 7
Ross, Emory, 41, 45, 49-50, 63, 65-66
Round Table Conference, 160n
Roussel, J., 165
Rubbens, Antoine, 152n
Rubber industry, 5-9, 123
Rural romanticism, 13-14, 121
Rutten, Martin, 12n-13n, 33, 37
Ryckmans, André, 135, 138, 143
Ryckmans, Pierre, 65, 68, 70, 105; and 1946 decree, 127, 128
Sacred Heart Congregation for the Propagation of the Faith (Propaganda), 3, 40
Sacred Heart of Jesus, the, 3
San Salvador, 1, 2
Savorgnan de Brazza, Comte, 2
Scalais, Felix, 86, 160n
Scheutist Fathers, 42, 69, 156, 163; Agence DIA, 154, 155; establishment of, 2, 3, 5; volunteer associations, 132, 133
"Secretaire Général en Belgique des Missions Protestantes au Congo," 91
Sendwe, Jason, 164
Senegalese, the, 52
Separation of State and Church, 60, 64, 160
Service de l'Enseignement, 75, 86
Service de l'Inspection, 92
Service Interfederale Belge d'Enseignement au Congo, 97
Sheppard, William, 9
Sigismundi, 81-82
Sita, Alphonse, 131
Six, Georges, 73, 133, 156n
Sjöblom, E. W., 5
Slave trade, 1, 4
Smet, Guy, 91
Socialist document of Reform 1956, 147, 148
Socialist Party (PSB), 7, 8, 72; and annexation, 74, 86, 88; in Belgian politics, 21, 22, 77; and Colonial Administration, 19, 26, 36, 76; and Concordat of 1953, 79, 81, 82; and Congolese political movements, 149, 151; and demands for reform, 20, 128, 147

Société Générale de Belgique, 20, 42
Sohier, Antoine, 100, 108, 119
Spaak, Paul-Henri, 78
Stanley, Henry Morton, 1, 2, 3n, 5
Stanley Pool, 2
Stanleyville, 47, 83, 141
Statistics: Catholic compared with Protestant, 26n, doctors, 49, members, 162n,
    missions, 55-56; Catholic Press, 146n-148n; CSC union strength, 128; educa-
    tional, 54, 58, 60n, 61n, 74n, 99; financial, 48, 49, 58, 99; population,
    26n, 104n; social centers, 122; strength of religious groups, 3n, 12n, 26n,
    113, 142
statut des villes, 151
Strausch, 94
Struye, 100
Subsidies, 22; to Catholic missions, 7, 9, 11; medical, 46-49
Sundkler, Bengt, 137
Synod of the Evangelical Churches of Belgium, 9
Synod of the Union des Eglises (the Synod), 91-92
Tempels, Placide, 109
Ten-Year Plan for the Economic and Social Development of the Belgian Congo, 85
Tezzo, Simon, 153n
Thirty-year plan for Congolese independence (A. A. J. Van Bilsen), 20n, 146,
    147, 148
Thompson, 102
Tibbaut, Emile, 12
Tilkens, Auguste, 79
Tippo Tib, 4
Tonsi (Mpadism), 138-139
Trappists, 3
Treaties, international, 39
Treaty of 1884, 4
Treaty of Berlin, see General Act of Berlin
Treaty of St. Germain-en-Laye, 79
Trockay, Fernand, 94
Tshuapa District (Equateur), 141
Ubangi Uelle District, 5
Uganda, 150n
UMHK, see Union Minière du Haut Katanga
UNELMA, see Voluntary associations, alumni
Unemployment, 69
UNESCO report, 122
Unilever, see Lever Brothers
Union Minière du Haut Katanga (UMHK), 45, 61, 62, 125
Unions, Belgian, 21; see also Voluntary associations
UNISCO (Union des Intérêts Sociaux Congolais), see Voluntary associations, alumni
United Nations, 140
United States, 4, 5, 7, 8, 10, 13, 20, 39, 53, 142
United Training College for the Upper Congo, 53
Universal Negro Improvement Association, the, 12n, 143n
University for Congolese (Kisantu), 69
University of Brussels, 74
University of Elisabethville, 74, 75
University of Ghent, 74

Political associations:

    Association des Parents d'Elèves des Écoles Catholiques de Léopold-
    ville, 159; Comité Mixte de la Ligue de Parents Chrétiens, 150;
    Fédération des Moniteurs Catholiques, 150; Intergroupe des Intérêts
    Chrétiens (IIC), 150; Mouvement National Congolais (MNC), 151, 152,
    157, 158, 162, 164; Renaissance Bakonga (Renaibako), 156

Political parties:

    ABAKO (Association Bakongo), 132, 140n, 143, 147, 151, 154-159, 163,
    164, 167, manifesto, 152-153, origins, 152; Balubakat, 157, 164;
    Lulua Frères (Parti de la Défense du Peuple Lulua), 157; Parti
    Solidaire Africain (PSA), 153, 160, 161n; Union des Croyants
    Congolais, 162n; Union Mongo, 157

Watchtower Bible and Tract Society, 140, 142

Weber, H., 32n

Weiss, Herbert, 116

West African Missionary Association, 7

White Fathers, 67, 114

Wide, E. R., 160n

Wigny, Pierre, 70, 74, 87, 100

World Council of Churches, 140n

World Missionary Conference, 1910, 53

Yava, Rodolphe, 88

Young, Crawford, 116

Yumba, Joseph, 153

Zangabie, Dominique, 146

Zanzibari Arabs, 1

Zimmer, Marcel, 94

Zulus, 137